MW00906962

The Wasnington Entrepreneur's Guide

2nd Edition

How to Start and Manage a Business in Washington

Dr. Paul Larson, University of Montana
Dr. Karl Vesper, University of Washington
Dr. Maury Forman, Washington State Department of Community,
Trade, and Economic Development

University Press
1719 Dearborn Avenue
Missoula, MT 59801
(800) 243-6840

The Washington Entrepreneur's Guide, 2nd Edition
How to Start and Manage a Business in Washington

ISBN 0 9624819 5 5

Published by:

University Press
1719 Dearborn
Missoula, MT 59801
(800) 243-6840

Washington Entrepreneur's Guide

Table of Contents

Authors

Paul Larson, Ph.D.

Dr. Larson is a Professor of Management at The University of Montana School of Business Administration. Besides teaching courses in entrepreneurship and business strategy, he has published books on entrepreneurship and speaks on management topics across the country. He writes a syndicated small business column and has consulted with a great number of Pacific Northwest businesses.

Karl Vesper, Ph.D.

Dr. Vesper received his Ph.D. from Stanford University in 1969. Currently, he has a three-way appointment as Professor of Management, Professor of Mechanical Engineering and Professor of Marine Sciences. An internationally recognized expert in the field of entrepreneurship, he has authored numerous books and articles.

Maury Forman, Ph.D.

Dr. Forman is the Manager for Education and Training for the Washington State Department of Community Trade and Economic Development. He received his Ph.D. from New York University in 1981. He is a frequent instructor on the subject of Starting a Home Base Business at workshops throughout Washington state. He has authored numerous books and articles.

Contributors

Dirk A. Bartram

Dirk Bartram is a partner with the Seattle law firm Helsell Fetterman LLP and practices business law exclusively. He has considerable experience consulting with businesses concerning the corporate, intellectual property, real estate and general business law. Mr. Bartram graduated Summa Cum Laude from Seattle University, Seattle, Washington and received his Masters Business Administration degree and J.D. degree with Honors from the University of Washington.

Lise Sellier Fitzpatrick

Lise Sellier Fitzpatrick is currently the customer service coordinator for the Trade Development Alliance of Greater Seattle, having previously worked for the Henry M. Jackson Foundation. Fitzpatrick holds degrees in International Finance and East Asian Studies from the University of Southern California.

Denferd W. Henke

Dan Henke is a partner with the Seattle law firm Helsell Fetterman LLP. His business practice emphasizes business planning, advice and negotiating and documenting commercial transactions. Mr. Henke works with his clients and their other advisors to select the proper business entity for the client's long term plan; to select appropriate methods to raise the capital necessary to allow the business to achieve the plan; to negotiate the client's significant contracts, sales, acquisitions and mergers; and to develop and execute an exit strategy for the client. Mr. Henke graduated Cum Laude from Dartmouth College in 1976 and received his law degree from the University of California, Berkeley, Boalt Hall School of Law in 1979.

David Harrison

David Harrison became the first executive director of the Northwest Policy Center in the fall of 1987. Since 1995 he has served as chair of the Center. The Center, established through a major grant from the Northwest Area Foundation, assists policy makers in Washington, Idaho, Oregon, Montana, and Alaska in devising strategies for maintaining a vital regional economy. He is also a Senior Lecturer at the University of Washington Graduate School of Public Affairs and has also served as its Associate Dean.

Jonathan Hayes, CFA

Jonathan Hayes is the Revenue Bond Programs Manager for the Washington Economic Development Finance Authority in the Department of Community, Trade and Economic Development. He is responsible for developing and managing the state's tax exempt and taxable industrial revenue and economic development bond programs which provide access to long term bond finance for eligible companies as well as providing technical assistance in the area of corporate and capital finance. Mr. Hayes has over twelve years' experience in the field of municipal and corporate bond finance. He has an MBA degree in Finance from Dartmouth College and holds the Chartered Financial Analyst designation.

Sam Kaplan

Sam Kaplan is the program and communications manager for the Trade Development Alliance of Greater Seattle, which promotes the greater Seattle area in the area of international trade and business development. He previously worked for U.S. Representative John Miller handling foreign affairs and trade issues. He has also worked as a free lance writer.

Michelle LaBrosse

Michelle LaBrosse, President of Success Connections, is a business innovation and development coach, trainer, publisher, and video producer. Her business is an evolution of Wired for Success, a finalist in the Bellevue Chamber of Commerce *Emerging Business Award for Business Innovation* in 1996. The firm was selected for her work in delivering business development education interactively on line. She has a B.S. in Aerospace Engineering and an M.S. in Mechanical Engineering.

Susan L. Peterson

Susan Peterson practices at the Seattle law firm Helsell Fetterman LLP primarily in the area of business law, with an emphasis on transactional work in the areas of real estate and business acquisitions, reorganizations and sales. Her secondary emphasis is in the area of business enterprises, including the choice of legal structure. Ms. Peterson graduated Cum Laude from the University of Washington in 1984. She received her J.D. degree, Cum Laude, from the Harvard Law School in 1987.

David Wingate
David Wingate has over 20 years experience in banking, commercial finance and rural economic development in the private sector. He currently works for the Department of Community, Trade and Economic Development Finance program. His responsibilities include helping small businesses gain access to capital with a priority on job creation and retention in timber dependent, high unemployment communities and businesses owned by women and minorities.

Acknowledgments

We are greatly indebted to the many people who have assisted in the writing and editing of this book. To each of them, we offer our deepest appreciation.

Lise Sellier Fitzpatrick, Jonathan Hayes, David Harrrison, Sam Kaplan, Michelle LaBrosse, and especially David Wingate for providing their expertise as contributors.

Neal VanDeventer and Russ Campbell for providing technical assistance.

Laura Myers for her extensive editing and typesetting contributions.

Gary Sorenson for a multitude of activities instrumental in completing the book.

Marcia Wingate for providing word processing and database input for the resource directory.

Shirley Gates for her keen eye in spotting errors in the original text of our drafts.

Catherine Gwinner, Karin Martin and Sheri McKeigue for their research assistance with the Business Resource Guide.

Margaret Schott and Leslie Nyitray from the Department of Licensing and Gary Grossman from the Department of Revenue for providing detailed information about their departments' entrepreneurial services.

Mike Fitzgerald, Sandi Benbrook, and Kathy Norwood Chance of the Washington State Department of Community, Trade and Economic Development for their continued support of education and training activities and materials for Washington entrepreneurs.

To all the small businesses and entrepreneurs who have helped make the state of Washington number 1 nationally in the creation of new companies. Their stories and experiences will help Washington continue to maintain that ranking.

Introduction

The first edition of *The Washington Entrepreneur's Guide* was published in 1993. A major strength of the book was its focus on the state of Washington and the information provided to readers specific to the state. In order to sustain those benefits, we decided to revise the book and include up-to-date information that would help Washington entrepreneurs start and build successful ventures. This second edition is the result of these efforts.

Besides providing current information on the economy, resource programs, and successful Washington companies, this second edition also has completely revised and updated computer spreadsheet templates. Readers will find them extremely useful in making financial projections for business plans.

The computer disk also includes important resources listed by county for the entrepreneur in Washington state. In addition to identifying the primary contact points of the Economic Development Councils and the Small Business Development Centers, we have provided a listing of local revolving and micro-loan programs, highlighting relevant information about each of them. This section is designed to help the entrepreneur quickly identify financial and technical assistance.

Chapter 3, which cover patents, trademarks and copyrights, was updated to include changes in laws in those areas. Chapter 5, which discusses licensing and tax regulations, has been brought up to date to reflect recent Washington state business legislation.

The chapter on raising capital (Chapter 7) has undergone significant revision. New loan and management assistance programs have appeared in the last couple of years, and we believe you will appreciate learning about them.

We hope you find the *Washington Entrepreneur's Guide, 2nd Edition* valuable in starting or managing your venture and wish you the best of luck. We welcome suggestions you may have for future editions of the book.

1

The Stages of Business Growth

"It takes twenty years to make an overnight success."
Eddie Cantor

Entrepreneurs thrive on growth. Growth brings challenges, variety, a sense of moving forward, and usually increased net worth. In fact, if your company is not growing it may be at risk. You may not be able to attract or retain quality managers and employees. The innovation of your company may stagnate. Competitors may move right past you. Your company may *have* to grow to be able to survive.

Although growth is wonderful, it brings with it problems. Cash flow is usually troublesome. Jobs don't get done because people are spread thin. Quality control can lapse because of the emphasis on getting more products out. People burn out because of the increased workload. If you grow too fast, the strain may destroy your company.

Your company may have to grow to be able to survive

The purpose of this chapter is to help you manage the growth of your company. Most growing firms pass through identifiable stages with predictable characteristics. This chapter describes the stages and the common pitfalls, so that you can anticipate problems and hopefully be able to avoid them. You want to enjoy the growth of your company, not be overwhelmed by it.

The Stages of Growth

Existence
The first stage of a small company is Existence. The basic questions at this stage are, "Do you have a viable product?" and "Will enough people buy your products to keep you alive?" The organization is made of yourself and any other partners and a few, if any, employees. You are involved in all aspects of the business,

At startup, *you* are the business

including product design, marketing, raising capital, etc. *You* are the business at this stage and it depends almost entirely on your energy and dedication. If you have a patentable product, this is the stage where you should should work on obtaining a patent. You also need to research the market to gauge what potential customers are looking for and to determine if enough people will buy from you so you can stay in existence.

Money is difficult to raise at this stage. Banks and venture capitalists are very leery of startup companies. The Small Business Administration (SBA) guarantees some loans to startup firms, but considerable equity and collateral are required. In many cases, the only sources of startup capital are your own resources and those of other individuals who are willing to back you.

Survival

Your business is able to survive if people start buying your products and you generate enough cash to continue paying the bills. At this stage you may hire a few people because you want to stop working sixteen hours a day. Although they may have some special skills for which you hired them, almost everyone in the company needs to be a "jack of all trades" at this point. You delegate some responsibility, but basically you make almost all decisions and you are still involved in all areas of the business. At this stage the company may be only marginally profitable, and you probably aren't able to pay yourself a decent manager's salary or a dividend check as an investor. Nonetheless, your business is generating enough cash to stay alive.

When you have a startup company, capital is hard to find

Capital is still difficult to raise at this stage. You at least have generated some sales, which bankers and venture capitalists appreciate. If you have a business plan that looks promising, you may be able to get a loan or equity financing at this stage from these sources.

You need to rise above the day-to-day pressures and write a longer-term business plan

The organizational structure is loose. You generally won't have set job descriptions, and people "chip in" on almost any job that has to be done. Planning emphasizes the short-term, usually pointed at staying in business another month. However, this is when you need to rise above the day-to-day pressures and write a longer-term business plan.

Early Success

You have reached the Early Success stage when your business consistently generates enough profits to pay you as a manager and investor. Usually the company has grown to the point that you can no longer make all of the decisions. Other people need to be promoted to management positions.

Now that you are in less need of capital, banks are happy to loan you money. If your company has the chance of significant growth, venture capitalists may be interested in investing. Cash flow may be an occasional problem, but it is not a constant worry.

Many businesses reach this stage and remain here for long periods of time. If you can find good managers, you may be able to spend much less time with the business. You may choose to disengage yourself from the business and pursue a more comfortable lifestyle, or you may decide to pursue other business ventures. You may decide to sell at this point and pursue something completely different. Or, if the opportunity is there, you may decide to forge ahead and really push the company to grow.

Many businesses remain in the Early Success stage for a long period of time

The success stage may be a real plateau and you will need to consciously commit to going beyond that point. For a retail store, it may mean opening several other outlets. For a manufacturer, it may mean design and production of new products after success with an initial product. For some ventures, the success stage may come very quickly and there is almost no time to think about ensuing growth–it just happens. Although the growth may come in different forms and at different rates, it poses similar problems to just about any firm experiencing it.

High Growth

In this stage, companies experience real growing pains. If you aren't aware of potential problems in advance and don't prepare for them, they can make your life miserable. The first realization you must make is that you have to delegate more responsibilities. You can't have your hand in every decision. You need to give subordinates authority and be able to trust their decisions. You must consciously take the role of a leader and manager and be less involved in the details of the company. If you haven't taken any management courses, you definitely should at this point. You need to be able to set goals, give feedback, and monitor performance. The need for *people* skills is critical. You may be the most technically knowledgeable person in your firm at this point, but if

In the High Growth stage, companies experience real growing pains

you can't relate well to people and manage them, they will be frustrated and your firm will lose productivity.

The organizational structure of your company needs to change as the enterprise grows. During the infancy of the firm, the few people involved worked on just about any job that needed to be done. Job responsibilities need to be better defined at this later stage. Job descriptions should be written so that employees have a clear idea of what is expected of them. Employees will become more specialized in their tasks. You may have to hire someone fulltime just to manage accounts receivable, for example. With this increased specialization, you need to promote communication between the different positions and departments so that people do not develop "tunnel vision". Many a company has been plagued by employees who believe that the company exists for the sake of the accounting department, or the sales department. You need to force the different specialists to communicate with each other and you also need to be a cheerleader to remind everyone of where the whole ship is headed. Overall, you are trying to bring structure to a growing organization whose natural tendency is to greater disorder. In the process, however, you are trying not to squelch the entrepreneurial spirit which brought about the growth.

The organizational structure of your company needs to change as the enterprise grows

Growth brings the need to hire or train a few specialists. With few exceptions, you need a skilled marketing person and a skilled finance person. If you are a manufacturer, you also need an experienced production manager. At the early stages one or two people may fill these roles. As growth occurs, each of these positions is so important that one person should be responsible for each area.

You need to set up a cash management system

In the frenzied atmosphere of a growing firm, you as a manager can be so consumed with the demands of everyday life that you don't allow time for long-range planning. A strategic plan and a marketing plan are extremely important during a period of growth. They both serve as road maps for where you are trying to go and they keep your energies focused on high priorities. Regardless of how busy you are, you must find time to formulate and update these plans.

A growing company usually has cash flow problems, even if it is profitable. Growing inventories, accounts receivable, and equipment expenditures cause cash flow problems. You need to set up a cash management system to avoid it. You also should have a financial management system. With the growing number of expenses of the business, you will be hard pressed to keep track of the financial condition of the company "in your head." A financial management system should include budgets, ratio analysis, and financial statement analysis. The purpose of these financial controls is to prohibit your accelerating train from running off of the track– a common occurrence for growing businesses.

Maturity

The Maturity stage is a second version of the Early Success stage. After dramatic growth, sales are leveling off. The company is on firm financial ground and cash flow is not usually a problem. The owner(s) has built considerable wealth and the company can usually run pretty well without the lead entrepreneur being there. Many entrepreneurs lose interest at this stage and seek to sell the business or get cash out of it. A common problem here is the direct opposite of that facing the high growth firm– how to get the large train accelerating again. The size of the organization inhibits its ability to innovate and move quickly.

A problem you face at maturity is how to get the train accelerating again

Conclusion

Most growing companies pass through recognizable stages. You, as the lead entrepreneur of your organization, need to be aware of them. Although the stages may be of different duration for different firms, the problems at each stage are fairly predictable. In this book, the chapters are presented in the order in which those issues normally surface in a growing enterprise. That order is:

As an entrepreneur you need to be aware of the growth stages of your company

Existence

1. Developing Business Ideas   Chap. 2
2. Patents, Trademarks, and Copyrights   Chap. 3
3. Marketing Research   Chap. 4

Survival

1. Regulations on Doing Business   Chap. 5
2. Choosing a Form of Business   Chap. 6

Early Success

1.	Raising Capital	Chap. 7
2.	Gathering Your Forces	Chap. 8

High Growth

1.	Strategic Planning	Chap. 9
2.	The Marketing Plan	Chap. 10
3.	Cash Management	Chap. 11
4.	Exporting	Chap. 12
5.	The Business Plan	Chap. 13

Maturity

1.	Harvesting a Business	Chap. 14

Don't be afraid to "jump ahead" of where your company is currently and read ensuing chapters. Some topics, such as Marketing Research and Cash Management, are always relevant, regardless of the stage of company development. These topics are merely presented at the earliest stages where the need for them is critical.

References

1. Baird, Bruce F. *The Technical Manager*. Belmont, California: Lifetime Learning Publications, 1983.

2. Churchill, Neil C. and Lewis, Virginia L., "The Five Stages of Small Business Growth," *Harvard Business Review*, May-June 1983, pp. 30-38.

3. Timmons, Jeffry A. *New Venture Creation*, 3rd Edition. Homewood, Illinois: Irwin, 1990.

4. Vesper, Karl H. *New Venture Strategies,* Englewood Cliffs, Prentice-Hall, 1990.

5. Vesper, Karl H. *New Venture Mechanics,* Englewood Cliffs, Prentice-Hall, 1993.

2

Developing Business Ideas

*"Everything has been thought of before,
but the problem is to think of it again."*
Goethe

To create a successful business, you must provide something that is unique. You will not succeed by being average. There are unlimited ways to differentiate your business. It can be the product itself, how it is marketed, the services provided, or the price you charge, to name a few.

To create a business you need to be three different people. You need to be a dreamer, a realist, and a critic. The dreamer in you will come up with an idea, the realist will figure out how to make it work, and the critic will let you know if a customer will like it.

However, every entrepreneur must recognize that there is a difference between good ideas and good businesses. Ideas are about 5% of the game. As an entrepreneur, your head is full of ideas, but many of them will not make good businesses. You need to focus on understanding the relationship of your idea (the dream) to the customer. If you have no customer, you have no business. Without a business, you have no dream.

A good idea and a good business are not the same

Knowing that an idea is merely the starting point of a successful business, take a look at how other companies have succeeded in differentiating themselves for their customers. The ideas presented below are only a few of the possibilities.

Ways to Make Your Company Unique

Quality

Quality is the obvious place to start. And when it comes to quality, few have traveled further than Paul Shipman who founded the Red Hook Ale Brewery. He began his company with the premise that beer in the United States could be made holding to the same strict standards to which fine European breweries have subscribed for centuries. That standard for craft brewing is derived from "Reinheitsgebot", the German purity law that was enacted in the 1500's. The Northwest entrepreneur went so far as to be the first to purchase new brewing equipment from Germany and use it in his facility in Freemont. Red Hook has gained a reputation of consistent quality by using carefully selected ingredients, highly trained brewers, and state-of-the-art brewing equipment.

> **You must provide something that is unique**

Quicker Response to Customers

Some industries, such as the cable industry, have traditionally had very slow response time for its customers. Summit Cablevision of Bellevue guarantees same-day service for repair problems as well as maintaining on-call service on Sunday. For installation, if they do not show up at the appointed hour they will install the cable for free. They also monitor phone calls to assure that incoming calls are answered within 30 seconds.

Less Maintenance to Customers

The Maytag repairman epitomizes this form of differentiation. Sell a product which requires less maintenance. If you are an oil driller and are working far from civilization (and from an oil rig repairman) a more dependable product is worth a lot of money.

Better Warranty

> **Listen to customers and dedicate yourself to meeting their needs**

The car industry has experienced "warranty wars." They are trying to gain your business by assuring you that you will not have to pay for repairs for a longer period of time. Forget the fact that they warrant only about two percent of the parts on the car. Customers pay attention to warranties in many industries. Make sure the quality of your product is high enough that product replacement costs will not break you.

Better Service

Tom Peters, author of *A Passion for Excellence*, says in his presentations, "It has gotten to the point that if you expect good service, people think you are some kind of weirdo!" Nonetheless, some companies excel in service. Nordstroms built its reputation around customer service. The basics of this approach are a willingness to listen to customers' concerns and a dedication to meeting their needs. Companies all over the country conduct service training that refer to the Nordstoms' model. You know you have been successful when your name is synonymous with better service.

Better Compatibility With Other Products
It is easy to think of similar products that are compatible with others. Computer hardware has to work with software. Microsoft of Redmond developed DOS and then signed a contract with IBM to include the product with every PC sold. It made Microsoft the leader in computer software. But what about something really unique? Wilson Marine of Seattle teamed up with Kenmore Air to fly parts for free to any boat that breaks down in their service area. It gives new meaning to the saying, "one if by sea, two if by air". If your product is more compatible with other units, you have a competitive advantage.

More Flexible Usage
An apple is used to keep the doctor away or just be eaten as a snack. But in Washington, where the apple is the number one agricultural product, entrepreneurs have thought of many uses for the apple. They have made Christmas wreaths and apple doll heads with this edible delight. Artists have had a field day with painting it and sculpting wooden replicas. Many people believe you can use the apple for all sorts of cooking as evidenced by the apple recipe book that includes such favorites as "Baked Beans and Apples", "Puchidee Apple Relish" or the "Truro Apple Foam Punch". And what is this country without the apple pie? The apple may not have as many uses as baking soda but if entrepreneurs develop a product with multiple uses, whereby their customer base expands, chances of success will be greater.

> **Consider developing a product with multiple uses**

Safer
Safety is a big issue these days, especially as government becomes more involved in legislating it and more people become lawsuit happy. Lenny Frasure of Highland Glass in Clarkston has developed and patented a safety window for the welded aluminum boats that are built in Asotin County. These are side-slider windows that do not shatter when the boats crash through the white water waves. Because of the safety of these windows, virtually every boat manufactured in the valley has them.

Healthier

Today's society is supposedly very health conscious. That is why creating a product that tastes good and is good for you is often a sure way to success. Pasta Mama's of Richland, a company that evolved from a home-base hobby by husband-wife entrepreneurs into a 25,000 square foot manufacturing and distribution center, has created the *Fried Dried Pasta*. This all-natural ingredient features 32 flavors and 13 different shapes and has no salt, no sugar, no eggs, and is low in fat. Sound terrible? It's not. Its customers are eating it up.

Create a product that is healthy and tastes good

Recycle

When Larry's Markets, a Seattle-based grocery store chain, started looking for 50 percent recycled plastic bags for its stores, it had to look no further than its back yard. American Plastic Manufacturing developed a product using recycled milk jugs.

Promote Athletics

The Northwest may be known for its inclement weather, but that does not stop Baden Sports of Renton from producing athletic balls. In fact, they have carved out a niche by supplying all types of balls to grade schools and high schools. That strategy has made them the largest ball maker in the Pacific Northwest and third largest in the country.

More Compact and More Portable

The battleground in electronics industries is over who can make products smaller and lighter. Notebook computers now have more power than desktop models had three years ago. Microsoft of Redmond is currently working on wallet computers that carry digital signatures, money, and theater or airplane tickets. You better start getting rid of all that spare change now. It may be bigger than your wallet.

Many industries are driven by the need for greater portability

More Attractive

The come-on "I am going to put you in the movies" may sound like a great line but that is what has happened to JanSport of Everett. The firm does not need much of an advertising budget because its back pack is so attractive that it has been prominently displayed on television programs such as *Northern Exposure, Beverly Hills 90210,* and the *John Larroquette Show* as well as movies such as *Jurassic Park* and *The Pelican Brief.* All this, for just a back pack.

Even if you don't change the functionality of a product, you can change its appearance. The trends in fashion colors change nearly every year, and if you keep producing with the same old colors you may be in trouble. With many generic products, packaging is what convinces a customer to purchase a particular brand.

In trendy industries, appearance is everything

Associate with Local Heroes

Why would anyone want to make a running shoe in Washington when Nike is right next door? Brooks Sports of Bothell felt up to the challenge. In fact its CEO, Helen Rockey, is a former Nike employee who intends on focusing on running and becoming a niche player. She intends to use local, high-profile runners to help market her shoe. She apparently is doing pretty well. The four-time winner of the Boston and New York Marathons, the current world record holder in the mile, and the 1983 winner of the Boston Marathon all run in her shoes.

More Status Appeal

Most companies would shudder to hear that they have the most expensive product in their field. Not Kliens Bicycles of Chehalis. In fact they even use that information in their marketing. Their bicycles are considered the "Cartier" of bicycles with costs ranging from $900 to $5,000. However, cost is not the only thing that gives them status appeal. Their bicycles are also known for their high performance, strength, efficiency and beautiful appearance. This is why the firm is one of the largest producers of custom quality bicycles in the United States, specializing in hand-built aluminum frame bicycles. Gary Klien came up with the idea as part of an entrepreneurial project at MIT. That school project has resulted in his exporting to more than 35 foreign countries.

More Convenient Hours

One occasionally sees businesses such as grocery stores and banks announcing new evening hours to provide more convenient access. They must balance the extra cost of operating such hours against the new business they get from additional customers. But even small businesses are trying to meet the time constraints of two-income families. Safeguard Pest Control of Edmonds provides extermination services when the customer wants rather than when the field person can get around to it. This endears the firm to working couples not able to be at home during the day.

Convenient hours help two-income families meet time constraints

Combine Fun With Education

Educational computer companies have been advertising their software as being so much fun that you will not even know that you are learning. Edmark Corporation of Redmond takes the opposite strategy in developing its product. They see kids as wanting to learn so they want their products to be rich educationally but also entertaining rather than the other way around. They measure their success by how much time the child is doing something to the software rather than how much time the software is doing something to the child. They go so far as to name their products Thinking Things and Science House. The result is that it becomes more fun for the child and the parent. It appears to be working. Their sales have gone through the roof.

People love to have fun

Promote Recreation

Washington is known world-wide for the sports, fishing, and water skiing boats made by Bayliner in Arlington and Tolleycraft in Kelso. K2 in Vashon Island manufactures fiberglass snow skis while four companies in Seattle– HO, O'Brien, Kidder, and Connelly– are the top four water ski manufacturers. Many of these products were developed in the entrepreneurs' garages while waiting for the rainy season to end.

Friendlier Environment

If you have ever ordered coffee from a Starbuck's store, there is a good chance that you may never have to make another order again. They not only try to remember your name, but they do a remarkable job of remembering your order. Double tall, non-fat, no foam? No problem. Double short mocha, half decaf, no whip with sprinkles? Coming right up. This friendly environment and service-oriented employees are some of the reasons why their outlets have become coffee houses rather than coffee stores.

A friendly environment brings customers back

Go Global

Some entrepreneurs realize that they cannot compete with the big companies domestically. That is what happened to Tim's Potato Chip. He knew that if he took his product nationally he would get gobbled up (no pun intended) by Frito Lay. So what did he do? He opened up a factory in Estonia, in the former Soviet Union, where Frito Lay wasn't.

Bob Walsh coordinated the Goodwill Games in Seattle. He noticed that one of the first places that Soviets went was to our pharmacies for vitamins. What did he do? He opened up a distribution center in the Soviet Union. Walsh vitamins are not only sold all over Russia but the Walsh Polyvit is the official vitamin of the Russian Olympic team.

Take your good idea to another country

Promote Local Products

Some people may fly Horizon Airlines because it flies all over the region. However, there are some people that fly the airlines because it serves fresh perked coffee from Starbuck's. Not only does it serve Starbuck's at its gates and on its planes, it also serves and promotes other Northwest entrepreneurs and their products as part of its in-flight service– from a mouth-watering pastry at a mom and pop bakery in Kent, (Kay's Gourmet Bakery), to local baseball hero cards (Pacific N.W. Trading Cards) in Lynnwood, to Talking Rain Water in Preston.

When all Else Fails...

When all else fails, you may want to consider making something with chocolate. It seems as if chocolate is one indulgence people are willing to pay for even in hard times. Don't believe that? Ask Seattle Fudge or Fran's Chocolate of Seattle, Boehm's of Issaquah or CBM Creative Chocolates of Seattle, Chuckar Cherry Company of Prosser or Spokandy, or Hallett Chocolate, or Treat Factory in Spokane. These are only some of the many chocolate factories that have started and prospered in Washington.

Getting the Wheels Turning

Sometimes all you need to create a unique product or service is a little prompting. The following approaches to innovation might work in your business.

Adapt Features of Other Products

Do you know where the idea of roll-on deodorant came from? From the ballpoint pen, of course. CAD-CAM robotics and other systems used in product design and development are often linked with special software so that various departments can work simultaneously on projects. Caddex Corp., of Woodinville, Washington, recognized that one big problem in such environments involved technical documentation. The company developed an electronic test and graphics editing system especially for technical documents. The software is an adaptation of the features of systems

A variety of creative ideas can be combined to develop new products already in use. The new product strengthens the weakest link in the manufacturing chain. Some of the greatest product breakthroughs have merely been adaptations of products in other industries.

Modify the Product

**Modify your idea
to make it
unique or more
efficient**

Stoddard-Hamilton Aircraft, Inc., of Arlington, Washington, sells build-it-yourself versions of two-seater airplanes. The company passes along the money it saves in assembly and product liability costs to consumers in the form of lower prices for its products. Robert Lynette, a Redmond, Washington consultant, modified an existing wind-powered, electric generator design by using a "teeter-totter" mounting. The result was a more efficient power generator that advanced the technology one step closer to becoming competitive in the marketplace.

Substitute Components

What do you get when you combine 15,000 old tennis shoes and 525 scrap tires? If you answered a basketball court, you would be correct. Satech, Inc. of Kirkland has built the first basketball court in the country made from recycled whole athletic shoes and tires. No more hardwood floors. This unique court at the Puget Sound Christian College Gymnasium is expected to reduce player injuries and improve athletic endurance.

Combine Features

**Recycled
components can
improve quality
and help the
environment**

You can no longer use parenting as an excuse for putting off your daily exercise. The Baby Jogger Company in Yakima has developed a baby stroller that enables parents to go hiking, exploring, and jogging while the child takes a nap or takes in the sights. One famous runner reported training with the baby jogger at a six minute mile pace while another woman won her women's division 5K race while pushing her daughter. To top it off, they even offer a lifetime guarantee on the stroller.

Revive What Is Dead

Some products seem to be resurrected periodically. Hula hoops come and go. So do skateboards, Black Jack gum, troll dolls, and short skirts. You don't have to invent something new, you just have to be there ready when it returns to popularity.

Copy the Trend Setters

You don't need to be creative to copy someone else. However, it does take ingenuity to know if a new idea will work somewhere else. The first quick oil change company in Seattle– Speedylube–

was inspired by a similar venture in Salt Lake City, and Pizza Pete was modeled after a restaurant seen in Cincinnati. Go to areas with reputations for setting the trends and keep your eyes open. Some of those ideas may work in this state and you could be the first to introduce them.

Conclusion

The one thing that each of these entrepreneurs had in common was that before they began their companies they had to be a dreamer, a realist and a critic. These characteristics not only stimulate creativity, but they also contributed to their success.

You cannot put a box around any of these personalities. In order to be creative, you need to look at your business from every angle. The ideas in this chapter will prompt the multiple personalities in you to think of ways of making your business unique and successful.

Be aware that the world is full of copiers (you were encouraged to do it yourself.) Therefore, any uniqueness you gain will probably only be temporary. You must therefore consistently search for new ways of standing apart from the pack. This is the fun of entrepreneuring.

Consistently search for new ways to stand out

References

1.   Baird, Bruce F. *The Technical Manager*. Belmont, California: Lifetime Learning Publications, 1983.

2.   Peters, Thomas J. and Austin, Nancy K. *A Passion for Excellence*. New York: Warner Books, Inc., 1985.

3.   Thompson, Arthur A. and Strickland, A.J. *Strategic Management*, Eighth Edition. Plano, Texas: Business Publications, Inc., 1995.

4.   Mattimore, Bryan W. *99% Inspiration: Tips, Tales and Techniques for Liberating Your Business Creativity*. New York, New York: AMACON, 1994

The authors appreciate the use of the film series, *Entrepreneurs and Innovators*, produced by UWTV and the University of Washington's Program in Entrepreneurship and Innovation, in identifying many of the entrepreneurs mentioned in this chapter.

3

Protecting Your Creative Advantage

"I gave up trying to keep others from copying us a long time ago.
Now I just try to remain a moving target."
Ken Thuerbach

Free competition is the backbone of America's capitalistic system.
From your company's perspective, though, you are wise to inhibit
competition by preventing other firms from copying you. There are
various means of doing this, and this chapter discusses four:
trademarks, copyrights, trade secrets and patents.

Trademarks

A trademark is a brand name, logo, or design used to identify or
distinguish products. Service marks are just like trademarks, except
they are used in connection with services rather than products.
Microsoft® is an example of a trademark. So is the waving, multi-
colored window pane for its *Windows®* product. *Nordstrom®* is an
example of a service mark for retail clothing store services.

A good mark can be essential to a business. It identifies and
distinguishes its products or services from the great works of others
offered to the consumer today. If the consumer instantly recognizes
your mark and associates it with positive qualities, you've achieved
a huge milestone. Once you've spent resources to develop mark
recognition, you don't want someone else using it or, even worse,
someone's lawyer telling you can't use it. The time to start
protecting your rights to a mark is before you even select it.

A good trade mark can be essential to a business

The authors would like to thank Mr. Dirk Bartram
of the Seattle law firm of Helsell Fetterman LLP for his
contributions to this chapter.

Selecting a Mark

The mark you select should satisfy two legal criteria. First, it must not infringe someone else's mark. Second, it should be of a type that you can prevent others from using.

Avoiding infringement. A mark will infringe if it is *likely to cause confusion* with a registered mark or an unregistered mark that is already in use. If the mark you are considering is similar in appearance, sound or meaning to an existing mark, and the two marks are used with similar products or services, the marks are probably confusingly similar. The following examples are real cases:

A mark will
infringe if is it
*likely to cause
confusion*

- *Brutus* for men's apparel infringed *Brut* for men's toiletries
- *Sleekcraft* for boats infringed *Slickcraft* for boats
- *Dream-Master* for mattresses did not infringe *Sleepmaster* for mattresses
- *E.L. Saturday's* for a restaurant-bar did not infringe *T.G.I. Friday's* for a restaurant-bar

If you think your proposed mark might infringe someone else's, pick another one. Better to go back to the drawing board now than be served with a lawsuit later that could shut down distribution of your product.

So, you ask, how do I find out if a confusingly similar mark is already in use? The most thorough way is to hire a professional trademark search firm. It will search for marks registered at the federal or state level, as well as unregistered marks. Most firms search for unregistered marks in trade journals, buyers' guides, catalogs, directories and other publications in industries related to yours. Search firms can be found in the yellow pages under "Trademark Agents and Consultants". The biggest drawback to hiring a professional search firm is cost. To complete a full trademark search in the U.S., most search firms will charge between $300-$500 for each mark. International searches will cost even more.

A professional
firm can search
for a similar
mark

A less expensive alternative is available. You can have the Patent Depository Library in the Engineering Library of the University of Washington (206-543-0741) assist you with a computerized search. It is free of charge. There's a problem, though, in relying exclusively on this search. The database includes only marks that are on file with the U.S. Patent and Trademark Office. If a mark is in use but the owner hasn't filed with the PTO, it won't be found in this search. That could spell trouble. Also, the database is about three months behind and is not as up-to-date as those used by most search firms. You should also call ahead for hours of operation because they vary based on the academic calendar year.

To keep your costs down without taking undue risk, combine both approaches. Have the mark searched at the Patent Depository Library first. If that search finds a confusingly similar mark, you will have avoided spending the $300-$500 to learn the same thing from a professional search firm. If the search is clean, then hire a professional search firm to do a more complete search for confusingly similar registered and unregistered marks.

You can do a trademark search on your own without too much difficulty

Picking a mark you can protect. Some trademarks are easier to protect than others. Descriptive marks– marks that describe something about the product– are difficult to defend. Examples are *Honey-baked Ham* for hams and *Quik Print* for fast copying services. Easiest to protect are arbitrary or fanciful marks which convey no information concerning the product or service, such as *Camel®* for cigarettes and *Kodak®* for film. The use of a personal name as a trademark can also be difficult to protect unless it has been in use as a mark for a significant period of time.

Registering a Trademark

Trademark rights arise from either (1) filing the proper documents with the Patent and Trademark Office (PTO) for a federal registration; or (2) actually using the mark. Federal registration is not required to establish rights in a mark, but it can provide you important benefits. For instance, a federal registration can give you nationwide rights (with certain qualifications) and provide you with certain advantages in any infringement lawsuit. The term of a federal trademark registration is 10 years, with 10 year renewal terms. You must use the mark "in commerce"– meaning international or interstate commerce– before a federal registration will be issued to you. The use must be a real commercial use in the ordinary course of trade, and not a transaction to merely establish use in commerce.

Arbitrary and fanciful marks are easiest to protect

An international class must be assigned to the goods or services identified in your application for registration. You can do it, or the PTO will do it for you. A table of international classes can be found in "Basic Facts About Registering a Trademark" from the U.S. Department of Commerce Patent and Trademark Office.

The cost of applying for a trademark registration depends upon whether you are already using the mark in commerce. If you are, you may file a "use" application for an application filing fee of $245 for each class of goods or services listed. You must file an "intent to use" application if you are not already using the mark in commerce but have a bona fide intention to do so. After filing an intent to use application, you must use the mark in commerce and submit an allegation of use within a specified period of time. The fee for an intent to use application is also $245 per class, and an additional $100 per class must be paid when the allegation of use is filed.

The cost of applying for a trademark registration varies

The symbol "®" can be used with your mark only after the registration has been issued. Prior to registration, you may use the "TM" symbol for a trademark, and the "SM" symbol for a service mark. These symbols will serve to alert the public to your claim to the mark before the registration is issued.

Using a Trademark

The successful trademark complements and distinguishes your company

The successful trademark is one that complements and distinguishes your company and product images. It should be used in all advertising, packaging, and correspondence. Maintain the same logo over time, since recognition is crucial. Register trademarks, since the registration discourages imitators and gives you increased legal clout. Be aware that trademarks do not provide ironclad protection. If you feel that someone has infringed on your trademark, *you* must initiate action, since the government won't do it on its own.

Copyrights

Copyright law protects "original works of authorship" such as computer software, books, designs, photographs, sculptures and other original works. It does not protect titles, names, short phrases or slogans. To protect the latter, you must look to trademark law. Copyright law gives the copyright owner the exclusive rights to copy, publicly perform or display, distribute or modify the copyrighted work. This protection extends to published and unpublished works. A copyright is in effect for the author's life plus fifty years.

The owners of all works published before March 1, 1989, were required to place a copyright notice on the work if they wished to claim copyright protection. It is optional for later works, but highly recommended because it informs the public that the owner claims copyrights in the work. If someone later infringes your work and it bears your copyright notice, a court will not allow the infringer to claim that he or she did not realize the work was owned by someone else. For all works except phonorecords and sound recordings, the notice should contain the following:

Your work is automatically copyrighted when you create it

> The symbol "©", or the word "copyright," or the abbreviation "Copr."
> The year of first publication of your work.
> The name of the owner of the copyright.

For example,   "© 1996 Megasoft Corporation".

For phonorecords and sound recordings, the copyright notice is the same except the ℗ symbol is substituted for the "©" symbol. All copyright notices must be placed in a location that gives reasonable notice.

Registration

No registration is required to secure a copyright, because you automatically acquire copyrights when you create an original work. However, registration is important to your legal rights. For instance, you can't sue for copyright infringement unless you have applied for copyright registration. In addition, if you register within three months after you publish the work or before someone infringes your work, you will be entitled to receive statutory damages and attorney's fees against the infringer. The threat of such awards provides a strong incentive for any infringer to avoid violating your copyrights.

Registration is important to your legal rights

The copyright registration filing fee is only $20. For copyright forms and information, contact the Copyright Office Forms Hotline at (202) 707-9100. Be sure to ask for Circular 1, "Copyright Basics." It provides an excellent overview of copyrights and the registration process.

Trade Secrets

Trade secret law might protect your information when trademark, copyright or patent law will not. To qualify for trade secret protection, the information must satisfy three requirements. First, it must be a secret. That is, it must not be known to or readily ascertainable from others. Second, it must be valuable. Third, the owner must have taken reasonable precautions to protect the information from unauthorized use or disclosure. Trade secret law can protect just about anything that meets those requirements. Examples are computer source code, customer lists, manufacturing processes, cost data, marketing analysis and preferred suppliers. No governmental registration or filing is necessary to protect trade secrets or to secure greater legal protection.

There are three requirements to qualify for trade secret protection

One drawback is that the owner does not have an absolute right to prevent disclosure or use of the trade secret. You can only prevent use or disclosure by improper means, such as a disclosure or use that is in breach of a confidentiality agreement, some uses or disclosures of trade secrets by a current or former employee, or industrial espionage. Trade secret law will not protect your secret from reverse engineering or development of the information from public sources.

One advantage of a trade secret is the duration of its protection. Protection will last as long as all three elements of a trade secret are satisfied.

Patents

If your business will be based on a novel invention, you need to become familiar with at least the basics of patent law. Patents are a complex subject, and this chapter can only provide an overview. A patent is "a right guaranteed by the government to a person or corporation which gives its holder the right to exclude others form making, using, or selling the invention claimed in the patent deed."

There are three types of patents

There are three types of patents– utility, design, and plant. A utility patent can be granted for a "new, useful and nonobvious process, machine, manufactured article, composition, or an improvement in any of these items." A design patent can be granted for a "new, original, and ornamental design for an article of manufacture". A design patent only protects the appearance of an article and not its structure or utilitarian features. Filing an application for a design patent is significantly easier than filing one for a utility patent. A plant patent can be granted to anyone who "has invented, or discovered and asexually reproduced any distinct and new variety of plant, including cultivated spores, mutants, hybrids, and newly found seedlings, other than a tuber-propagated plant or a plant found in an uncultivated state." Utility and plant patents are in effect for seventeen years from the date of issue, while design patents are in effect for only fourteen years.

A patent may be compared to a hunting license. It enables you to legally "go after" a patent infringer through a suit filed in court. The government does not seek out patent infringers; rather, you must take action against them. In such a suit, you ask the judge to order that the infringer no longer make, use, or sell the invention claimed. You also typically ask for monetary damages to compensate for the loss of income sustained during the period when the patent was infringed.

The government does not seek out patent infringers

Be aware the patent is merely a license to sue, not a guarantee that the suit will be successful. There are many reasons why the suit might not be successful, including the fact that the patent might be shown by the infringer to be invalid, despite having already been issued by the government! Even if your law suit is successful, the legal fees– $50,000 or more is typical– for pursuing infringement action could be greater than the infringer is ever able to pay. And this says nothing for the loss in your time and energy during what may be a very long, frustrating process, particularly if more than one infringement action needs to be filed at the same time.

You have to spend a significant amount of money to obtain a patent, even if you do a large amount of the work yourself. You can perform a search yourself, otherwise you may pay someone else from $400 to $1000. Depending on the complexity of the patent application; you may pay an attorney from $1000 to $5000 to prepare the patent application. The cost can go considerably higher.

The cost of a patent can get very high

Fewer than one patent in ten pays for even its own filing cost, let alone a significant profit to its inventor. A patent is *no guarantee of commercial success.* Most people who file patent applications are not business people– they are inventors. A patent is only a starting point in the entrepreneurial process.

This introduction is not intended to dissuade you from pursuing a patent. It remains one of the best forms of insurance available to inventors and companies which generate proprietary products or processes. You need to be aware, however, that receiving a patent requires money and effort, and that you still have a long way to go in building a successful business.

The Patent Process

A patent is only a starting point in the entrepreneurial process

To be eligible to receive a United States patent, you must file a patent application *within one year* of the date on which you first publish, publicly use, sell, or offer your invention for sale. To be eligible for most foreign patents, you must file your application *before* you take any of the above steps. Patent materials are submitted to:

Patent and Trademark Office (PTO)
Washington, D.C. 20231

Once you file a patent application, you usually have to wait between one and three years for the Patent Office to review and decide whether or not to grant you a patent. By filing a patent you establish *potentially valuable* rights against any inventor who later conceives of the same invention and applies for a patent on it. However, during this waiting, or "pending" period, *you have no legal rights to file a suit against an infringer.* You may send the infringer a warning letter, but you only receive your right to sue when the patent is issued.

You only receive the right to sue an infringer when the patent is issued

If you plan to have your invention manufactured by another company or plan to sell your invention outright to them, filing for a patent may be a precondition for that company to look at your invention. They will usually insist that you sign a waiver agreement, which states that they will only respect the rights to your invention to the extent to which these rights are covered by the "claims" in your patent. Consequently, if your patent claims prove to be deficient, your protection may be limited or non-existent.

How Much Can You Do Yourself?

You can do it all yourself in spite of the fact that the legalities can be complex, but you need to be willing to invest a significant amount of time learning the process. You read about prison inmates who take law bar examinations without ever going to law school. They just read all the materials in the prison library. By the same token, you can teach yourself the field of patent law. However, most people turn the whole process over to an attorney and hope that the costs do not become exorbitant. They do not wish to become bogged down in all of the legalities of writing a good patent application.

It is not difficult to write a patent application; however, writing one that *really protects you* is a fine art. This is where the experience of a good patent attorney is invaluable. If you are serious about doing it yourself, you should get the book *Patent It Yourself* (see citation at the end of the chapter). It is a complete guide to the patenting process. Even if you hire an attorney to do your patent work, knowing this material can help you facilitate his work and can reduce your cost.

A good patent attorney can help you write an application that really protects you

Conclusion

Trademarks, copyrights, trade secrets and patents can be valuable property for your company. Take the necessary steps to register rights in that property. Realize, however, that in almost all cases *you* must initiate action when you think there is an infringement. Legal action is often slow and almost always costly, but if you register your rights in a timely manner you will usually have the right to seek attorney's fees from an infringer. If you have information that does not qualify as a patent, trademark or copyrightable work, consider protecting it as a trade secret.

You **must initiate action when you think there is an infringement**

References

1.   Jones, Stacy V. *The Inventor's Patent Handbook.* New York: The Dial Press, 1969.

2.   Levy, Richard C. *Inventing and Patenting Sourcebook.* Detroit: Gale Research, 1990.

3.   Pressman, David. *Patent It Yourself.* New York: McGraw-Hill Book Company, 1979.

4.   Richardson, Robert O. *How to Get Your Own Patent.* New York: Sterling Publishing Co., 1981.

5.   Russell, J. Thomas et al. *Kleppner's Advertising Procedure*, 10 Ed. Englewood Cliffs, New Jersey: Prentice Hall, Inc., 1986.

6.   Samuels, Jeffery M. *Patent, Trademark, and Copyright Laws*. Washington, D.C.: The Bureau of National Affairs, Inc., 1987.

7.   *General Information Concerning Patents*. Washington, D.C.:   U.S. Department of Commerce, Patent and Trademark Office, 1989.

4

Marketing Research

*"You don't become successful in business by trying to be successful;
you become successful by meeting customers' needs."*
Peter Drucker

One of the most common reasons businesses flounder or fail is that management is not in touch with what customers want. The company makes products that management wants, but not necessarily what people are willing to buy. The basic purpose of marketing research is *to give management a clear idea of who customers are and what they want.* Market research also provides information on the size of markets and whether or not they are growing.

Although market research should be an on-going project, it is especially critical in the following circumstances:

Marketing research helps you know your customers and what they want

- As a business is being planned, before the doors open;
- Before new products are introduced;
- When sales are declining; and
- When new competitors enter the market.

The market information you gather helps you formulate a marketing strategy, which describes how to design, price, promote, package, service, and distribute products or services.

Types of Marketing Research

The two major types of marketing research are *qualitative* and *quantitative* research. In general, qualitative research uses a small sample and does not employ statistical analysis to arrive at conclusions. It typically costs less, is more appropriate at early stages of the research process, and provides less precise conclusions than does quantitative research. Quantitative research draws from a large enough sample so that researchers can analyze responses

The two major types of research are qualitative and quantitative

quantitively and employ statistical techniques. The primary types of qualitative research in this chapter are:

- Expert interviews;
- Case studies; and
- Focus groups.

The main forms of quantitative research are:

- Secondary data studies;
- Experiments; and
- Questionnaires.

All of these research methods are described in this chapter.

The research method you choose should be based on the type of information you want to get

The research method you choose should be based on the type of information you want to get. Although the qualitative methods can generate in-depth information, it may be biased. In expert interviews, case studies, and focus groups you are hearing from only a few sources. If you feel confident of those sources, the research may be valid. In many cases, however, the opinion of a few is not representative of the way the entire market might respond, and therefore you have faulty information. Because quantitative techniques gather information from a greater number of sources, the data might be more reliable. In many cases, qualitative techniques initially generate ideas, and quantitative techniques are then used to substantiate initial qualitative findings.

You can do research yourself, but it requires considerable time

The second issue in choosing a research method is how much money you are willing to spend. You can do any of the research methods yourself, or you can hire a marketing research consultant. A consultant typically charges $50/hour or more, so the research can easily cost $5000. Expert interviews, case studies, and secondary data are research methods you can do yourself if you have the time. Focus groups, questionnaires, and experiments are more involved. You can do them yourself, but you must learn the techniques and invest quite a bit of time in the research process. The information in this book describes each of these research techniques, but you would be wise to read other books that describe research techniques in more depth.

Qualitative Research

Expert Interviews

An *expert interview* is a discussion with someone who knows much about the industry you are researching, perhaps a person who has competed in the industry for a long time. In some cases, a person with such experience may not be threatened by a newcomer to the industry and will "spill his guts." You may have to talk to quite a few people before you find one willing to share her experiences, but your efforts will be rewarded if you perservere. Be honest when you approach such people and communicate your intentions of starting a business. They will quickly decide whether they want to talk to you. If you misrepresent the fact that you are a potential competitor, they will see right through you.

An expert may not be threatened by a newcomer

There are other places to search for experts. *Adjacent industries* are possibilities. Assume that you make furniture and want to find out more how to market it. If you call other manufacturers and ask them for help, they may not respond, especially if you have similar products. An industry adjacent to furniture building would be the lighting industry. Typically, lamps and furniture are sold in the same stores and through the same channels. If you spoke to a lighting manufacturer, they would not be afraid of giving you information because it would not be used competitively against them.

Retailers, sales reps, suppliers, and industry associations, as well as customers, can be experts on an industry. If you make furniture, speak to the most prominent furniture retailers about customers and their buying habits. Sales reps are independent business people who sell different manufacturers' products, usually to retail outlets (see Chapter 10). Since they are in contact with a large number of manufacturers and retailers, they often know the industry very well. If there are only a few suppliers to your industry, they often can tell you a lot about it. If you want to open a pizza restaurant, the few suppliers of food products to your area will be able to tell you quite a bit, including sales trends, which of your competitors does the most business with them, etc. Industry associations usually gather statistics on the industry and survey customers. The officers of an association, especially if they were involved with the research, are often experts on an industry. Experienced customers can tell you a lot about an industry. If you make boats, talk to some old-timer on the lake who has been buying boats for fifty years. He'll know a lot

Experts in an industry can be found in many places

about the industry and customers. In an expert interview, you are seeking information from someone who knows your industry.

Focus Groups

Researchers use focus groups to generate ideas or gather information about customers. The advantage of a focus group over interviews with individuals is that the people can respond to each other. One of them may bring up a point that another had not thought about, and thus the group can provide depth of information that individual interviews cannot. A focus group is usually comprised 6 to 12 consumers and meets for up to two hours. In many cases a focus group is conducted as initial research. With the ideas generated from the group, a questionnaire is designed and customers are surveyed so that responses from a larger number of people are obtained.

> **Researchers use focus groups to generate ideas or gather information about customers**

Just about *any* business can get a group of its present or potential customers together and quiz them as to their product preferences, views about competitors, and buying habits. If you own a fitness center, call 12 members, offer them a free lunch, and tell them you want their honest opinions about your center and fitness in general. Many customers are anxious to express their opinions on any topic.

You need to plan a focus group. Invite 6 to 12 people. A group less than six tends not to have the interaction and idea generation that you would like. A group of more than 12 becomes hard to manage and some people do not get much chance to participate. In general, you should try to have groups that are relatively homogeneous. For the health club, you might want to have separate groups for aerobics and weight lifters. If those two differing groups were together, they might be reticent to voice their true opinions (like weight lifters wanting to tear out the dance floor so that more weights could be added). You therefore first need to decide if you need several focus groups for the different types of customers that you serve. Strangers in focus groups tend to be less inhibited and express their opinions more freely. Try not to assemble a group of people who know each other well.

> **The advantage of a focus group is that the people can respond to each other**

A focus group needs a *moderator*. She introduces the general topics for discussion and brings the discussion back on track if it wanders. The moderator should blend into the group and not appear different from the group. For example, male groups usually have male moderators and young groups usually have young moderators, etc. Although the moderator needs to have a well thought-out plan for the session, she tries to play a minor role and let the discussion sustain itself on the various topics introduced. She should attempt to tone down those who are outspoken and tend to dominate discussions. You should not have an employee of your company be the moderator. You want people to express honest opinions, including negative ones, and many are reticent to do so knowing a member of the organization is present.

Most focus groups are recorded on a tape recorder. This relieves the moderator or anyone else of having to take notes during the session. Some focus groups are video-taped, which helps you to review participants' reactions and gestures. Some professional marketing research firms have special rooms equipped with cameras and one-way mirrors, so that you see observe people's reactions "live." A problem with this is that some people become inhibited with a camera pointing at them or knowing that someone is watching them.

Focus groups are excellent tools for gathering in-depth information on a variety of topics. You can usually obtain much richer data from these than from questionnaires. Their primary drawback is the sample size. You may get good information, but is it representative of all customers? To substantiate findings in focus groups, surveys are usually performed afterwards.

The primary drawback of a focus group is its sample size

Case Studies

A *case study* is an in-depth research project of a particular person or situation. The advantage of this technique is the depth of information obtained. The disadvantage, similar to focus groups, is that you are studying only one or a few subjects and therefore the results may be biased. Assume that you manufacture fishing poles and you want to understand the mind set of potential customers. In a case study approach, you would pick one or only a few persons and seek to understand all of their considerations in purchasing a new fishing pole. Perhaps you would go fishing with them and quiz them about what features they like and dislike in poles. Perhaps you would talk to them about the poles they own and what their thought process was in deciding to buy them. Perhaps you would go with them to a local fishing shop and ask them about the products there and how they are merchandised. In a case study, you try to determine *all* of the relevant variables that affect your subject and the decisions that they make.

A case study gives an in-depth look at a particular person

Assume that you own the same fishing pole company and are perplexed by the fact that some retailers to whom you sell are able to move many poles while others move almost none. A case study approach to this problem would be to go to both a retail store that has high sales and to one that has low sales and observe how the poles are sold. Do salespeople push them? Where are they displayed in the store? What competitive poles are stocked? These are only a few questions to be answered which could explain the different sales levels. The basic approach of a case study is to study only a few units but obtain in-depth information.

Quantitative Research

Secondary Data

Secondary data contain research information which is gathered by someone else but that you are able to use. The advantages of secondary data are that they are not expensive and in most cases are accurate (but check the sources). The disadvantage is that you rarely can find just the information you are looking for– you have to settle for what you get.

Secondary data usually relate to industry structure. They include statistics on total industry sales, number of businesses, industry payroll, etc. These describe more the *suppliers* in the industry than the consumers. Some people believe that marketing research relates strictly to users of products and services, and therefore this type of information should be considered *industry structure*. Whether the information describes customers or the industry, it is still helpful to you in formulating a marketing strategy. Therefore, it is included in this chapter on marketing research. You will see reference to the same information in other sections that deal with industry structure.

> **Secondary data contain research information which is gathered by someone else but that you are able to use**

The U.S. Government publishes incredible amounts of information, some of which is valuable to certain businesses. The Census Bureau publishes business industry statistics every five years in the *Census of Retail Trade, Census of Wholesale Trade, Census of Service Industries, Census of Manufactures, Census of Mineral Industries, Census of Construction Industries*, and *Census of Agriculture*. Each census provides data on the number of companies, sales, number of employees, total payroll, expenses, and other statistics. They are provided for the entire U.S., by state, and by county. State and county statistics are reported in large, general industries. Federal statistics are cited by specific, narrowly defined industries. Besides the business censuses, the U.S. Government also publishes the *Census of Population* and the *Census of Housing*. All U.S. Census documents are available at different libraries in Washington which

> **The U.S. Government is an excellent source of data**

are designated Official U.S. Publication Depositories. The Internal Revenue Service publishes extensive financial information on industries in the *IRS Source Book of Statistics of Income*. Contact your local IRS office to obtain the book.

Industry Studies. There are two primary sources of industry studies. The first is exhaustive, book-length reports that are usually done by economists. You can look for such references in the card catalogs of major libraries. If you have access to a database system which provides references to other libraries, you can often get the study on "inter-library" loan from another library.

> **There are two primary sources of industry studies**

The second type of industry study is much shorter, typically done by consulting or investment companies. Examples of such companies are Wall Street research houses, Arthur D. Little, Stanford Research Institute, Business Trends Analysts, Business Communications Company, Martin & Martin, E.R.C. statistics, and others. Business Trend Analysts, Inc. in New York, prints a listing of over 150 industry studies that it will sell. The cost of such studies ranges from $1,000 to $2,000. Business Trend Analysts, Inc.'s phone number is (516) 462-2410.

Company Directories. Several directories publish information on both public and private U.S. companies. The *Thomas Registry of American Manufacturers*, the *Dun & Bradstreet Million Dollar Directory* and *Middle Market Directory*, *Standard & Poor's Register of Corporations*, and the various Moody's publications list companies by industry. Some give limited financial information. Check your local libraries for these directories. Dun & Bradstreet compiles credit reports on all companies of significant size and charges a fee to member companies which want the information. You need to use this information with caution. It is not audited and some is self-reported, therefore there can be errors in the information.

> **Several directories publish information on both public and private U.S. companies**

Company Documents. Some companies publish annual reports which contain company information. Write to the company and ask them to send one. If a firm has publicly traded stock, it must file Securities and Exchange Commission (SEC) quarterly report 10-Q and annual report 10-K. These are public information and can be obtained by contacting the SEC. The companies are required to provide complete financial data and also operating information.

Business Information Guides. Several guides to sources of business information are published. The following three are some of the more widely distributed ones:

Where to Find Business Information: A Worldwide Guide for Everyone Who Needs the Answers to Business Questions. This reference book lists over 5,000 publications of current interest.

An Annotated Guide for Harvard Business School Students. It is a superb guide to most of the business reference books found in libraries.

Encyclopedia of Business Information Sources. By industry, this book lists sources of information, trade associations, trade journals, and other pertinent industry information.

Check your local library to see if it has one of these information guides. If not, you should encourage them to borrow it from another library through their lending program or purchase one of them. They are very helpful in finding industry information.

Financial Information Sources. Several companies publish industry financial data, which includes financial ratios and common-size financial statements. Most libraries will have one of the following sources of financial information.

Several companies publish industry financial data

- Robert Morris Associates
- Dun & Bradstreet
- Standard and Poor's

Databases. On-line computer databases are becoming increasingly popular. Some of them contain information on specific industries. The following resources provide information on databases:

Directory of Online Databases

Information Industry Market Place: An International Directory of Information Products and Services

Trade Associations. Just about every industry has one or more trade associations whose purpose is to promote the entire industry. They typically publish trade publications. The associations often conduct industry surveys and then print the results. Contact any associations in your industry and see what information they have available. If you are unsure what associations exist in your industry, consult the *Encyclopedia of Associations*, the *Directory of Directories*, or the *National Trade and Professional Associations of the United States and Canada and Labor Unions.*

Experiments

An experiment is a situation where you manipulate a variable, hold others constant, and look at the effect on another variable. For example, assume you are trying to decide between two different types of packaging for a model boat kit you are manufacturing. You decide to try the first type of packaging at Lake City Hobby in Seattle and the second type at the Hobby Hut in Renton. After three months, with permission of the stores, you reverse the arrangement to see whether one type of package tends to sell better in both stores. If so, and other factors seem to be equal, you adopt that package design for the ensuing production runs. The advantage of the experiment over other research techniques is that you can try different marketing approaches in a "live" situation. Asking people what they would do is one matter. Observing what they do is another. Like other research techniques, an experiment allows you to test different marketing approaches on a smaller scale before trying them on a broader scale.

The advantage of the experiment is that you can try different marketing approaches in a "live" situation

Experimental Variable. There are three general classes of experimental variables: independent, dependent, and control. In the boat example, the independent variable was the one you manipulated, which was the packaging of the boat. The dependent variable was the one which you observed to see the effects– sales of the boat. Control variables are other factors which can affect the dependent variable, but you try to keep them constant.

The key to a successful experiment is to control other "confounding" factors to ensure that changes in the dependent variable (sales) are due only to changes in the independent variable (packaging). To control such factors as well as possible, several steps might help. First, the stores should be comparable in sales, merchandise selection, type of customers and levels and types of advertising. Second, the experimenter in this case should make sure that the boat models were similarly priced and displayed in both stores. Third, the local economies of the stores should be assessed for similarity during the test period, including possible seasonality effects to assure that differences in sales were not the result of differences in those factors. Fourth, the experimenter should check to be sure that competing brands of boats were not introduced at just

The key to a successful experiment is to control other "confounding" factors

one of the stores and not at the other during the test. Fifth, the experimenter should also make sure that salespeople promoted the boats similarly at both stores. Failure to control for possible differences in such variables between stores can yield misleading results.

A variety of marketing questions might be answered through properly controlled experiments. Product features might be changed and customer reaction assessed. Prices can be changed. Different types of promotion might be used. In similar market areas, you might try newspaper advertising in one and television advertising in the other. If you are considering hiring inhouse salespeople, try one or two in a few areas to see how they do. Perhaps you are considering direct marketing your products and have obtained a large mailing list. Rather than mail to all of the people on the list, which is costly, mail to a small experimental group and gauge the response.

Marketing questions may be answered through properly controlled experiments

A multitude of experimental designs exists. Some have only two groups. One receives the experimental treatment (change in price, packaging, etc.) while a control group does not. Some designs can have as many as eight groups. To select a design, you must study a marketing research text which discusses in detail experimental design. Several books are listed in the bibliography at the end of this chapter. Marketing research consultants can assist you in design or they can perform the entire experiment for you, if you are willing to pay the fees. Experiments need to be carefully designed. You can do it yourself, but you need to be well versed in the different possible approaches.

Questionnaires

A questionnaire, or market survey, is a tool for gathering information about current or potential customers. It is one of the most widely used forms of marketing research. A questionnaire is usually considered quantitative research, which lends itself to statistical analysis, if a large enough sample size is used. A survey can range from an exhaustive phone survey of your current nationwide customers to a one page questionnaire that customers fill out while in your store. Information gathered from a questionnaire is used to formulate the marketing strategy for the firm, which includes how products are designed, priced, promoted, packaged, serviced, and distributed.

A questionaire is a tool for gathering information about customers

Steps in Questionnaire Development. Listed below are the traditional steps in questionnaire development:

1. Decide on Purpose of Questionnaire
2. Select Sampling Method
3. Decide Number and Types of Questions on Each Topic
4. Design the Topic Sequence
5. Write Questions and Response Categories
6. Decide on Layout and Format
7. Pretest and Revise

The sequence may vary somewhat on different projects, and in many cases it is a cyclical process– you proceed through several steps, then go back and revise what you did previously. For example, you may have decided that questions concerning customers' opinions of competitors should come near the end of the survey. However, after writing out the questionnaire you find that respondents cannot answer some other questions relating to the entire industry until they have thought about competitors. Therefore, you may need to back up and redesign the questionnaire so that competitor questions come earlier in the survey.

The process of designing a questionnaire is a cyclical one

There are many books and references on writing questionnaires. You can obtain a short handbook entitled *How to Write a Questionnaire* by contacting:

University Press
1719 Dearborn
Missoula, MT 59801
(800) 243-6840
Cost: $7.00

Before you begin a survey research project, you should read this or the many other references on questionnaire development.

Internet Market Research

Many product positioning ideas can be obtained inexpensively by "seeing" what other people are doing and by communicating with them about their interests. The World Wide Web and the other features of the Internet are incredible tools for finding out what other people are doing and for getting feedback on your ideas.

You can search the World Wide Web for similar products or service ideas through any of the numerous search engines. You can find information on the web by typing keywords into a "search engine" and it will search all the websites on the web looking for information that matches your keywords. There is a website that contains many of the most popular search engines on the web. To get there, enter http://www.search.com.

Much research can be done on the Internet through newsgroups or websites

Additionally, there are numerous newsgroups and listservs done over the Internet for many different topics. Many of them may have participants from your target market. You can find lists of listservs and newsgroups on all the major on-line services. Additionally, many of the major on-line services have their own bulletin boards and forums on topics that may be of interest to your target market. Most listservs and newsgroups do not have joining restrictions, but you do have to use discretion in using these to actually market your product or service. Most people do not mind offering information but do resent being pitched through this forum, and many listservs and newsgroups will remove you from the list if you do this.

Conclusion

Marketing research is especially critical at early stages of growth

Marketing research is important at all stages of company growth, but it is especially critical at early stages. As a young firm, you cannot afford to make marketing mistakes. Blunders can put you under. The purpose of marketing research is to understand your customers and what motivates them to buy. Since your customers' tastes and motivations change over time, the need for research is on-going.

References

1. Brownstone, David M. *Where to Find Business Information: A Worldwide Guide for Everyone Who Needs the Answers to Business Questions.* New York: Wiley, 1982.

2. Daniells, Lorna M. *An Annotated Guide for Harvard Business School Students*, revised edition. Boston: Baker Library, Graduate School of Business Administration, Harvard University, 1979.

3. Luck, Adele K., Wales, Mary F., and Rubin, Cynthia B. *Marketing Research.* Englewood Cliffs, New Jersey: Prentice Hall Inc., 1982.

4. Marlow, Cecilia A. *Directory of Directories.* Detroit, Gale Research Co., 1991.

5. Parasuraman, A. *Marketing Research.* Reading, Mass: Addison-Wesley Publishing Co, Inc., 1986.

6. Timmons, Jeffry A. *New Venture Creation,* 2nd Edition. Homewood, Illinois: Irwin, 1990.

7. *Annual Statement Studies.* Philadelphia: Robert Morris Associates, 1991.

8. *Encyclopedia of Associations,* 31st Edition. Detroit: Gale Research Co., 1996.

9. *Encyclopedia of Business Information Sources,* Eleventh Edition. Detroit: Gale Research Co., 1996.

10. *Encyclopedia of Information Systems and Services.* Detroit: Gale Research, 1989.

11. *Directory of Online Databases.* Santa Monica, California: Guadra Associates, 1989.

12. *Dun and Bradstreet Million Dollar Directory,* 1996 Edition. New York: Dun and Bradstreet, 1996.

13. *Industry Norms and Key Business Ratios.* New York: Dun & Bradstreet, 1989.

14. *Information Industry Market Place: An International Directory of Information Products and Services.* New York: R.R. Bowker, 1982.

15. *National Trade and Professional Associations of the United States and Canada and Labor Unions.* Columbia Books, 1996.

16. *Standard & Poor's Register of Corporations, Directors, and Executives.* New York, Standard & Poor's Corp., 1996.

17. *Thomas Register of American Manufacturers,* 76th Edition. Thomas publishing Co., 1989.

5

Regulations on Doing Business

"It is better to beg forgiveness
than to ask permission in the first place."
Unknown

Most entrepreneurs smile and nod when they read the above quote. There are times, however, when this philosophy will backfire on you. You may be ignorant of the Internal Revenue Services' rules, but the IRS will fine you heartily when it finds you out. You can face severe consequences if you break certain laws regulating businesses. You don't need to be a business law specialist to start a business, but you do need to be aware of some of the basics. The first section of this chapter describes the licenses and registrations which you are required to obtain. The second section describes the taxes which apply to your business.

You can face severe consequences if you break certain laws regulating business

Licenses and Registrations

Federal Requirements

All businesses except sole proprietors with no employees are required to have a Federal Employer Identification Number (EIN). Go to your local IRS office or call the IRS at (800) 829-3676 to obtain your EIN, for which there is no charge. The IRS and the Social Security Administration use this number to identify your business on all returns, statements and other documents. If you are a sole proprietor with no employees, you will use your Social Security Number for these purposes.

If you have employees, you need to obtain an employee identification number

The authors would like to thank Ms. Susan Peterson
of the Seattle law firm of Helsell Fetterman LLP for her
contributions to this chapter.

State Requirements

Master Business License. All businesses operating in Washington–including sole proprietors, partnerships, corporations and limited liability companies– must obtain a Master Business License. The state has implemented a one-stop registration service. By completing a three page Master Business Application and making a single payment, you satisfy all state requirements that most businesses must meet. Included are your registration with the Department of Revenue (for B&O Tax, Retail Sales Tax and any other applicable state taxes), registration for State Unemployment Insurance, registration for Industrial Insurance (also known as worker's compensation) and Trade Name Registration. Upon filing the application and paying the $15.00 fee, you receive a nine digit Unified Business Identification Number (UBI Number) which is used by all state agencies to identify your business. Your actual business license will follow in the mail. You can obtain your Master Business License by contacting any of the 48 local UBI Service Offices located at the departments of Employment Security, Labor and Industries, and Revenue or by contacting:

> Department of Licensing
> Business License Services
> Olympia, Washington 98504-8006
> Telephone: (360) 753-4401

Last year the Business License Services unit answered approximately 133,000 calls. The best time to call is between 8:00 and 9:00 a.m. and between 4:00 and 5:00 p.m.

In addition, the Business License Services department will provide you with a personalized Licensing Packet. The packet will indicate all State licensing requirements for your particular business (including any that are specific to your business or industry) and the location of the applicable state offices in your area. For example, contractors and engineering firms are subject to additional licensing requirements.

To obtain your packet, call 360-753-4401. Describe the business operation you wish to begin. You will be asked the following information:

- Under what type of business ownership will the business operate?
- Will you be hiring any employees?

You must obtain a Master Business License

The Business License Service will provide you with a packet that indicates licensing requirements

- Where is(are) your geographical area(s) of operation?
- What type of service will be provided or what type of goods will be manufactured or sold?
- Will you be doing business under a name other than the full legal name of the business owner?

Complete the Master Business Application and return all forms to the Master Licensing Service or any UBI office.

Trade Name Registration. If your business is operating with a business name other than your legal name, you must register the trade name with the Master License Service of the Department of Licensing. This can be accomplished on the application for your Master Business License. Registration of the trade name gives notice to other businesses that a particular trade name is being used in Washington and assists the public in determining the identity of the business owner. You may call MLS at 1-900-463-6000 to find out whether a trade name is registered in Washington, and/or the names and addresses of the owners or parties of interest in a business. Each call costs $4.95 for the first minute and .50 for each additional minute. Last year there were 25,948 search requests answered. The registration fee for the trade name is $5.00. The trade name registration is good until canceled and need not be renewed. If your company is incorporated, you need not register the name. Trade name registration is not a substitute for seeking a federal trademark registration (see Chapter 3).

> **If you want to protect your business name, you should register it as a trade name**

Local Requirements

If your business is located within the city limits of a municipality, you may need a city business license. This is the city's way of ensuring that zoning, fire, and building regulations are observed. Fees are usually assessed by the size of a company. You can obtain information on city business license requirements by contacting your City Hall and asking to be connected with the licensing division.

> **You may need a city business license**

In addition, counties in Washington require certain types of businesses to obtain county licenses. Call your county office and ask for the licensing division. They will ask you what type of business you own and will let you know if it needs to be licensed through them.

Annual Licensing and Fees

All organizations registered with the Secretary of State must annually pay a license fee and/or file a list of officers and directors (known as the annual report) with the Corporations Division of the Secretary of State.

All organizations registered with the Secretary of State must pay an annual license fee

For corporations that are "profit", the renewal fee is $50.00 plus a handling fee of $9.00. There is no annual report fee. There is no annual corporate license for nonprofit corporations, but there is an annual report fee of $10.00. Limited liability companies and partnerships must annually pay a license fee and file a list of members and managers.

All licenses obtained through the Master License Service are renewed at the same time each year. The business will receive a notice listing all your renewable licenses about 45 days before they expire.

Taxes

Federal Income Tax

All businesses must comply with the federal income tax laws. You are required to pay estimated federal income taxes quarterly, based on projected profits. This is the IRS' way of getting periodic payments from you instead of waiting (and hoping) to receive one big check on April 15th of the following year. You are allowed some latitude if you underestimate taxes and pay the difference when you file your return for the year, but you are fined if you underestimate by too large of an amount. While individuals pay taxes based on a calendar year with returns due April 15, certain businesses may choose to be taxed based on a fiscal year that is different from the calendar year. Federal income tax returns for those businesses must be filed on the 15th day of the third month after the end of the fiscal year.

All businesses must comply with federal income and Social Security taxes

Internal Revenue Service forms and other useful information are available from the IRS in their Business Tax Kit, which is available by visiting your local IRS office or calling (800) 829-3676. For assistance on federal tax questions, call (800) 829-4059.

State and Local Taxes

Washington State has approximately 360,000 registered businesses. Sixty thousand of those businesses pay 98 percent of all the taxes collected.

Business and Occupations (B&O) Tax. Washington does not have a state income tax, but it does have a state Business and Occupations Tax. You are required to pay this tax for the privilege of engaging in business activities within the state. The tax is based on the gross sales, gross receipts or gross income of your business. The rate of tax depends upon the type of business activity you are engaged in. 1995 tax rates ranged from .011 percent to 3.3 percent. In addition, a surtax equal to 4.5 percent of the tax payable is imposed for the period from January 1, 1995 thorough June 30, 1997. However, several categories of businesses are exempted from the surtax.

There is a B & O tax credit available for some small businesses. The credit applies to businesses with a B &O tax liability of less than $70 for monthly filers, $210 for quarterly filers, or $840 for annual filers. The maximum credit is $35 per month, $105 per quarter and $420 per year. For assistance in computing the credit, you can refer to the Special Notice published by the Washington Department of Revenue on this subject. In addition, various other deductions and exemptions are available. For more information, contact:

The rate of the B&O Tax is based on the type of business activity in which you are engaged

Department of Revenue
Taxpayer Information Division
General Administration Building
P.O. Box 47478
Olympia, Washington, 98504-7478

In addition to the tax credits, the legislature has also recognized the importance of removing unnecessary burdens from small businesses that are trying to establish themselves. Therefore, effective July 1, 1996, 140,000 small businesses across the state– those businesses with annual gross revenue of under $24,000 will no longer have to file a tax return. The new law will provide much desired relief for entrepreneurs starting new businesses. Previously, the tax credit for many small businesses canceled out taxes owed to the state. However they still had to file a tax form. The result was wasted effort on everyone's part.

There is a B&O tax credit available for some small businesses

The Department of Revenue estimates the loss to the state will be about $700,000 but the new law will allow the department to concentrate on enforcing tax compliance among larger businesses rather than bringing in more revenues. The small businesses can then concentrate their money and energy on developing a larger client base and providing service to their customers. Small service oriented businesses will benefit the most from this new law. Retailers who gross less than $24,000 will also benefit from the new law but will still have to file tax forms to remit sales tax to the state.

Retail Sales Tax. If your business involves retail sales, you are required to collect the Retail Sales Tax at the time of sale and forward it to the Department of Revenue with your B&O tax. The state tax rate is 6.5 percent, and local governments impose from .5 percent to 1.7 percent of additional tax. State and local retail sales taxes are collected and forwarded together. The Retail Sales Tax applies to the selling price of tangible personal property and selected services purchased by consumers. It is imposed on retail sales of personal property to consumers, rental or leases of tangible personal property (such as equipment, machinery and lodging), and specified services. Food products and manufacturing machinery and equipment are two major exemptions. In addition, a variety of other exemptions and deductions are available.

> **If your business involves retail sales, you are required to collect the Retail Sales Tax**

Use Tax. Use tax is due on the use of any tangible personal property within the state when Washington state retail sales tax was not paid at the time of the purchase or manufacture of the property. Use tax rates are the same as those for retail sales tax.

Property Taxes. In Washington, real property taxes are administered at the county level. The real estate tax covers buildings, structures and other improvements, as well as the land itself. Real property taxes are levied as of January 1 each year, but are payable in two equal installments. You are required to pay at least half of the property taxes by the end of April and the remaining amount by the end of October. Total property taxes are determined by the sum of regular and special levies. Regular levies cannot exceed $10 per $1000 of property value, and there is a six percent limit on the annual increase in regular levy revenues, excluding new construction. Special levies (school, fire, sewer etc.) require the approval of 60 percent of voters.

> **Real property taxes are administered at the county level**

In addition, you are taxed on the personal property owned by your business. Personal property includes items which are generally moveable such as furniture, business machines, non-attached mobile homes, commercial boats, equipment and supplies. The tax is imposed as of January 1 of each year. You are required to submit an annual property listing no later than March 31 of each tax year; the county assessor's office will mail the necessary forms by January 1. Personal property is subject to the same tax rates as real property,

> **You are also taxed on the personal property owned by your business**

and like real property taxes, personal property taxes are payable in two installments, by the end of April and the end of October.

You should contact your county assessor's office for more information on real and personal property reporting requirements, and to determine if you are eligible for any exemptions.

Employment Taxes

If you have any employees, you are required to comply with government regulations covering withholding, social security payments, unemployment insurance, and workers' compensation insurance. You should obtain IRS Publication 15 *Employer's Tax Guide*. It describes in detail the taxes summarized here.

First, you must determine if your workers are "employees" as defined by the state and federal agencies. If you can categorize your workers as "independent contractors" rather than employees, you need not be concerned with these taxes and regulations. The IRS, however, is making a concentrated effort to distinguish workers. Here is why:

You pay less taxes when you have independent contractors

Independent Contractor	Company Employee
Can deduct work expenses	First 2% of work expenses, not deductible
Makes quarterly estimated tax payments	Taxes withheld by employer
Pays full social security and Medicare taxes	Pays 1/2 of taxes; Rest paid by employer
May be able to deduct part of residence as home office	Hard to qualify for home deduction
Can shelter 15% of income, up to $30,000	Retirement savings usually capped at $9500 or less
May be able to hire family members as employees and deduct their salaries	No deduction for paying salaries to other people
Can deduct work related travel	Can deduct only unreimbursed travel

Source: Ernst and Young

The Internal Revenue Service uses a 20 part test to see if a person is an independent contractor or an employee. Workers are generally considered employees if they:

1.   Must comply with the employers' instructions for work.
2.   Receive training from or at the direction of the employer.
3.   Provide services that are integrated into the business.
4.   Provide services that must be rendered personally.
5.   Are aided by assistants who are hired, supervised, and paid by the employer.
6.   Have a continued working relationship with the employer.
7.   Must follow set hours of work.
8.   Work full time for an employer.
9.   Do their work on the employers' premises.
10. Must do their work on a sequence set by the employer.
11. Must submit regular reports to the employer.
12. Receive payments of regular amounts at set intervals.
13. Receive payments for business or traveling expenses.
14. Rely on the employer to furnish the tools and materials.
15. Lack a major investment in the facilities or equipment used to perform the services.
16. Cannot make a profit or suffer a loss from their services.
17. Work for one employer at a time.
18. Do not offer their services to the general public.
19. Can be fired by the employer.
20. May quit work at any time without incurring liability.

Source: Internal Revenue Service

> **The IRS uses a 20 part test to see if a person is an independent contractor or an employee**

> **You may need to set up a federal deposit account for withholdings**

In sum, anyone who performs services for you is an employee if you, as the business owner, can control when, where and how the individual's work is done. IRS Publication 539, *Employment Taxes,* gives examples of the employer-employee relationship. If you want a formal decision as to whether a worker is an employee, file form IRS Form SS-8, *Information for Use in Determining Whether a Worker is an Employee for Federal Employment Taxes and Income Tax Withholding.* Call (800) 829-3676 for any of these IRS forms.

Federal Income Tax Withholding. You are required to complete IRS Form W-4 form for each of your employees, which allows you to calculate how much federal income tax should be withheld from that employee's paycheck. If the total amount of payroll taxes you remit to the IRS per calendar quarter (including Social Security and Medicare, discussed below) exceeds $500, you need to set up a federal deposit account with a local bank. Depending on the amount that you are depositing, federal guidelines determine how often you must make deposits. It ranges from monthly to every three days. The IRS supplies coupons that must be filled out when you make deposits. The bank sends the money directly to the IRS. At the end of each quarter, you file IRS Form 941 which summarizes the amounts that you withheld.

Social Security and Medicare. You are also required to withhold Social Security and Medicare taxes from your employees' paychecks, and to pay an equal amount on your employees' behalf. In 1995, employers were required to withhold 6.2 percent of the first $60,600 of salary or wages for Social Security, and 1.45 percent of all income for Medicare. Equal amounts were required to be paid by the employer. Certain restrictions apply, so be sure to review the IRS' Social Security rules.

> **You are also required to withhold Social Security and Medicare taxes from your employees' paychecks**

If you are a sole proprietor or a partner in a partnership, you are hit hard with Social Security taxes on the net income of your business. You, personally, are required to pay both the employer's and the employee's half of Social Security and Medicare payments. In 1995, sole proprietors' and partners' contribution rate for Social Security was $12.40 percent on the first $60,600 of income, and for Medicaid, 2.90 percent of all income. You are required to remit your Social Security and Medicaid taxes quarterly along with your quarterly estimated federal taxes.

Unemployment Insurance. Unemployment insurance is administered at both the state (SUTA) and federal (FUTA) levels. The insurance provides payments to employees who have been terminated or in certain circumstances have quit a job. FUTA and SUTA payments are due quarterly; you have one month to pay at the end of each quarter. If you have a Federal Deposit Account, you can deposit FUTA in the account along with the appropriate coupon. The SUTA tax rates are based on your experience as an employer, the rate paid by the former business owner, or the average tax rates for businesses in your industry. SUTA taxes are remitted to:

> **Unemployment insurance is administered at both the state and federal levels**

The Employment Security Department
P.O. Box 9046
Olympia, WA 98507-9046
For information, call (360) 902-9360

However, various exemptions are available. You may not have to pay unemployment insurance on the following types of employment:

There are some types of employment where you may not have to pay unemployment insurance

- Family employment, spouse or unmarried children under the age of 18 (for sole proprietors only)
- Insurance agents, insurance solicitors or real estate salespersons paid by commission
- Outside salespersons of merchandise who are paid solely by commission
- Casual labor not in the usual course of your trade or business
- Corporate officers
- Certain beauty and barber shops
- Musicians and entertainers, if exempted by written contract
- Students on small farms
- Spouse and unmarried children under age of 18 of corporate officers on a small farm
- Spouses and unmarried children under age of 18 of sole proprietors regardless of size of farm

Your responsibilities in the unemployment insurance program are discussed in a booklet entitled *Unemployment Tax Information* available at any Employment Security District Tax Office.

Industrial Insurance. Industrial Insurance (workers' compensation) is a state-mandated insurance program that provides compensation and medical benefits to employees injured on the job. When you carry this insurance, you are protected from any legal action for work-place injuries suffered by your employees. If you fail to carry this insurance, you may be subject to severe penalties. Washington law requires all non-exempt employers to cover full-time, part-time, seasonal, or occasional employees with this insurance. In addition, you can elect to include yourself as one of the insured parties.

You *must* provide Industrial Insurance for all employees

You can obtain workers' compensation insurance through the state program or through self-insurance. It is not possible to substitute private insurance. To qualify for self-insurance, employers must meet minimum financial requirements, demonstrate the ability to make prompt payments, and maintain an active safety program. Due to the high cost of medical care, most employers cannot afford the risk of self-insurance. The state program's insurance rates are set by industry classification.

The Washington Department of Labor and Industries requires you to fill out their forms and pay a deposit to begin coverage under the state workers' compensation insurance program. Thereafter, you submit a payroll report within a month of the end of each quarter. To register with the state program or to receive information on exemptions, contact:

Department of Labor and Industries
P.O. Box 44000
Olympia, WA 98504-4000
(360) 902-4200

For more information on the industrial insurance program, you may request a booklet entitled *The Employers Guide to Industrial Insurance.* The book is also available at local offices of the Department of Labor and Industries. Labor and Industries offices are listed in the white or blue pages of the telephone book under Washington, State of.

You can obtain workers' compensation insurance through the state program or through self-insurance

Conclusion

This chapter has provided a brief overview of some of the key business regulations that will affect your business, including licensing and registration, federal taxes, state and local taxes, and employment taxes. Make sure that you abide by the regulations which apply to your company. You can write away directly to these programs for information and forms. Otherwise, accountants and business lawyers usually stay current with these programs and can streamline the process for you.

Be sure to abide by the regulations that apply to your company

There are many other legal issues that arise when operating a business in Washington state. Bookstores usually carry several basic business law books, which can be helpful resources, and from time to time you may have to call upon an attorney well versed in business law.

References

1. *Operating a Business in Washington State: A Business Resource Guide.* Department of Licensing. Olympia, Washington, 1995.

6

Choosing a Form of Business

"It was a friendship founded on business, which is a good deal better than a business founded on friendship."
John D. Rockefeller

One of the decisions you must make early in the life of your firm is the legal form of business. Sole proprietorships, partnerships, corporations and limited liability entities are the four primary forms or organization, and there are several types of partnerships and corporations. There is no *one best* form of organization; it depends on the company and its owners' situation. A description of each of the legal forms is given below along with the considerations in choosing between them.

There is no *one* best form of business

In a *sole proprietorship*, there is one person who owns and controls the business. She alone receives the profit or loss from the company and is personally responsible for the debts. Profits are taxed at her individual income tax rate.

A *partnership* is owned by two or more persons. The most common form of partnership is a *general partnership*, in which all partners legally share equal right to manage the business. Each partner has responsibility for *all* debts of the firm. A partnership agreement dictates management responsibilities, how profits are to be distributed, and other issues important to the partners. The partnership itself is not taxed, rather profits are allocated to each of the owners and they are taxed at individual tax rates. Figure 6-1 the end of this chapter lists common issues addressed in partnership agreements. Some business people state that the only issue of

In a partnership, profits are allocated to each of the owners and they are taxed individually

The authors would like to thank Mr. Danferd Henke of the Seattle law firm of Helsell Fetterman LLP for his contributions to this chapter.

critical importance is a provision for breaking up the partnership. If the business is doing well, most issues can be worked out between owners as they come up. However, if the business is doing poorly and somebody wants out, partners wish they had clearly spelled out how to break up the partnership fairly.

A *limited liability partnership* is a partnership registered as such under the laws of the State of Washington. The general partners of a limited liability partnership are not liable personally for the debts of the partnership arising from the omissions, negligence, wrongful acts, misconduct or malpractice committed by the other partners, employees, and agents of the partnership. Accordingly, only the partner's investment in the partnership is exposed to the risk of such claims or debts. The limitation on liability for negligence and malpractice make this entity of particular appeal to professional service partnerships, although to take advantage of this form the professional limited liability partnership must have the prescribed level of errors and omissions insurance. A general partner of a limited liability partnership remains jointly and severally liable for all other debts and obligations of the partnership, however. In all other respects, this entity resembles a general partnership.

> **The general partners of a limited liability partnership are not personally liable for certain types of debts**

A *limited partnership* has a general partner who is responsible for all debts of the partnership and who manages the company. There are one or more limited partners who are liable for no more than their investment and who do not participate in the day-to-day management of the firm. In the 1970's and early 1980's, limited partnerships were used frequently as tax shelters, but current tax laws have restricted this usage. You should consult an attorney experienced in partnerships to set up a limited partnership.

A *corporation* is a legal entity separate from its owners, who own shares of stock in the company. A company must comply with fairly stringent regulations in the state in which it is incorporated. Shareholders generally are not responsible for debts of the company beyond their investment in stock and are, therefore, insulated from claims against the company. Corporations are taxed on the income they make, plus dividends which are disbursed to the shareholders are taxed, resulting in "double taxation." The "regular" type of corporation (as opposed to the special types described below) is called a "C" corporation.

> **A corporation is taxed at two levels, resulting in "double taxation"**

An "S" corporation is a special type of corporation which receives special tax treatment. If a corporation qualifies for "S" status from the Internal Revenue Service, it is taxed like a partnership whereby corporate income "flows through" to shareholders and is taxed at individual rates. The corporation itself is not taxed, thus avoiding double taxation. To be considered an "S" corporation, a firm must:

- not have more than 35 shareholders (75 shareholders for tax years beginning after 1996);
- not have any non-individual shareholders (other than estates & trusts and in taxable years beginning after 1997, certain tax exempt organizations);
- not have a nonresident alien as a shareholder; and
- not have more than one class of stock.

An "S" corporation receives special tax treatment

A *closely held corporation* is a corporation in which 5 or fewer persons own more than 50% of the stock and that meets other requirements for being considered "closely held". The purpose of this designation is to allow smaller companies to incorporate more easily and have fewer reporting requirements. A closely held corporation could also have "S" tax status. The firm could, therefore, provide advantages of incorporation to owners, such as limited liability, while avoiding double taxation and burdensome reporting requirements. The "S" and "closely held" designations have made incorporation more attractive to smaller firms.

A *limited liability company ("LLC") is* a flexible entity designed to combine the benefits of partnership with those of the corporate form. The members of a limited liability company are personally liable for the obligations of the limited liability company only to the extent that shareholders of a corporation would be under analogous circumstances. The limited liability company may have any number of members (provided there are at least two) and any number of classes of members. The members may be individuals or any form of entity including corporations. The manner in which the LLC must be managed may be decided by the agreement of the members. The income of the LLC is taxed at the member level, thus avoiding the double taxation of the corporate form. Members may personally deduct their shares of the LLC's losses to the extent of their tax bases in the LLC.

LLC's offer advantages of both corporations and partnerships

Choosing a Legal Form of Business
The choice of legal form of organization depends on a variety of factors, the most important typically being:

- liability of the owner(s);
- tax considerations and distribution of profits and losses;
- ability to raise capital;
- expense and complexity of organizing the business;
- amount of government regulation and reporting requirements;
- management control.

Each of these factors is discussed below. Be aware that the laws change frequently for some of these factors, and consultation with legal, accounting, and/or tax professionals is a good idea.

Liability of the Business Owner

Most businesses with high-growth potential choose to incorporate or form limited liability companies for one overriding reason – limited liability. A shareholder in a corporation or a member of a limited liability company is not liable for more than his investment in the corporation or the LLC. Creditors cannot seek individuals' assets for repayment of corporate or LLC liabilities. With proprietorships and partnerships, owners are personally liable. In fact, general partnerships make each owner liable for debts for the entire company.

Laws affecting choice of legal form of business change often

Be aware that the corporate and LLC forms primarily protect you from liability suits. If your business is sued by customers, employees, or anyone else, your personal assets are protected. (They can also sue you personally, however, under some circumstances) These forms provide protection against creditors seeking to claim your personal assets because of your business debts; however, most banks require a *personal guarantee* to back up loans to corporations and LLC's. If you give a guarantee, the corporate and LLC forms will not provide you protection against creditors, to the extent of the guarantee.

Tax Considerations and Distribution of Profits/Losses

Tax laws change frequently; therefore, you should consult an accountant or tax attorney about current tax considerations. One tax law has remained unchanged for a long period of time: owners of "C" corporations can be taxed twice, which is not the case for owners of proprietorships, partnerships, and limited liability companies. The corporation is taxed on net profits, and if dividends are declared to shareholders, each owner is taxed on his return. If a corporation has "S" status, however, this disadvantage disappears and it is taxed similarly to a general partnership or limited liability

Banks may require personal guarantees on loans when you are incorporated

company. Since a corporation is a legal entity separate from its owners, profits of the company do not "flow through" directly to owners for taxation purposes. Owners are taxed only when dividends are declared, and owners cannot deduct company losses against their individual income. An "S" designation allows losses from a company to be applied towards owners' individual returns, reducing their tax liabilities. In summary, a "C" corporation is taxed differently than a proprietorship, partnership, or limited liability company, whereas an "S" corporation is treated the same.

Amount of Government Regulation

Corporations are required to comply with a large number of laws, whereas partnerships, limited liability companies, and proprietorships are not highly regulated. Furthermore, if a corporation issues publicly traded stock (see Chapter 7), the reporting requirements can be overwhelming. If, however, a corporation is "closely held," the reporting requirements are reduced. Therefore, unless a corporation is "closely held," it has significantly more reporting requirements and is more closely regulated than proprietorships, partnerships and limited liability companies.

Partnerships, LLCs, and proprietorships are not regulated as highly as corporations

Ability to Raise Capital

It is usually difficult for any business, regardless of the legal form of organization, to raise capital at startup. In the long run, the corporation is best organized to raise capital, followed by a limited liability company, followed by a partnership, followed by a proprietorship. The "C" corporation has the ability to sell stock to a relatively large number of investors (see Chapter 7 for a discussion of "going public"), and with a large equity base, corporations have less difficulty in obtaining loans. Limited liability companies and partnerships allow a company to have more than one owner, allowing it to raise more money than a proprietorship (unless Bill Gates is the proprietor). Proprietorships can raise only what the owner has to invest or what the firm can borrow.

The corporation is best organized to raise capital

Management Control and Decision Making

A sole proprietor has complete authority to run the business as he sees fit, which many entrepreneurs appreciate. The drawback is that the entrepreneur is then responsible for doing just about everything in the company at startup, and that can be overwhelming. In a partnership, all owners have equal right to manage the company, regardless of what percentage of ownership they have, unless otherwise agreed in a written partnership agreement or if it is a limited partnership. The decision-making process can become cumbersome. Unless specifically noted otherwise in the partnership agreement, each general partner can act on behalf of the other general partners, legally binding them without their knowledge. The advantage of the partnership is the pooling of skills and knowledge, which may be essential for the company to grow.

In a limited liability company, management is vested in the members, unless the certificate of formation assigns that right and obligation to a manager. If a manager is in charge, then no member of the limited liability company, acting solely in her capacity as a member, is an agent of the LLC. The limited liability company is a quite flexible entity. Its management may be as the members agree in a limited liability company agreement.

In a corporation, there is a distinction between management and shareholders, although in smaller corporations there is usually a significant overlap. The shareholders elect a board of directors who make general policy decisions and hire managers to conduct the business' affairs. The articles of incorporation usually include clauses on what types of decisions the board and managers can make. The advantage in this area of the corporation, like a partnership, is the involvement of different people in the decision-making process, although it can be cumbersome. In a corporation, an owner cannot legally bind another owner, as in a partnership.

The sole proprietorship is the easiest legal structure to set up

Complexity and Expenses of Organizing the Business

A sole proprietorship can be started simply and cheaply. All that needs to be done is to get proper licenses (see Chapter 5) and a tax identification number (if employees will be hired). A general partnership agreement can be simple; in fact, legally it does not have to be written. An agreement should be written, however, for the partners' protection, but it does not have to be filed with any government agency. However, you must register your limited liability partnership with the state to take advantage of that form. You must register a limited liability company with the Corporations Division of the Secretary of States office through a certificate of formation and you should have a limited liability company agreement reflecting the members' allocations of rights and obligations. On average, the Division registers more than 11,000 organizations each year. There are about 100,000 profit corporations and limited partnerships and 28,000 non profit corporations currently registered in the State of Washington.

You would be wise to consult an attorney to draw up a partnership agreement

The last section of this chapter shows typical issues addressed in partnerships. You don't have to consult an attorney to draw up a partnership agreement, but you would be wise to do so after you have drafted an agreement. The corporation is the most expensive, time-consuming legal form to organize. The fee for filing Articles of Incorporation for profit corporations is $175. The annual renewal fee is $50. Attorney's fees for incorporation and LLC formation range from $500 and up, depending on the complexity of the organization.

Forms for incorporation are available from:

Corporate Division
Secretary of State's Office
505 East Union, 2nd floor
P.O. Box 40234
Olympia, WA 98504-0234
(360) 753-7115

That office can also let you see the Business Corporation Act, Title 23b Revised Code of Washington (RCW).

Registered Agents

All corporations and limited liability companies doing business in Washington must have a registered agent with a Washington State address. The registered agent may be an individual or any other organization qualified by the Corporations Division to do business in Washington.

The registered agent receives license renewals and other notices and forwards them to the organization. The agent also accepts legal papers served on the corporation. The organizing documents or application to do business in Washington must contain or be accompanied by a statement signed by the registered agent indicating consent to serve.

All corporations and LLCs doing business in Washington must have a registered agent

Other Considerations

There are other factors that may affect the choice of legal form of business, including provisions for retirement plans and fringe benefits. The regulations in both of these areas are quite complex and change frequently. Consult an attorney familiar with business law.

The Seven Commonly Asked Questions

1. Can a Business become a corporation by just completing a Master Business Application?

   No. Articles of Incorporation must also be completed and filed with the Secretary of State's Corporations Division.

2. If a master business application is filed in another agency first, is the customer guaranteed that their chosen corporate name will be available?

   No. Only the Corporations Division can determine if a corporate name is available by checking that name with other corporate and limited partnership names and name reservations on file.

3. What happens if a non-corporate Washington business with a UBI decides to incorporate?

   If the change in ownership structure is within 60 days of the original application and if permission is obtained from the Department of Revenue supervisor, the business may keep the UBI it has been using. Otherwise, anytime a business ownership structure changes, it must apply for a new UBI.

4. How is the filing date determined for Articles of Incorporation?

   The filing date is the date the articles are received in the Corporations Division with 1) legal requirements met and 2) the applicable fees.

5. Why can't administratively dissolved corporations with the same name and owners keep the same UBI once the reinstatement period has expired?

   Under law, a corporation is treated like a person --- it has a life of its own. After the reinstatement period expires, the law defines the corporation as dead. Once the corporation is considered "dead", it cannot be resurrected. The owner must create a new person with a new UBI.

6. What is a foreign corporation? Does it register with the Corporations Division?

   It is a corporation formed in a jurisdiction other than Washington. Foreign corporations file with the Corporations Division, filing applications for a Certificate of Authority to do business in Washington.

7. What is the procedure if duplicate UBI numbers are found for a corporation?

> Call the corporate help desk for assistance. This is a complicated and detailed process and is best handled by a division staff person.

Compiled by Secretary of State's Office Corporations Division

Summary

The choice of legal form of business depends on a variety of factors. In general, most entrepreneurial firms with good growth potential would be well-advised to go ahead and incorporate, especially if they can receive "S" and "closely held" status, or form a limited liability company. The primary advantages of the corporate and LLC forms are the limitation of personal liability and the ability to raise capital. If "S" status is obtained, there are no tax disadvantages for the corporation, and if "closely held" status is obtained, the amount of regulation for the corporation is greatly reduced. The use of the LLC form reduces regulation even more.

In general, you would be well-advised to go ahead and incorporate

References

1. Kamoroff, Bernard. *Small Time Operator*, 2nd Edition. Laytonville, Cal: Bell Springs Publishing Company, 1979.

2. *A Guide to Starting a Business in Minnesota*. St. Paul: Minnesota Department of Trade and Economic Development, 1988.

Figure 6-1. Possible Issues in Partnership Agreements [2]

1. Name of the partnership.
2. Duration of the partnership.
3. Location of its place of business.
4. Capital contribution of each partner.
5. Whether partners may make additional contributions.
6. The level at which capital accounts of partners must be maintained.
7. Participation of each partner in profits and losses.
8. The amounts of any regular drawings against profits.

9. Duties, responsibilities, and sphere of activities of each partner.
10. Amount of time to be contributed by each partner.
11. Prohibition of partners' outside business activities which would compete with the partnership business.
12. Name of the managing partner and method for resolving management disputes.
13. Procedure for admitting new partners.
14. Method of determining the value of goodwill in the business, in case of death, incompetence, or withdrawal of a partner or dissolution of the partnership for any other reason.
15. Method of liquidating the interest of a deceased or retiring partner.
16. Age at which a partner must withdraw from active participation, and arrangements for adjusting his or her salary and equity.
17. Whether or not surviving partners have the right to continue using the name of a deceased partner in the partnership name.
18. Basis for expulsion of a partner, method of notification of expulsion, and the disposition of any losses that arise from the delinquency of such a partner.
19. Period of time in which retiring or withdrawing partners may not engage in a competing business.
20. Procedures for handling the protracted disability of a partner.
21. How partnership accounts are to be kept.
22. The fiscal year of the partnership.
23. Whether or not interest is to be paid on the debit and credit balances in the partners' accounts.
24. Where the partnership cash is to be deposited and who may sign checks.
25. Prohibition of partners' selling or pledging their interest in the partnership except to other partners.
26. Identification of material contracts or agreements affecting the liability or operation of the partnership.

Comparison of Types of Business Forms
In Washington State

	LIMITED LIABILITY COMPANY (RCW Ch. 25.15)	LIMITED PARTNERSHIP (RCW Ch. 25.10)	S CORPORATION (RCW Title 23B)	C CORPORATION (RCW Title 23B)	LIMITED LIABILITY PARTNERSHIPS (RCW Ch. 25.04)
NON-TAX CONSIDERATIONS					
Classes of Ownership Interest	Multiple classes permitted	Multiple classes permitted	Only one class of stock permitted (different voting rights are permitted)	Multiple classes permitted	Multiple classes permitted
Number of Owners	Need at least two; otherwise unrestricted	Need at least two; otherwise unrestricted	Maximum 35	Unrestricted	Need at least two, otherwise unrestricted
Types of Owners Allowed	Unrestricted	Unrestricted	Only individuals (except non-resident aliens) and certain trusts	Unrestricted	Unrestricted
Affiliated Group Membership	Unrestricted	Unrestricted	Prohibited	Unrestricted	Unrestricted
Who Manages	Flexible: default is all members; may specify manager or members in operating agreement	General partners manage; limited partners may have personal liability if they exceed "safe harbors" of RCW 25.10.190	Directors and officers; shareholder vote required for major transactions	Directors and officers; shareholder vote required for major transactions	General partners manage

	LIMITED LIABILITY COMPANY (RCW Ch. 25.15)	LIMITED PARTNERSHIP (RCW Ch. 25.10)	S CORPORATION (RCW Title 23B)	C CORPORATION (RCW Title 23B)	LIMITED LIABILITY PARTNERSHIPS (RCW Ch. 25.04)
Owners' Liability for Entity's Contractual Liabilities	Members and managers are not personally liable for contractual obligations of entity	General partners are personally liable for all obligations of partnership; limited partner is not personally liable unless participates in management and contracting party reasonably believes limited partner to be general partner	Directors, officers and shareholders are generally not personally liable for contractual obligations of corporation	Directors, officers and shareholders are generally not personally liable for contractual obligations of corporation	General partners are personally liable for all obligations of the partnership, other than those arising from negligence, omission, wrongful acts, misconduct, or malpractice
Owner's Liability for Entity's Tort Liabilities	Members and managers are liable for their own torts, but generally are not liable for tort obligations of entity

Note special rules for professional LLCs | General partners are liable for all partnership torts; limited partners are liable for own torts but not for partnership torts | Directors, officers and shareholders are liable for own torts, but generally are not liable for corporation's torts | Directors, officers and shareholders are liable for own torts, but generally are not liable for corporation's torts | General partners are personally liable for all obligations of the partnership, other than those arising from negligence, omission, wrongful acts, misconduct, or malpractice |
| Is an Ownership Interest a Security? | Under Howey test, LLC interest might not be security if holder is actively involved in LLC's business | Limited partnership interest is a security in most cases; under Howey test, general partnership interest is usually not a security | Corporate shares are securities | Corporate shares are securities | Under Howey test, general partnership interest is usually not a security |
| Transferability of Ownership Interests | Unless LLC agreement provides otherwise, assignee may become member only with consent of all members | Unless limited partnership agreement provides otherwise, assignee may become limited partner only with consent of all partners | Restricted only by shareholders agreement | Restricted only by shareholders agreement | Unless partnership agreement provides otherwise, assignee may become partner only with the consent of all the partners |

	LIMITED LIABILITY COMPANY (RCW Ch. 25.15)	LIMITED PARTNERSHIP (RCW Ch. 25.10)	S CORPORATION (RCW Title 23B)	C CORPORATION (RCW Title 23B)	LIMITED LIABILITY PARTNERSHIPS (RCW Ch. 25.04)
Events Triggering Dissenters' Rights	Merger only	Merger only	Merger, share exchange, sale or exchange of substantially all assets	Merger, share exchange, sale or exchange of substantially all assets	None
Dissolution	Occurs automatically upon event of dissociation of any member unless within 90 days all remaining members agree to continue or LLC agreement otherwise specifically authorizes continuation	Occurs automatically upon event of withdrawal of general partner unless there is a remaining general partner and all partners agree to continue or partnership agreement otherwise specifically authorizes continuation	Life of corporation may be perpetual	Life of corporation may be perpetual	Occurs automatically upon event of withdrawal of general partner unless there is a remaining general partner and all partners agree to continue or partnership agreement otherwise specifically authorizes continuation
Method of Formation	File certificate of formation	File certificate of limited partnership	File articles of incorporation	File articles of incorporation	File application for registration
Qualification to Do Business in Other States	Authorized to do business in other states with LLC statutes; unclear in states that have no LLC statute	Authorized to do business in other states	Authorized to do business in other states	Authorized to do business in other states	Authorized to do business in other states
Annual Reporting Requirements	Must file annual reports and pay annual license fees	None	Must file annual reports and pay annual license fees	Must file annual reports and pay annual license fees	Must file annual reports and pay annual license fees

	LIMITED LIABILITY COMPANY (RCW Ch. 25.15)	LIMITED PARTNERSHIP (RCW Ch. 25.10)	S CORPORATION (RCW Title 23B)	C CORPORATION (RCW Title 23B)	LIMITED LIABILITY PARTNERSHIPS (RCW Ch. 25.04)
FEDERAL INCOME TAX CONSIDERATIONS					
Owner Basis for Entity Debt	LLC debt is non-recourse to members (in absence of guaranties). Therefore, basis attributable to any debt will generally be allocated to members in accordance with their respective shares of income or gain.	Basis attributable to nonrecourse debt will generally be allocated in accordance with manner in which partners share income or gain. Limited partner will not receive basis for recourse liabilities in excess of their capital contributions and contribution obligations.	Corporation's debt does not increase shareholder basis in shares	Corporation's debt does not increase shareholder basis in shares	Partner will not receive basis for recourse liabilities in excess of their capital contributions and contribution obligations
Deductibility of Losses of at Owner Level	Member may deduct member's allocable share of losses to extent of member's basis in membership interest, which includes member's allocable share of LLC debt	Partner may deduct partner's allocable share of losses to extent of partner's basis in partnership interest, which includes partner's allocable share of partnership debt	Shareholder may deduct shareholder's allocable share of corporation's losses only to extent of shareholder's basis in shares, which does not include any allocation of corporation's debt	No flow-through of losses	Partner may deduct partner's allocable share of losses to extent of partner's basis in partnership interest
Distributions to Owners	Nontaxable to extent of member's tax basis in membership interest	Nontaxable to extent of partner's tax basis in partnership interest	Nontaxable to extent of shareholder's tax basis in shares	Generally taxable to extent of corporation's earnings and profits	Nontaxable to extent of partner's tax basis in partnership interest

	LIMITED LIABILITY COMPANY (RCW Ch. 25.15)	LIMITED PARTNERSHIP (RCW Ch. 25.10)	S CORPORATION (RCW Title 23B)	C CORPORATION (RCW Title 23B)	LIMITED LIABILITY PARTNERSHIPS (RCW Ch. 25.04)
Levels of Tax on Entity's Income	Income tax only at member level	Income tax only at partner level	Generally income tax only at shareholder level	Income tax at both corporate and shareholder levels	Income tax only at partner level
Special Allocations of Income/Loss	Permitted (subject to § 704(b) regulations)	Permitted (subject to § 704(b) regulations)	Prohibited	Not applicable, corporation pays tax on corporation's income and receives tax benefits from any losses	Permitted (subject to § 704(b) regulations)
Gain on Liquidation	No tax at entity level; nontaxable to member to extent of member's tax basis in membership interest	No tax at entity level; nontaxable to partner to extent of partner's tax basis in partnership interest	Generally no tax at entity level; gain flows through and is taxed to shareholder (increasing shareholder's basis in shares)	Taxed at corporate level	No tax at entity level; nontaxable to member to extent of member's tax basis in membership interest
Inside Basis Step-Up Following Transfer of Ownership Interest	Permitted with § 754 election	Permitted with § 754 election	No step-up	No step-up	Permitted with § 754 election

* For LLCs and limited partnerships this assumes the entity is organized to lack at least two of the following four "corporate" characteristics: (1) limited liability, (2) centralized management, (3) continuity of life, and (4) free transferability of interests.

7

Raising Capital

"A banker is a person who is willing to make a loan if you present sufficient evidence to show you don't need it."
Herbert V. Prochnow

Your business needs money as much as it needs good people and good products. Growth requires capital. Unless you have a lot of money to put into the business yourself, you will have to find sources of capital. This chapter describes different sources of capital and how to approach them.

Don't try to raise money just for the sake of raising money. Some people feel like they don't have a bona fide business unless they borrow some money or get people to invest in their company. Raising money in either way can be expensive and each method brings with it additional risks for you and your business. If you can avoid borrowing or bringing in investors, you are better off. Unfortunately, most businesses cannot avoid doing one or the other.

Don't try to raise money just for the sake of raising money

You have probably heard how difficult it is to raise money for a new or small company. One hears two conflicting stories. The newspapers run stories about entrepreneurs exasperated at how difficult it is to get bank loans. Some business people feel that Washington bankers are especially conservative. But on the other hand, you find people who say, "If you have a good plan, there is money out there. You just need to know where to look and how to ask for it." There is some truth to both of these arguments. With a good business plan and knowledge of where to look for money, your odds of being able to raise capital should be greatly improved.

The authors would like to thank Mr. Jonathan Hayes of the Washington Economic Development Finance Authority, Mr. David Wingate from the Washington State Department of Community, Trade and Economic Development and Messrs. Danferd Henke and Dirk Bartram of the Seattle law firm of Helsell Fetterman LLP for their contributions to this chapter.

Have A Plan

The most common difficulty that entrepreneurs face is not having a business plan or having an inadequate one. Your business plan is your company's sales tool to potential capital sources— make it the best that you can. You will probably only have *one* shot at any given capital source. If you go in with an inadequate or poorly thought-out business plan, your creditability as a business manager may be severely damaged, and it is unlikely that you will get a second chance.

Your business plan is your company's sales tool to potential capital sources

Remember, you are going into business to *make money*. You may have additional reasons, especially for choosing the particular type of business that you have, but if you aren't focused primarily on the profitability of your venture, you will find it very difficult to attract outside capital in any form.

Recognize the risks involved in your venture— especially if it is a start-up. Most entrepreneurs severely underestimate the returns necessary to compensate for the risks involved in a new business. Statistically, eighty percent of new businesses fail in the first three years. That's not a comforting situation for a potential lender or investor. You will need a high degree of security (for borrowed money) or high potential returns (for equity capital) to compensate for these risks.

Due Diligence Works Both Ways!

When a potential investor or lender looks at your venture, they go through a process called *due diligence*— it's a thorough investigation of all aspects of your business to determine if everything is as you say it is and if your plans and projections for the future are sound and reasonable. Entrepreneurs often neglect to do their *own* due diligence, however. When you set out to raise capital, find out everything that you can about your potential capital sources— their background, what other companies/industries they have helped finance, what the experiences of those companies have been, what the track record for their portfolio has been, what kind of ongoing support (managerial or additional stage financing) can be expected, etc... Get references, *and check them out!* True financial professionals will expect you to ask these questions. If there is any balking at providing answers, politely go somewhere else for your financing requirements.

Make sure to do your own due diligence

Your Best Source of Capital

It's yourself– your own savings, personal assets, and your business' earnings. Part of your business plan will be getting the initial start-up capital together. Your own savings is the only source that you can count on. It may take years of no fancy vacations, no new car, scrimping and saving on everything to put it together. How badly do you want to own your own business? One partnership starting a delivery service met every Wednesday night for five years. At each meeting, each partner put $10 in the kitty. At the end of the five years, they had enough to buy their first truck.

Another advantage of relying on your own resources is that strings are not attached. Described below are several methods of using your own personal resources.

You **are your best source of capital**

- *Cash.* Cash from savings and retirement accounts is the most common form of equity for small start-up businesses. Cash can also be generated from the sale of assets you do not need– what lenders often refer to as "toys". If you have a 401k retirement program, you can borrow from it without paying a penalty, and the interest you pay is tax deferred income added to your retirement fund.

- *Personal Debt.* You can also raise equity for your business through personal borrowing. While this is debt, commercial lenders will perceive it as equity in your business. This is important because business lenders usually want to see as much equity in a new business as the amount of their loan. Lenders consider a new business a start-up and businesses that have been in operation for less than three full tax reporting years. The payment requirements on all personal debt can have a negative effect on a business loan application if it significantly affects the amount the owners will have to draw out of the business.

When you rely on your own resources, there are no strings attached

- *Friendly Debt.* The most attractive type of personal loan is "friendly debt" because usually it has a long term and relatively low, fixed rate. This means lower monthly payments. "Friendly debt" is borrowed from relatives and friends. Often this type of loan can be unsecured. Also, when things do not go as planned, "friendly" lenders are often more flexible creditors.

- *Home Mortgage.* This is a loan secured with the owner's residence. In small, closely held businesses, it is likely that banks, the SBA and most commercial lenders will want the owner's residence as additional collateral for their business loan. By obtaining a residential mortgage or home equity loan, the owner will raise additional cash for the business and benefit from the lower, fixed rate and long term.

Other Personal/Consumer Loans can be obtained from credit unions, banks and finance companies. These will generally be secured by other personal assets, such as a car, boat or other real estate. Both credit union and bank consumer loans will often have a fixed rate and lower rate than commercial loans. If your business needs small amounts of capital, credit cards are another alternative. They are relatively easy to obtain, unsecured and have reasonable rates if you take the time to shop around. The disadvantage of credit cards is their short term. Most credit card minimum payments are based on a three year payoff.

The Primary Source of Capital Investment Funding

It's retained earnings– the profits that a business makes that are reinvested in the company. According to statistics from the Federal Reserve Bank, *77 percent* of all capital investment by American businesses is funded by retained earnings. Don't feel bad if you didn't guess this; even many financial professionals overlook this source of funds. Increasing your profits is the best thing you can do to improve your capital funding situation. A profitable growing company doesn't need as much outside funding as a company that is less profitable. And when it does need outside funding, it can get it on much better terms.

Retained earnings are the primary source of capital

Outside Sources of Capital– Debt vs. Equity

Unless you can talk someone into *giving* you money, you need to decide whether you want debt or equity capital. When you borrow money, it is called *debt*. You are required to pay back the money by a certain date and under certain terms. The people who loan you the money do not own a part of your company, although they may have the right to take the business if you do not meet the terms of the loan. Debt financing is *not* risk capital! Lenders are not interested in taking on much risk– they are interested in getting their loan repaid. Don't ask them to "believe" in you– that's the job of equity capital. Lack of understanding of this point is one of the main reasons for entrepreneurs' dissatisfaction with their banking relations.

You need to decide whether you want debt or equity capital

Equity financing involves giving up part ownership of your company. You do not make set payments to investors, rather they share in the profits of your firm. The amount of money they invest and the percentage ownership of the company that you give to them are negotiable.

Debt financing has some advantages over equity financing. The most important is that you do not give up any ownership of the company. Many entrepreneurs give up significant portions of their company at startup for relatively small investments. These people later regret having given up equity which later is worth a lot of money, since the value of the company has increased substantially. Once you give up ownership, the only way to get it back is to buy it, which may become very costly. Second, debt capital is usually much cheaper than equity. Interest costs are lower than the returns that equity partners will expect. Interest costs are also a tax-deductible business expense; distributions to equity participants are not. If you borrow money, the origination fees are usually less than those associated with equity financing. Third, since you do not give up ownership in debt financing, you do not have to deal with other partners and their ideas on running the business.

Equity financing involves giving up part ownership of your company

Equity financing also has some advantages over debt financing. First, it may be less risky to the business. Equity financing does not require set payments on certain dates. This takes the pressure off you to have enough cash to meet those payments. You also do not run the risk associated with variable interest rate loans. If the economy turns downward or your sales are lower than expected, a bank is not waiting to repossess the business. Second, equity investors are willing to give money to riskier business situations, in return for higher returns than a banker would demand. Banks do not usually loan money to startups or to businesses which they consider to be risky. Therefore, equity financing may be the only alternative. Third, you can generally raise larger amounts of money through equity investments than through debt (but there are all sorts of exceptions). Fourth, equity finance is more conducive to business growth than debt is. Funds paid out to make interest and principal payments on your company's debt are not available for reinvestment in the company. If debt service payments consume too large a portion of a company's cash flow, the company's growth can be stopped in its tracks. Potentially profitable opportunities can be lost and competitors can overtake the company. Loan documents usually contain restrictive covenants. These are intended to preserve the lender's security interests, but they can also greatly limit the company's freedom of action in pursuing new ventures. Fifth, your co-owners will frequently bring very valuable managerial and

Equity and debt financing both have advantages and disadvantages

specialized talent to your venture– talent that otherwise might be far beyond your ability to pay for it.

Entrepreneurs often worry that they will be pushed aside and lose control if they give up sizable amounts of their equity. This can be over-emphasized, however. Bill Gates has given up a very large proportion of Microsoft's equity over the years without losing any real control. Remember that due diligence works both ways; if you have done *your* due diligence properly, the potential of loss of control should not be a significant concern. If the added investment results in growth of the firm, your ownership interest may still be worth considerably more than you began with. 10 percent of a $10 million firm is worth much more than 100 percent of a $100,000 firm.

Debt Financing

There are various types of debt financing for your business. Loans from banks are the most common, but leases, trade credit, loans from finance companies, and special loan programs, including Economic Development Financing programs are other possibilities. Each is described in this section.

Bank Loans. Bankers are infamous for being conservative. You need to understand why they are forced to be that way. They borrow money from depositors and loan it out to businesses. If they borrow it at 7 percent and loan it out at 10 percent, their *spread* is three percent. What happens if a business they loan money to does very well? They get their three points. What happens if the business goes bankrupt? They may lose their total investment. If a bank makes 100 loans and only four of them go bad, it may appear that the bank is doing a good job; but a bank that had 4 loans out of 100 go bad would soon be out of business. A loss ratio of 4 percent is larger than the bank's 3 percent spread (profit margin). Bankers are also under pressure from government loan evaluators. If the evaluators rate many of their loans as being quite risky, the bank is severely hampered in making loans. Yes, banks are conservative, and you cannot expect them to make a loan in a situation they consider to be quite risky.

Types of Bank Loans. Banks make different types of loans and the terms of a loan are generally dictated by what the money is used for.

Short-term loans are used to finance assets which become cash in the short term (one year or less). For example, seasonal fluctuations

> **Remember that due diligence works both ways**

> **You cannot expect a bank to make a loan in a situation they consider to be risky**

in inventory are usually financed by short-term loans. You need money to buy inventory before the heavy selling season begins. Once you have sold the inventory and collected on it, you should be able to pay the bank back. Short-term loans are usually used to finance inventory, accounts receivable, and other situations where cash is needed for only a short period of time.

Some people do not understand why a bank gives a series of short-term notes instead of issuing longer-term debt. Banks want to match the term of the loan to the source of repayment. Consider the service station owner who borrows money to fill his underground tank with gasoline. The bank loans him the money for the gas, requires him to repay the loan when the tank is empty, and then will turn right around and re-loan the money to refill the tank. The bankers aren't stupid. If they gave a long-term loan for gasoline, chances are cash would eventually be used for a new pickup truck or a new hoist. Then there wouldn't be enough money to purchase gasoline when the tank becomes empty again. The bank would then be asked to make another loan. Short-term loans are used to finance assets that become cash in the short term. The source of repayment for short term loans is the sale of inventory and collection of receivables.

Short-term loans are used to finance assets that are liquidated in the short term

A *line of credit* is a short-term loan, usually due within a year, because money can be borrowed, paid back, and then borrowed again. A bank typically allows a certain credit limit (with some restrictions) up to which you may borrow. When you have the cash, you pay the loan back down, but you still retain the right to borrow again if the need arises. Like other short term loans, a line of credit is usually secured with short term assets, inventory and accounts receivable, and is used to provide the seasonal cash needs of the business. Normally the bank will review and renew the line of credit each year after receiving annual financial statements. Most banks require the balance on a line of credit to be paid off (cleared) at least once a year for a period of at least seven days. This type of loan alleviates the pressure to go to the bank every time you need to borrow money– the credit is already established. Banks are very selective as to whom they will give a line of credit. Do not use operating lines of credit to buy long term assets. As with other short term loans, the source of repayment for short term loans is the sale of inventory and collection of receivables.

A line of credit is a short-term loan

Intermediate term loans are used to finance assets such as automobiles, furniture, and equipment. These are assets which are used for several years but wear out. You typically have one to five years to pay off this type of loan. The source of repayment is net profit and depreciation, a non-cash expense.

Long-term loans are usually paid off over long periods of time, anywhere from six to twenty-five years. Because of the risk to banks of interest rate fluctuations, they are offering fewer of these loans. They are also making payment schedules more compressed. You don't see too many loans with terms longer than ten years these days. Long-term loans are used to purchase real property– land and buildings. The banks are willing to loan over longer periods of time on these assets because they feel confident that the assets will retain their value if they need to be repossessed. In general, banks are willing to make long-term loans on long-term assets. Like intermediate term loans, long term loans are paid from profit and depreciation.

> **Intermediate term loans are used to finance assets which are used for several years but wear out**

Choosing a Banker. You should spend some time choosing a banker. It is a shopping process, which you should do before you urgently need the money. Nothing will turn a banker off more quickly than a frantic applicant. There is an old saying that it is easiest to get a loan when you don't need it. Once again, don't borrow just for the sake of borrowing, but do project your cash needs. Well in advance of when you need the money, talk to different banks.

Of course you want a loan with the best terms, but there are other factors to consider as you shop. Try to find a bank that can handle your needs as you grow. If you are right up against a bank's upper lending limit, you *may* have to shop for another bank in the future (most small banks have the ability to find other banks to "participate" with them when loans go over their lending limit). Also, try to find a bank that has lending experience in your industry and in working with young, growing companies. The bankers will understand the seasonal and cyclical variations that affect your need to borrow. Lastly, try to find bankers with which you have "good chemistry." You're dealing not with just a bank, but also with bankers. Their commitment to you may be invaluable. You can evaluate some of these issues simply by dealing with the bank. You may need to talk to outsiders to get accurate information on some issues. Fellow entrepreneurs, accountants, attorneys, and consultants can give you their assessments. Ask for small business references from the bank and talk to some of their current loan holders. Don't think that you should bank with the first institution

> **You should spend some time choosing a banker**

that agrees to give you a loan. As with any product that you are selling, it doesn't hurt to let people know that others are interested in what you have to sell. Shop around. Have some alternatives.

Talk to both large and small banks. Larger banks have more capacity, but are often more conservative in their lending policy, and decision making is usually centralized. This means the people who make the decision to lend are usually a long way from your business. Smaller community banks are usually more familiar with your business and decisions are generally made closer to home, sometimes at the branch where you bank.

Approaching a Bank. At the same time you are shopping for a bank, you are selling yourself. Yes, bankers do have common criteria they use in deciding whether to give a loan. However, their rules can bend if they "like what they see." The way you present yourself is as important as what you present.

> **Talk to both large and small banks**

Try to get an introduction to a banker as opposed to calling him "cold." If someone he knows introduces you and puts in a good word for you, the door is opened. Try to complete a business plan (see Chapter 13) even for a bank loan. If yours is a startup business, you *need* to present a complete plan. Whatever written materials you present to a bank, make sure they appear professional, complete, and accurate. Your plans and projections should state your assumptions and they should be reasonable ones. The banker with whom you have face-to-face discussions likely will not be the sole decision maker about your loan. You will want to leave those persons who will only read about your business with a good impression as well.

> **The way you present yourself is as important as what you present**

The banker will be trying to assess your business acumen and ability to repay the loan. If you have a partner, accountant, or employee who can provide support and expertise, have them come to meetings with the banker. One of the concerns that bankers have is whether you, as an entrepreneur, can stay focused and pay attention to the financial end of the business. If you do not have strong financial skills, bring someone involved with your business who can emphasize the finances of the company. Avoid talking about the spectacular new plans for growth that you have and all of the new products or acquisitions that you are considering. The banker will fear that you will go off half-cocked and not keep track of finances. Emphasize the fact that there will be more than adequate cash flow to make loan payments. This is what they are concerned with.

What Bankers Need to Know to Give You a Loan. All bankers will want you to give them some basic information before they consider giving you a loan. Make sure you have answers to these basics (a good cash flow projection will help answer many of them):

- How much money do you need to borrow?
- When do you need the money?
- How will you earn the money to repay the loan?
- What will you use the money for?
- When can you repay the money?
- What collateral can you pledge to secure the loan?

> **Always bring personal and business financial information when you talk to your banker**

Always bring personal and business financial information with you when you talk to your banker about a loan. Generally a banker will want to see three years of business financial statements, three years of business and personal tax returns and a current personal financial statement. Bankers will expect anyone with 20 percent or more ownership in the business to personally guarantee a loan. If you appear unwilling to guarantee, a banker may question your commitment to the business.

The Bank's Decision. Each bank approaches lending decisions in its own somewhat subjective fashion. However, banks have traditionally evaluated the "5 C's of Credit" in determining whether to give a loan: Character, Capacity, Capital, Conditions, and Collateral. These criteria are standard enough in the banking world that each merits a description.

> **Banks have traditionally evaluated the "5 C's of Credit" in determining whether to give a loan**

Character. The banker will try to determine if you are a trustworthy person. Have you paid back previous loans on time? What does your personal and business credit report show? Do you have the reputation of being an honest business person? Are you open and honest in your dealings with the loan officer? This criterion is the most subjective of the five, and yet one of the most important. Bankers know that when it is all said and done, your integrity will determine to a large degree whether or not the loan will be repaid.

Capacity. The banker evaluates whether the business has enough historical cash flow to repay the loan. If it does now, you will need to present a cash flow projection for him to make such a decision. In decades past, bankers were not as concerned with this aspect as they now are. Previously, if the loan was backed up by plenty of collateral, the decision to loan was easy. Recently, however, banks have become much more careful. In most cases, bankers don't want to have to sell your collateral becasue you can't make your payments. By their own admission, they are lousy salespeople and they would prefer you stay in business and make loan payments than for them to sell your collateral. They evaluate capacity through your projected cash flows.

Capital. The banker evaluates how much money you, or other investors, have in the business. The bank does not want to become an owner of the business; it wants to remain a lender. If it puts the majority of money into the business, it begins to feel more like an owner. Bankers want to ensure that the business owners put an adequate amount of capital into the firm for two reasons. First, if they do have to sell your collateral, they normally can't get a very good price for it. Therefore, they want a cushion. Your investment provides that. Second, an investment on your part tells them that you are committed personally to the venture. It is amazing how much more committed people become once their own money is tied up in a project. Different banks and loan programs require varying levels of owner investment. The range may be anywhere from 30 percent up to 50 owner investment. In very few situations can you expect to borrow all of the money you need. You need to put in a substantial amount yourself or get others to invest.

> **The bank does not want to become an owner of the business; it wants to remain a lender**

Conditions. The banker evaluates the overall economy, your industry, and your competitive position before making a loan. If your business is highly dependent on the national economy and the forecast for it is down, you probably won't get the loan. Likewise, if companies are struggling in your industry and/or they usually react aggressively to a newcomer, the banker may be hesitant to make a loan. It is your job to point out the promise of the proposed business in the business plan.

Collateral. Bankers want to know what they will get from you if you are unable to repay the loan. If you have a startup business, they are very serious about collateral. If you borrow money for inventory, they usually want more than the inventory itself as collateral for the loan. They don't have much faith that they could sell it for enough to recapture the value of the loan. Therefore, they ask for secondary means of collateral, either other assets of the business or your personal assets. If you are at startup, you will almost always be required to pledge personal assets as collateral. Beyond that, you may be asked to give a personal guarantee, which

> **Bankers don't want to have to sell your collateral because you can't make your payments**

allows the bank the right to seize assets not already pledged as collateral if you default on the loan. They can even garnish your future wages. It is not easy to risk losing your house, other personal assets, and even future wages, but you almost invariably will be required to do it.

Negotiating the Deal. A bank loan should be negotiated. The first time you deal with a bank, you may feel like you need to accept whatever they offer. Remember that they are a business and are trying to make the best deal for themselves. In most cases, they have some bend in them. Many an entrepreneur is ecstatic at receiving a loan, signs on the dotted line, and later regrets they didn't read the loan agreement more closely and negotiate it. First, banks will look to tie up as many of your assets as they can as collateral, including assets you will acquire in the future. You will probably have to do this to get your loan, but you may lock yourself out of any further loans down the road because no assets are free to be used as collateral. You may be able to negotiate a partial release of collateral in the future when you need collateral for a future loan, but this is not a certainty. Make sure you know what assets you are tying up in a loan agreement.

> **Make sure you know what assets you are tying up in a loan agreement**

You may be able to negotiate a loan without a personal guarantee or with a limited guarantee, particularly if your business is established and you have successfully completed several loan transactions with the same bank. Most lenders have a guideline for closely held businesses that owners with 20 percent or more interest in the company must guarantee.

> **You may be able to negotiate in advance "skip payment" months**

Depending on the type of business you own, you may be able to negotiate in advance "skip payment" months. If your business is a highly seasonal one, with resulting wide variations in monthly cash flow, the bank may agree to let you skip payments in the low cash-flow months (the bank will continue to charge you interest, however) and increase payments in high cash-flow months. You should negotiate forms like these before the loan is finalized, rather than during its course.

Most loans are written with certain *restrictions*. After giving you a loan, bankers want you to operate in a fashion that preserves the safety of the loan. They may require that you not take on any further debt, not make dividend payments, nor pledge your assets to anyone else without their prior consent. They may require you to maintain cash reserves or working capital at certain levels, submit

The Washington Entrepreneur's Guide

periodic financial statements to them, maintain insurance on key people, or comply with other restrictions. *Make sure you know what the restrictions are.* They can be negotiated. You may not be able to change a lot of them, but you want to make sure you don't get boxed into a corner by a restriction of which you were unaware. By the same token, make sure that what the banker tells you is documented in the agreement. In Washington, oral promises about your loan are not enforceable. That warning will be stamped all over your loan documents. If a banker agrees to a condition or term of your loan that is or may become critical to you, make sure that promise is in writing. For example, if they tell you that you can have a line of credit up to a certain amount, make sure it is written in the loan agreement. Don't sign the loan form until you have had an accountant and/or an attorney review it. Your banker may not be working for the bank when you need him to verify a verbal agreement.

Most loans are written with restrictions

Developing A Relationship With Your Banker. After receiving a loan, most entrepreneurs contact their bankers on only two occasions: when they need more money or when they are unable to make a payment. These are not the banker's favorite visits. *Do not surprise your banker!* Send him financial statements, new product releases, favorable newspaper articles about your business or products, etc. Invite him to your office or plant for a tour and discuss how the business is doing. Ask for advice on running your business (you don't have to listen). After all, a banker spends most of his time in his office looking in on businesses from the outside. He gets excited when he feels like he is an insider. Make him feel like a part of your team, not an adversary. This will be important when you do go in to borrow more money or call to say that you will be late with a payment. A strong relationship won't get you a loan the bank views as too risky and it won't save you from being assigned to the special credits branch of the bank if you do not perform your obligations, but it may make a lot of difference in borderline situations.

A relationship with your banker may make a lot of difference in borderline situations

Once you have the loan, make the payments on time. Don't take the loan for granted and don't treat the payments as something to get around to a few days late. The bank will be tracking your performance. If you need to apply for another loan later, the bank will view a record of timely payments as evidence of your character and capacity. Conversely, your record of late or missed payments will speak volumes to the banker about the degree of risk associated with your proposed loan.

Although you want the banker to feel like an insider, you also should be careful to document your interactions with him. After any meeting in which you discuss terms of your loan, you should write a letter *to your banker* stating your understanding of the discussion and keep a copy in your file. Some business people have been shocked when their bank apparently changed the terms on loans, to the business people's disadvantage. If you have no record of dealings with your banker, you may not be able to justify your position.

Once you have the loan, make the payments on time

Special Credits. The "Special Credits" or "Non-performing Assets" department is the internal division to which a bank will assign a loan it views as troubled. There are circumstances under which a bank will view a loan as troubled even if the borrower is current with all payments. The Special Credits bankers are experts at seeing to it that the bank gets repaid, at whatever the cost to you or your business. Their tactics may range from the seemingly benign offer to you to provide advice on maximizing cash flow to the aggressive and sudden cancellation of your financing vehicle. The bank may demand additional collateral, new loan terms, or immediate repayment of a part of the balance of your loan in return for not canceling your line of credit immediately or otherwise calling your loan. What often occurs is that the borrower will provide the additional collateral or make a substantial early repayment, only to have the bank cancel the financing a few months later anyway. If you should ever learn that a bank has or is about to assign you to its Special Credits department, consult your attorney immediately. You will need to know what your rights are under the loan documents and the law before you begin to negotiate a "work-out" of your problems with the bank.

The Special Credits bankers are experts at seeing to it that the bank gets repaid

Governmental Programs

Small Business Administration (SBA) Loans. The SBA offers a variety of loan programs (see Chapter 16, Business Resources, for a detailed description). The great majority of its loan work is guaranteeing loans (SBA 7a Program), not loaning money. Most commercial banks are qualified SBA lenders and can process loan applications and have loan guarantees approved by the SBA. The guarantee assures the lending institution that if a borrower defaults on the loan, the government will cover the bank's losses up to 75 percent of the value of the loan over $100,000 and 80 percent on loans under $100,000. Loan guarantee fees range from 2 percent

The SBA offers a variety of loan programs

(loans under $80,000) to 3.75 percent on loans over $500,000. This program obviously reduces the risk to the bank. Loans are still through the bank; they are just guaranteed by the SBA.

Over the last decade, the SBA 504 loan program has become more popular with lenders and businesses. This program allows 90 percent financing of business expansions, but is limited to fixed asset acquisition (land, building and equipment). The SBA sells bonds to fund up to 40 percent of a project, a bank makes a direct loan for 50 percent and the business must put 10 percent equity into the projects. The bank's risk is reduced because the 40 percent SBA bond portion takes a second position behind the bank. The advantage to the business is receiving the low, fixed rate bond financing and the ability to conserve working capital to finance growth.

Most commercial banks are qualified SBA lenders and have loan guarantees approved by the SBA

In the eyes of a borrower, the SBA loan looks like any other bank loan. However, the guarantee allows the bank to charge a slightly lower interest rate than they would have otherwise (the maximum rate on an SBA guaranteed loan is 2.75 percent over prime). Or perhaps the bank is led to make a loan to a company that it would not have if the guarantee had not been available. In the last several years the SBA guarantee to any one business has ranged from $500,000 to $750,000.

Washington has a very active SBA lending program. Most commercial banks are qualified SBA lenders. If your bank is not, contact the Community Development Finance program at (360) 753-0325. The SBA itself can also tell you which banks it most frequently works with. District offices in or close to Washington are:

In the eyes of a borrower, the SBA loan looks like any other bank loan

Seattle District Office- Western Washington
1200 6th Ave., Suite 1700
Seattle, WA 98101-1128
(206) 553-7311 – General Information
(206) 553-7070 – Recorded Information

Spokane District Office – Eastern Washington
W. 601 1st Avenue, 10th Floor East
Spokane, WA 99204
(509) 353-2800   Fax: (509) 353-2829

Portland District Office
220 SW Columbus St., Suite 500
Portland, OR 97201-6695
(503) 326-2628   Fax: (503) 326-2808
Wahkiakum, Cowlitz, Clark, Klickitat, Skamania

SBA Internet & Bulletin Board Information
SBA Home Page: http://www.sba.gov
SBA Gopher: gopher://gopher.sba.gov
File Transfer protocol: ftp://sba.gov
Telnet: telnet://sbaonline.sba.gov
SBA Electronic Bulletin Board: (900) 463-4636

> **The USDA has a guarantee program for businesses in areas with a population of less than 50,000 people**

USDA Rural Development Business & Industry Guarenteed Loans. The USDA has a guarantee program very similar to the SBA for businesses in areas with a population of less than 50,000 people. Most commercial banks are qualified lenders and can process loan applications and have loan guarantees approved by the USDA. This guarantee program will guarantee 80 percent of the loan from $200,000 to $5,000,000. The loan guarantee fee is 2 percent, less than current SBA fees. For more information contact Community Development Finance (360) 753-0325 or:

USDA Rural Business Services
P.O. Box 2427
Wenatchee, WA 98807
P# (509) 664-0241

Non-Traditional SBA Lenders. There are two kinds of non-traditional lenders, SBA qualified finance companies and "out of area" bank SBA Centers. There are fourteen *SBA Qualified Finance Companies* which were licensed by the SBA during the Carter Administration. Historically, the most active has been *The Money Store*, which is the largest SBA lender in the country. During the last five years, other SBA finance companies have entered the Washington market, including AT&T Capital, GE Capital Small Business Finance, and Associates Commercial Capital Corp. These companies compete with each other and banks to make SBA guaranteed loans. They will compete both on interest rate and approving loans which banks may not approve.

"Out Of Area" Bank SBA Centers & Aggressive SBA Lenders.
These lenders have also become more common and competitive
during the last five years. These are commercial banks who have
specialized in SBA guaranteed loans as a market niche. Like the
SBA qualified finance companies, they can be very competitive as
to the credits they will approve and the interest rate they will charge.
Some of these lenders include (location is headquarters of bank):
Olympic Bank in Sequim, 1st Community Bank of Washington in
Lacey, City Bank in Lynnwood, Pioneer National Bank in Yakima,
Sterling Savings in Spokane, North Cascades Bank in Chelan, Bank
of Grays Harbor in Aberdeen, North Sound Bank in Poulsbo,
Centennial Bank in Olympia, ABC Bank in Boise, Idaho and Zion's
Bank in Salt Lake City, Utah.

Economic Development Financing

Economic Development Lenders include local, regional and state
revolving loan fund programs. Over the last decade, with bank
small business loans being harder to obtain, these revolving loan
funds have become an important source of financing for
entrepreneurs, particularly in rural areas and for women and
minority business owners.

> **"Out of Area" lenders have become more common and competitive during the last five years**

Economic development lenders are primarily non-profit
corporations, though some are local or state government programs.
Their mission is to :

1) create and retain jobs
2) diversify local and state economies
3) encourage economic growth

Most revolving funds are financed with loan and/or grant funds
from federal, state and local governments. Some receive loan
capital and operating funds from private corporations (often banks),
foundations, and religious charitable organizations. They do not
compete with private lenders, rather they make loans more
attractive to other lenders by filling "gaps" in financing proposals.

> **Economic development lenders are primarily non-profit corporations**

Revolving funds all have their own loan policies, eligibility criteria
(both borrower and use of loan proceeds), rate and loan terming.
Refer to the Finance section in Chapter 16 of this book, or on the
computer disc, or contact either Community Development Finance
or your local Economic Development Council for more contact
information on the revolving funds serving your area.

While each revolving fund is tailored to local economic needs and the goals of funding sources, they have some requirements in common which you should be aware of when considering them for part of your financing proposal:

- Positive Net Worth/Equity Requirement– After a loan is made the business must have a positive net worth. If the business equity is in the red, new equity capital must be part of the proposal. Usually owner capital of at least 15 percent of the loan request is required, and often up to 20 percent or more of the whole proposal.

All revolving funds have some requirements of which you should be aware

- Matching funds– Most revolving funds require other lenders to be involved in the financing proposal. Normally a one-to-one match, but sometimes more. This means for every dollar of revolving funds loan there must be one dollar of other loan funds. Matching loan funds can come from any of the debt sources in this chapter including banks, seller contacts, trade creditors and often, but not always, leases.

- Job Creation and/or Retention– Most revolving funds require one job to be created or retained for each $20,000-$35,000 of their loans. This means a full time job (FTE). Two half time jobs equal one FTE. To qualify as a job retained, it must be shown that the job will be lost if the business does not get the loan.

Revolving Fund Loans are attractive for several reasons:

- Rate– Usually fixed, and often below market. A general range is from 9-12 percent. Most common rate is 10 percent fixed.

- Long term– Usually longer loan term than banks, but often not as a long term as SBA or RDA on real estate and equipment.

- Subordination/Equity– revolving funds can take a second position behind banks to appear almost like equity, even when their loan is made to the business. Most SBA and USDA loan officers will usually accept this if other credit criteria are met. Revolving funds are NOT unsecured lenders and will usually want to have a first position on some business or personal assets, though generally their collateral requirements are less than other lenders. If the loan is made to the individual owner, not the business, and is secured by personal assets, it should be considered as equity by other lenders. The most common asset to be pledged is the owner's home, either a first or second mortgage.

Local Decision Making. Most revolving fund loans are approved by a loan committee made up of local business people who know the local market, often the borrower, and have a strong interest in supporting local business. Many other lenders have decision makers located in other areas.

Loan limits vary, but most revolving funds can lend up to $150,000.00 and have a minimum loan of between $10,000.00 and $25,000.00. See the Business Resource Guide or the computer disc for details of these programs and others.

Micro-Loan Funds. Micro lending has become a popular economic development tool over the last five years. The target market for these loan funds includes very small existing and start up and home based businesses. The idea came from Asia, where very small loans would be made to people in impoverished villages. Most of these early successful model funds were managed by a cooperative made up of the villagers who would borrow money.

> **Most revolving fund loans are approved by a loan committee**

There are many definitions of a micro-loan. Many banks consider a commercial loan under $100,000 a micro loan. Micro loan funds make loans as low as hundreds of dollars and as high as $25,000. Each has their own limits and target market. See the Business Resource Guide or the computer disc for details of these programs and others.

Washington State Development Loan Fund (DLF) /Community Development Block Grants (CDBG)

Community Development Block Grants are federal grants. The State of Washington and larger metropolitan communities use a small portion of these federal grants to fund economic development loan programs. The State of Washington Development Loan Fund is a revolving loan program similar to those described above, but designed for larger projects. The DLF can fund up to 30 percent of a project with loans generally up to $350,000, but with special approval loans can be made up to $700,000. Community Development Block Grant funds, through the Washington Development Network, are also used by the state to provide loan capital to local revolving and micro-loan funds. See the Business

> **Community Development Block Grants are federal grants**

Resource Guide in this book, for details of these programs and others, or call Community Development Finance at (360) 753-0325.

Minority And Woman Owned Business Programs

The State of Washington has two primary finance programs for certified minority and woman-owned businesses. The DLF (state revolving fund) has a special loan program for certified businesses which can make loans where other financing is not available. This program can finance up to 100 percent of a project for loans up to $50,000. The second is the Linked Deposit Program. Certified businesses can obtain a 2 percent lower interest rate from participating banks. For information on certification as a minority or woman owned business and other programs or call:

Washington State Office of Minority and Woman Business Enterprises
406 South Water
P.O. Box 41160
Olympia, WA   98504-1160
Phone # (360) 753-9693   FAX# (360) 586-7079

> **There are two primary finance programs for certified minority and woman-owned businesses**

Business Assistance Center, Minority and Woman's Business Programs
Washington State Department of Community, Trade, and Economic Development
2001 Sixth Avenue
Suite 2700
Seattle, WA 98121
Phone #: (206) 389-2561

For more information on the financing programs, call community Development Finance (360) 753-0325

Many local revolving and micro loan funds identify minority and woman owned business as a priority sector.

Seller & Dealer Financing

One of the most common methods of getting into business for yourself is to purchase a business, or some of its assets, from the current owner. The typical assets which sellers are willing to finance include land, buildings, equipment and rolling stock (cars, trucks, forklifts etc.). Sellers usually want cash for inventory and keep the business' cash and receivables.

The major advantage of seller financing is that the terms of sale are negotiable. Negotiable terms include interest rate (often fixed and lower than other lenders); length of the loan (often a longer term than banks or other lenders are willing to provide); and cash down payment (many sellers are willing to take little or no down payment, depending on how strong an incentive they have to sell). If the incentive to sell is strong enough, the seller may be willing to subordinate their loan to others.

One method of getting into business is to purchase a business from the current owner

The seller is not always the current business owner, and seller financing is not just for start-up businesses. Land and buildings are often financed with a seller's Real Estate Contract. This type of financing is used for relocation and/or expansion of existing businesses as well as new owners and start-ups. Small business owners also purchase equipment and rolling stock from private owners or other businesses.

Most, but not all, sellers would prefer cash. As a small business owner, you should always ask the seller if they are willing to sell on contract. If they are, be prepared to negotiate terms. Do not always accept the first offer. One strong motivation for sellers to offer contract terms is to defer capital gains taxes. This is usually more relevant to land and buildings, which appreciate in value, and less true for equipment and rolling stock.

You should always ask the sellers if they are willing to sell on contract

Dealer Financing. Excellent financing terms for equipment and rolling stock can often be obtained from the dealer. Equipment and commercial vehicle dealers often have arrangements with lenders to finance their sales to small businesses. The most common forms of dealer financing are with a Conditional Sales Contract or a Lease. While this is not always the most attractive financing, in many cases dealers can offer better terms than a small business owner can obtain directly from their banks. As with other seller financing, it is always wise to ask the dealer what financing is available– then compare it to offers made by other lenders.

Trade Credit
Trade credit can be used to finance inventory. It is a short-term loan from suppliers. Most suppliers will sell to you on credit; however, a new company has to work at getting it. Suppliers want to know the names of other companies with which you have accounts, so they can check with them to see if you have paid your bills. At startup, of course, you have no accounts. You need to get a few key accounts, and thereafter the others will fall into place.

Trade credit can be used to finance inventory

Offer to go on a COD basis with a major supplier. After several purchases, they will grant you credit. You then have them to list as a credit reference.

Listing yourself with Dun & Bradstreet often gives you credibility. They provide credit and financial information to member companies. Your suppliers could therefore check with D&B about your credit. To list your company, contact the D&B office at 1-800-234-3867.

Be aware that trade credit is short term. Most companies give you thirty days to pay for purchases, sometimes you get up to sixty or ninety days. You probably will not have liquidated your inventory that quickly. You therefore need to find another way to pay the bills. Line up another source in advance. Don't get behind in your payments. Your inventory is the lifeblood of your business. If you get put on COD terms or suppliers refuse to ship to you because you are behind on your bills, your company is severely hampered. You may have great difficulty reestablishing trade credit once it is taken away.

Be aware that trade credit is short term

Trade credit can also be costly. Most suppliers give you a discount if you pay early. A common credit term is 2/10 net 30. This means that you have thirty days to pay the bill, but if you pay within ten you get a 2 percent discount. If you don't pay early and take the discount, you are paying the equivalent of 36 percent interest on the borrowed amount. If you have the cash, you should pay early. It will improve your profits.

Trade credit can also be costly

Commercial Finance Companies
Finance companies will sometimes give loans to businesses which banks consider too risky, particularly in capital intensive industries which require a heavy investment in equipment, such as logging and heavy construction. They will also tend to specialize in industry sectors banks consider high risk, such as motels. Historically, they are not as concerned with your ability to repay as they are with their ability to liquidate your assets if they get them back. Over the last five years some finance companies have become more oriented to cashflow lending and more competitive on the rates they charge, and generally have a lower fee structure.

Finance companies are typically willing to loan on equipment, inventory, and accounts receivable. A finance company cannot loan against them if a bank already has claimed them as collateral.

Finance companies will generally lend 70-80 percent on receivables, 40-50 percent of the liquidation value of inventory, and 60-70 percent of the liquidation value of assets. The equipment loans are usually for five years, while the receivables and inventory loans are for one year. Finance companies usually write stringent prepayment penalties into loan agreements. They don't want you to turn around and refinance the assets with a bank as soon as the opportunity arises.

Finance companies loan on a percentage basis of the liquidation value of assets. While finance companies don't like to get assets back much better than do banks, they are much better and experienced at getting rid of assets. They are willing, therefore, to make riskier loans if they feel that they can get their money out at auction. If you can't get banks to give you a loan, consider finance companies. Be ready to pay the price, however. Their interest rates are 2 to 6 percentage points higher than the banks'. Also, finance companies may be very aggressive about enforcing their rights against you and your collateral if you fail to perform your obligations.

> **Finance companies will sometimes give loans to businesses which banks consider too risky**

Leasing

Most finance companies are willing to provide lease financing and many commercial banks have leasing and/or commercial finance company subsidiaries. The advantages of leasing include low down payment, longer terms, tax benefits, better rates and lower fees. Not all lease programs have some, or all of these benefits, and need to be carefully reviewed and compared to other financing options.

There are many kinds of leases and they can be flexible in how they are structured. Sometimes leases are treated as loans with the lessee capitalizing the asset like a purchase, depreciating the asset and showing lease payments as principal and interest payments (capital lease). In other cases, the lessor will depreciate the equipment and the lease payment will be fully written off as an operating expense (operating lease). After receiving a quote on lease financing, you should check with your accountant to determine if the lease is a "capital" or "operating lease". Whether a lease is considered an operating or capital lease can have a significant effect on the income tax your business will pay.

> **Finance companies loan on a percentage basis of the liquidation value of assets**

Industrial Revenue Bonds

Lease programs need to be carefully reviewed and compared to other financing options

Industrial revenue bonds are a form of *security*. They are a type of debt financing available to smaller (under $10 million project size) *manufacturing and processing* companies. Commercial, retail and service companies cannot use this type of financing. Financing proceeds can be used for land (a maximum of 25 percent of the borrowing), buildings, and new equipment. Working capital cannot be financed through this method.

Industrial revenue bonds are a form of security

Industrial revenue bonds are issued through state and local financing authorities. Payment of principal and interest is the responsibility of the borrowing company; however, the issuing governmental authority does not provide any funds nor does it provide any guarantee of the debt. The borrowing company must be creditworthy in its own right; usually some form of credit support, such as a letter of credit, will be required to support the bond issue. The advantage to the borrowing company is that this type of financing permits the company to borrow at tax-exempt rates, which provide a great savings in interest costs over conventional financing means. Historically, the all-in annual borrowing cost (including the cost of the letter of credit) for industrial revenue bonds has averaged 1½ percent below prime. It also permits the company to borrow long-term at fixed rates, something not possible from other sources.

This type of financing permits the company to borrow at tax-exempt rates

While issuance costs generally restrict the attractiveness of industrial revenue bond financing to projects larger than $1.5 - $2 million, some issuing authorities such as the Washington Economic Development Finance Authority (WEDFA) in Washington state have equipment finance programs to make tax-exempt financing available for equipment purchase projects as small as $250,000.

For more information on industrial revenue bonds and other bond finance programs, contact:

Washington Economic Development Finance Authority (WEDFA)
1000 Second Avenue, Suite 2700
Seattle, WA   98104-1046
(206) 587-5634
(206) 389-2819 fax

Conclusion on Debt Financing

Debt financing enforces a set payment schedule upon your business. If you don't make payments according to the loan agreement, you risk losing the business and whatever else you pledge against the loan. With a loan, however, no one else becomes an owner of the business. It is also more difficult to sustain a high growth rate for your business with debt financing than it is with equity financing. Shop around for a bank that can meet your long-term needs, and be prepared when you go in to ask for a loan. *Prepare your business plan.* The SBA may help the bank in making a loan to you. Ask your banker if they are certified with these programs. If banks are unwilling to give you a loan, consider finance companies. You *may* have to pay higher interest rates, though. If your project will create or retain jobs, call Community Development Finance at (360) 753-0325 to obtain help structuring your proposal and determining what type of loan and/or lease programs you are eligible for and make the most sense for your business. Lastly, trade credit can provide you with short-term credit. Don't depend on it for long-term financing of your business.

> Debt financing enforces a set payment schedule upon your business

Equity Financing

Any time someone invests money in your enterprise with the expectation of realizing a profit from that investment, they have just bought a *security* from your company, and both state and federal securities laws are applicable to the transaction. This is a point which cannot be overemphasized! Most equity and many kinds of debt fall into this category. Compliance with securities laws can be complex, and the assistance of a transaction advisor, such as a knowledgeable attorney or accountant, is a wise precaution. This may seem like overkill when it is just your oldest friend investing $10,000 for 10 percent of your profits. However, doing it right at the beginning can save you many headaches– and a lot of expense– later. Beyond the fact that violation (even if inadvertent) of securities laws can lead to severe penalties, both civil and criminal, any problems in your capital structure will have to be fully resolved before a public stock offering can be made. Even if you aren't now thinking of ever doing a public offering, you do not want to create potential problems for yourself.

> Most equity and many kinds of debt fall into the category of security

Equity Investors

An equity investor becomes part owner of your business. She doesn't require a set payback schedule, rather she shares in the business profits and growth in equity. There are different generic types of equity investors. The simplest type is a "friendly investor," such as a relative or friend who believes in you, gives you money, and takes a share of the business. Second, wealthy individual investors– usually known as "angels"– have provided the funding for many start-up ventures. They are people with significant means and an interest in being a part of high opportunity ventures. Third, venture capitalists are professional fund managers who seek to invest in high-growth ventures. Fourth, stock offerings make stock available to a large number of investors. A public stock offering allows stock to be traded by investors in different markets. All these forms of equity investment are discussed in this section.

> An equity investor becomes part owner of the business

Types of Equity

Common Stock. The most basic form of equity is common stock. Common stockholders may receive dividends and other distributions from the company. They are entitled to vote for members of the board of directors and to vote on major decisions regarding the company, such as sale of all of its assets, merger, or dissolution. Common stockholders generally take the greatest risk, because their rights to receive profits are subordinated to lenders and preferred stockholders. However, they also have the potential for the greatest profit if the business does well.

> The most basic form of equity is common stock

Preferred Stock. Preferred stock is usually issued to investors who don't want the risk of common stock. Risk is reduced by giving the preferred stockholders preferential rights over common stockholders. For instance, preferred stockholders are usually entitled to receive dividends before any are received by the common stockholders. They also usually have a priority to the proceeds upon any sale of the company. Frequently, that priority is equal to the amount of the preferred stockholders' investment plus any unpaid dividends.

> Preferred stock is usually issued to investors who don't want the risk of common stock

Sometimes preferred stock is convertible into common stock. Preferred stockholders convert if the value of the common stock received in the conversion will exceed the preferred stock's liquidation proceeds and dividends. Convertibility enables the preferred stockholders to obtain a higher rate of return if the business does well. Preferred stockholders might also receive redemption rights. Generally, these rights allow a shareholder to force the company to redeem preferred shares if the company is not sold or doesn't conduct a public offering within a specified period of time after the shareholder's investment.

Registration rights are another benefit preferred stockholders sometimes receive. These rights, which are triggered when the company goes public, allow the preferred stockholders to have their common stock registered after the preferred stock has been converted. The filing and preparation costs of registration are borne by the company. This is a valuable right to the investor, because it allows the investor to sell in public markets without paying all of the expense of a securities registration, which is considerable.

Convertibility enables the preferred stockholders to obtain a higher rate of return if the business does well

Warrants. A warrant is a contract right to purchase the company's common stock in the future at a fixed price, usually at or above the current per share price. These are often packaged with subordinated debt or preferred stock to give the investor a greater return if the business does well.

Duties to Other Shareholders– Sharing Control

Having other shareholders creates significant new legal obligations for the entrepreneur. He or she must obtain their approval of any transaction the entrepreneur has with the company after fully disclosing the terms of the transaction to them. In addition, the entrepreneur, when acting on behalf of the company, is required to act prudently, in good faith and in a manner he reasonably believes to be in the best interests of the company.

The owner/company lease is an example of a transaction affected by these new obligations. For tax reasons, business owners often lease real estate to their company rather than having the company directly own the property. Often the lease terms are more favorable to the lessor than in an arms' length transaction. After other shareholders are admitted, they must approve renewal of the lease after they are fully informed of the renewal terms.

Having other shareholders creates significant new legal obligations for the entrepreneur

Having other shareholders also requires the entrepreneur to share control of the business. Unless there is an agreement otherwise, minority shareholders will be entitled to vote for the directors of the company. In most situations, they will also be required to approve any sale or merger of the company or to amend the company's governing documents.

Shareholder Agreements

Before you sell equity in your company, you and your investors should sign a shareholder agreement drafted by an attorney who has a thorough understanding of corporate law. Shareholder agreements prescribe what happens to shares after a stockholder dies or withdraws, how directors will be elected, and how the shareholders will make important decisions affecting the company's future. Most agreements also prevent shareholders from selling their shares to third parties without first offering them to the existing shareholders.

Securities Laws

It's crucial that you comply with federal and state securities laws when selling equity. If you don't, your investors can require you to buy back their investment with interest, and you may become subject to administrative or even criminal proceedings.

Don't think that securities laws only apply to stock sales by publicly traded corporations. Under federal law, securities are any investment of money in a common enterprise with the expectation of profits that are generated through the efforts of others. Under Washington law, securities include any investment of money, property or even services in the risk capital of a venture with the expectation of some valuable benefit. Under these definitions, securities laws will apply even when one old college buddy gives you $2500 to put in your new software company, and you promise a share of any profits.

There are two major types of securities laws: those that require registration or allow an exemption from the requirements, and those that prohibit fraud.

Registration. Prior to the offer or sale of securities, the seller must file a registration statement unless it has an exemption. The purpose of the registration statement is to disclose all of the information needed by the average investor to determine whether the securities offered are a good investment. A registered securities offering requires vast amounts of time and is very expensive. Fortunately, exemptions from registration requirements are available for non-public offerings. (Exemptions are discussed below in more detail under "Private Placements".) Remember, every sale of securities must either be registered or qualify for a registration exemption, whether the sale is to the public, a small number of investors or a venture capitalist.

Anti-fraud. The anti-fraud rules prohibit the "making of any untrue statement of a material fact or the omission of material facts which are necessary to make a statement not misleading." This means that, when selling or even offering to sell a security, you must disclose to the investor all facts that a reasonable investor would consider important when making an investment decision. These rules apply to the offer and sale of registered securities, as well as offers and sales of stock that are exempt from the registration requirements. This means that even if your sale is exempt from the registration requirements, you must still comply with the anti-fraud rules. Usually, this means you will need to have a lawyer to prepare a document for your investors which thoroughly discusses your company and the proposed investment.

> A registration statement should disclose all information needed by an investor to determine if the securities offered are a good investment

Types of Equity Offerings

There are several different types of equity offerings. Non-public offerings, also called "private placements," include offerings to "friendly investors," such as relatives, friends or associates who give you money and take a share of the business. Private placements are also offered to wealthy individual investors who have an interest in being a part of high opportunity ventures. Another type of offering is venture capital placement. It is a specific type of private placement with professional fund managers who seek to invest in high-growth businesses. Finally, a public stock offering allows stock to be traded by investors in public markets. All of these forms of offerings are discussed in this section.

When you seek equity capital, you need to be aware of the criteria investors use. Two critical criteria are stage of development and growth potential. The stages of development are similar to those presented in Chapter l, The Stages of Business Growth. Each is described below:

> When you seek equity capital, you need to be aware of the criteria investors use

- *Seed Stage.* This is the idea stage of the business. Work is done completing product development. The stage ends when the business plan is written.

- *Startup Stage.* The owner(s) actively pursues the business and seeks to make sales. The stage ends when commercial interest is shown in the product.

- *First Stage.* The organization becomes established. Sales are made. The organization has sufficient cash flows to survive.

- *Rapid Growth.* Sales of the company increase dramatically.

Investors also classify companies according to the potential that they demonstrate. These are:

Investors also classify companies according to the potential that they demonstrate

- *Stable Small firms.* These companies have annual sales of $1 million to $5 million. They have little potential for growth because of either choice, market size or circumstance.

- *Foundation firms.* These companies have annual sales potential of $5 million to $20 million and have growth rates of ten to twenty percent per year.

- *High Growth firms.* These companies have sales potential exceeding $20 million and grow in excess of thirty percent per year.

Figure 7-1 shows what type of equity investments are generally available to companies depending on their stage of development and growth potential of the firm.

Figure 7-1. Equity Capital Available for Different Ventures

Stage of Development	Stable Small Firms	Foundation Firms	High-Potential Firms
Seed	Personal Savings	Personal Savings Friendly Sources	Personal Savings Wealthy Individ Venture capital
Startup	Personal Savings	Wealthy Individuals	SBIC's Venture Capital Wealthy people
First Stage	Personal Savings Friendly Sources	SBIC Wealthy Individuals	Venture capital Wealthy Individ
Rapid Growth	Personal Savings Friendly Sources	Venture Capital Public stock	Venture capital Public stock

Private Placements
In private placements, shares are offered to a small number of people, usually no more than 20-40. Private placements include offerings to friendly sources as well as to investors who are not family or friends but who have significant assets, cash flow or both.

Friendly Sources. High potential firms such as Netscape are very much the exception. Most companies in Washington or any other state are essentially Stable Small, and will not grow beyond $1 million in annual sales. These companies do not have a realistic chance of attracting money from wealthy individuals, venture capitalists, or a public stock offering. Usually owners of these firms must rely on their family and personal acquaintances for investment capital. For those companies that do have the potential of significant growth, however, each of the following alternatives is a possibility.

Private placements include offerings to friendly sources as well as other investors

Wealthy Individual Investors. These fall into two types. First is the "one shot"– these investors are actually buying themselves jobs. Frequently they are mid-career managers who have been "right sized" from their previous company and are using their severance package and personal savings to bankroll their second career. These people will often consider types of companies and industries that other "angel" or early-stage equity investors would not. They will, however, also expect to be heavily involved in the running of the company and to be able to reap at least a living wage-equivalent return on their investment.

Wealthy investors fall into two types

The other typical investor group includes people with considerable wealth who are interested in investing in startup or early stage companies that they consider promising (often termed "angels"). There are approximately 250,000 of these individuals in the United States. The best estimate of the size of this market is that $10-20 billion is invested annually into approximately 30,000 ventures in this country. This compares to approximately $4-5 billion annually into approximately 3 thousand enterprises by the venture capital industry.

In general "angel" investors are looking for much the same type of company as are the venture capitalists– high growth potential with a five to ten year cash-out. To a large degree, they are in competition with the venture capitalists. Because of this, an area such as the Puget Sound with its large population of Microsoft millionaires, will often have a relatively small number of venture capital sources.

"Angel" investors often look for "psychic" income beyond just the balance sheet and income statement– the chance to help other entrepreneurs, assist with inner city problems or MWBE (Minority and Woman Business Enterprises), for example. These factors are only frosting on the investors' cakes. "Angels" did not become highly affluent by being fools and the entrepreneur should expect their due diligence to be as thorough as any other capital source.

Finding "angel" investors is not easy. They do not generally publicize their interest in investing in new companies. They would be inundated with business plans if they did, which is the last thing that they want. The best way is to "network" with as many professionals, business attorneys, accountants, commercial real estate brokers and other business service providers as possible. Blow your own horn as much and frequently as possible. Some areas will have business forums which allow entrepreneurs to get up and tell their story in front of venture investors. One such in the Puget Sound area is:

"Angel" investors look for companies with high growth potential and a five to ten year cash-out

> MIT Enterprise Forum of the Northwest
> 217 Ninth Avenue North
> Seattle, WA   98109
> (206) 623-8632

In recent years, computer-based "matching" services to bring together entrepreneurs with potential investors have been formed in different parts of the country and overseas. The Western Investment Network (WIN) is one in Washington state. WIN will only deal with firms seeking to raise less than $1 million and requires that an entrepreneur have a transaction advisor– usually an experienced securities attorney or accountant. The entrepreneur submits a business plan and application with $100 application fee to WIN. WIN gives the plan a thorough "scrub"; the plan is then re-submitted with a $650 network fee. WIN will then circulate a précis of the plan to those investors in its database whose investment criteria are met by the proposed venture. This protects the investor from being buried in business plans and ensures that they will only see those proposed ventures in which they might have an interest. Investor interest varies according to the potential enterprise and cannot be guaranteed. Typically, however, about three potential investors will be sufficiently interested to want to learn more about the venture. WIN can be contacted at:

Finding "angel" investors is not easy

> Western Investment Network
> 411 University Street, Suite 1200
> Seattle, WA   98101
> (206) 467-0212
> (206) 463-6386 fax

The Washington Entrepreneur's Guide

Securities Laws Exemptions for Private Placements of Equity.
Private placements must qualify for an exemption from both the
federal and state registration requirements. One frequently used
state exemption in Washington is referred to as "Regulation D",
because it is similar to a federal exemption of the same name. You
can qualify for the state exemption under one of three rules:

1. *Rule 504.* For offerings of $500,000 or less to 20 or
   fewer investors. No commissions can be paid on the
   sales. Each investor that is not accredited (see
   definition below) must meet either a "suitability" or
   "sophistication" requirement. The suitability
   requirement is satisfied if the investment is not
   excessively large when compared to the investor's
   remaining assets. The sophistication requirement is
   met if the investor has the knowledge and experience
   in financial and business matters, either alone or with
   a representative (such as an accountant or other
   financial advisor) to be able to evaluate the relative
   risks and merits of the investment.

> **Private placements must qualify for an exemption from both the federal and state registration requirements**

2. *Rule 505.* For offerings of $5 million or less to not
   more than 35 purchasers who aren't accredited, and
   any number of accredited investors. Each non-
   accredited investor must meet either the suitability or
   sophistication requirement.

3. *Rule 506.* For offerings of more than $5 million to no
   more than 35 non-accredited investors, and any
   number of accredited investors. The non-accredited
   investors must meet the sophistication requirement.

Accredited investors include:

- Any individual whose individual net worth, or
  joint net worth with that person's spouse, exceeds
  $1,000,000;

- Any individual who had an individual income in
  excess of $200,000 in each of the two most recent
  years or joint income with that person's spouse in
  excess of $300,000 in each of those years, and has
  a reasonable expectation of reaching the same
  income level in the current year;

- Directors, executive officers, or general partners of the company or partnership selling the securities.

- Certain financial institutions, trusts and other organizations

Under this exemption, there can be no general solicitation of investors or advertising. No commissions may be paid in Rule 504 offerings. In Rule 505 or 506 offerings, commissions may be paid only to registered broker dealers. Under any of the alternatives, you must provide the investors with full disclosure about their potential investment, and Rules 505 and 506 have very specific disclosure requirements, including audited financial statements if you offer to non-accredited investors. You must insure that your investors are not currently intending to resell their securities. You must also file certain forms with the state and federal securities regulators.

The requirements of the federal Regulation D exemption are similar to the Washington exemption. Other Washington and federal exemptions might also be available for your offering.

Under this exemption, there can be no general solicitation of investors or advertising

Private placements are much easier than public offerings, but they aren't without problems. It is difficult to persuade brokers to sell the stock. Even sales commissions of 15 to 20 percent may not motivate brokers to market the stock. Second, purchasers of privately placed stock may not sell their stock for two years. Third, the securities regulations are complex. In choosing an attorney to help with a private placement, it is crucial to select one who has extensive experience with them.

Venture Capital
The term "venture capital" refers to professionally managed funds that invest in smaller, privately held companies. Venture capitalists look for companies that will grow dramatically. Most hope to "cash out" of the investment in a three to ten year time period.

A *Small Business Investment Company* (SBIC) is a venture capital company that's certified through the Small Business Administration (SBA). These firms must invest in enterprises that meet SBA guidelines. SBIC's are eligible for SBA loans to finance the investments. They operate very much like any other venture capital company, though they tend to make more debt investments. At present, there are four SBICs in the state of Washington, as listed in Chapter 16.

The Pros and Cons of Venture Capital. Venture capital may be the only source of funds for an enterprise. Banks are usually hesitant to loan to young, growing companies. Venture capitalists understand that they are taking on high risk, but they are betting on a "big win." They may invest when no one else is willing to. Another advantage is that venture capital investment doesn't require scheduled fixed payments like debt. Lastly, venture capitalists often provide management assistance to the company. Although some entrepreneurs regard this as a burden, in many cases the assistance is of very high quality. Venture capital's biggest disadvantage is that it usually requires the entrepreneur to give up a significant measure of ownership and control.

> **Venture capital refers to professionally managed funds that invest in smaller, privately held companies**

Closing a venture capital deal is a long shot. Roughly 60 percent of the proposals are rejected after a brief reading. About 25 percent are reviewed in some detail, then turned down. 15 percent are investigated thoroughly, and only a third of those get investment offers. Of these, only half result in venture capital financing. Thus, only 2 to 3 percent of all proposals are successful.

> **Venture capital may be the only source of funds for an enterprise**

Searching Out Venture Capital Firms. There are about 600 private venture capital companies and SBIC's in the United States. Many are concentrated in Silicon Valley near San Francisco and on Route 128 near Boston. They tend to specialize in certain stage financing and on certain types of industries. *Pratt's Guide to Venture Capital Sources* is probably the most authoritative directory of venture capital companies. It describes the type of investments venture capitalists are seeking. Check your local library for this book, or contact the publisher:

Venture Economics, Inc.
40 W. 57th St.
New York, NY 10019
(201) 622-4500

Like SBIC's, venture capital firms tend to come and go locally, sometimes as branch offices of venture capital firms in other cities. Three associations can also provide information on sources of venture capital:

> **Closing a venture capital deal is a long shot**

Western Association of Venture Capitalists
3000 Sand Hill Road
Building 1, Suite 190
Menlo Park, CA 94025
(415) 854- 1322

National Venture Capital Association
Suite 700
1655 North Fort Myer Drive
Arlington, VA 22209
(703) 351-5269

National Association of Small Business Investment Companies
(NASBIC)
1199 North Fairfax St., Suite 200
Alexandria, VA 22314
(703) 683-1601

What Venture Capitalists Evaluate. Each venture capital company has its own criteria for evaluating potential deals, but the following are nearly universally considered:

> **Each venture capital company has its own criteria for evaluating potential deals**

Management Abilities. Venture capitalists look first to see who is involved in your venture and what their skills are. Venture capitalists like to back people who have had previous success in other ventures. They think this factor is more important than the business opportunity itself. They want to see evidence of marketing, finance, and operations management experience. Review Chapter 8, Gathering Your Forces, on how to build a management team.

Nature of the Product and Industry. You need to have a unique product or service and the ability to maintain a competitive advantage.

Return on Investment. Investors are willing to look at risky ventures if they believe they can obtain high returns. You won't get much attention if you project profits to be slightly better than what the bank can guarantee. Figure 7-2 shows the rate of return that venture capitalists typically seek. They range from a minimum of 25 percent to greater than 60 percent.

Before jumping to the conclusion that venture capitalists are the newest breed of robber barons, understand that the odds are against them. Typically, five of every ten deals backed by venture capital go under, three are marginally profitable, and two turn out to be winners. They don't win frequently, so when they win they must win big.

Figure 7-2. Returns on Investment Typically Sought by Venture Capitalists

State of Business	Expected Annual ROI	Expected Increase in Initial Investment
Startup	60 %+	10-15 times
First Stage	40-60%	6-12 times
Second Stage	30-50%	4-8 times
Third Stage	25-40%	3-6 times
Turnaround	50%+	8-15 times

Schilit, 1987, p. 78

Harvest Options. Venture capitalists don't want to own a piece of your company indefinitely. You must show them a "harvest option"– that is, how they will eventually get their money out of the investment. Refer to Chapter 14, Harvesting a Business, for means of cashing out of a business.

> **Investors are willing to look at risky ventures if they believe they can obtain high returns**

Approaching Venture Capitalists. The way you approach venture capitalists is important. Don't mail a business plan to every venture capital company for which you find an address. Do your homework. Find out which venture capital companies consider the stage of development and type of industry that you are in. Try to get an introduction through a third party.

Write a good business plan! You're tired of hearing that, but it can't be overemphasized. You may have a great idea and opportunity, but if the business plan doesn't communicate that well, venture capitalists won't consider you. Chapter 13, The Business Plan, details information you should include. Make sure you have a clear executive summary that grabs attention. Sometimes investors won't read the rest of the business plan because the summary doesn't capture their interest. Since they are usually evaluating management, competitive advantages, return on investment, and harvest potential, highlight them.

> **The way you approach venture capitalists is important**

Conclusion on Venture Capital

Venture capital is not easy to get. To have a chance, you need to show solid management, a promising competitive position, high returns, and an exit strategy. Make sure that you really need the money or that you can't borrow the money, because the venture capitalists will want a big chunk of your business. Prepare a good business plan and send it to firms that are willing to consider companies in industries like yours and that are at your stage of development.

Issuing Stock

A public offering ("going public") is the sale of shares to a large number of buyers. Any company seeking to "go public" must endure a rather tortuous preparation process that is heavily regulated by the Securities and Exchange Commission (SEC). In addition, you'll have to find an underwriter to market the stock. An underwriter may choose to do so on a "firm underwriting" basis (which guarantees the sale) or a "best efforts" basis (which does not). Very few startup or small companies are able to interest underwriters to handle initial public offerings on either basis, especially the first. When they do succeed in public offerings, however, they usually gain a substantial infusion of cash and their founders usually experience a great increase in wealth as a result.

Securities Laws Exemptions for Public Equity Offerings. Small stock offerings can take advantage of simplified registration and filing requirements. In Washington, if you are planning to sell $1 million or less of stock in any given year, you may be able to use the ULOR (Uniform Limited Offering Registration– also known as SCOR, Small Corporate Offering Registration) registration filings. ULOR offers a simplified fill-in-the-blanks disclosure format. The ULOR format has also been adopted by the Securities and Exchange Commission as an alternative format for securities exempted from normal registration under Regulation A. "Reg. A" exemptions are available for stock offerings of $5 million of less. The assistance of a qualified transaction advisor– either a securities attorney or experienced accountant– is strongly advised in preparing filings and public offerings under either of these programs.

There are pros and cons of going public, and they need to be weighed carefully.

Pros. Public stock offerings can raise large amounts of capital for a company. The typical IPO brings in between $500,000 and $10 million. As a company founder, you have liquidity, because you now will be able to sell shares on the stock market, though you won't be able to sell some shares for at least two years. Your equity in the business increases substantially. The increased equity usually allows you to raise further capital through borrowing. Having a publicly traded stock can help bring recognition to your company.

Cons. The expenses of a public stock offering are significant. Attorney, accountant, and underwriter fees and printing costs are tremendous. These expenses can range from seven to twenty percent of the value of the offering, depending on its size. Some of the parties are willing to take some of the stock instead of being paid cash.

As a publicly held company, you must file quarterly disclosure documents with the SEC. The red tape and paperwork can be overwhelming. It can take an extra full-time person just to handle the SEC reporting requirements.

You will no longer have the ability to run the company as freely as you used to. Boards of directors typically take far more active roles once a company is publicly held. There is pressure on you to produce profits in the short-term, which may reduce your long term success. In general, you are going to be distracted from running your business by the need to respond to stockholders.

If the stock is successfully sold in the initial public offering, the next question is whether the market for it will be active so that shareholders can sell their shares and, they hope, make a profit in the process. Existence of a secondary market to provide liquidity for your stock can be crucial to acceptance of your offering. This is partly a matter of number of shares and number of shareholders that you have. The Pacific Stock Exchange (PSE) has established a SCOR Marketplace for listing of SCOR and Reg. A securities. Contact the PSE at 1-800-TALK-PSE for listing information. Shares for which there are relatively strong markets are usually listed on the NASDAQ or other stock exchanges and can be found listed in most newspapers' financial pages. Examples of some Washington startups which have "gone public" and achieved active markets include Aldus, Costco, Egghead, Nordstrom, QFC, Safeco, Starbucks, and others including such giants as Boeing and

In general, you are going to be distracted from running your business by the need to respond to stockholders

Weyerhaeuser. Initially, it is the size a company's profits are expected to become that determines whether the market will buy, not the size or even existence of its profits at the time it goes public. McCaw Cellular, for example, had no profits when it became publicly traded. Heart Technology similarly went public entirely on anticipation of a future expected to be vastly greater than the company's present performance.

The Key Players. There are several key players in an initial public offering. The first is you, the lead entrepreneur. You have the most at stake and therefore will sweat the most blood. Every entrepreneur who has gone through the IPO process attests to the stress and long hours involved. You need skilled outside advisors in the process. The three main players are the attorney, the underwriter, and the accountant.

There are several key players in an initial public offering

The attorney. You must have a good attorney to get through this process, and you must be willing to pay for the considerable amount of time that he puts in. Attorneys may accept stock in partial or full payment for their services. Ideally, you would like an attorney who is well acquainted with your industry and has handled previous IPOs. There have been enough public offerings by Washington firms so that the larger law firms in Seattle have partners with experience in handling them.

The underwriter. An IPO can be handled either by an investment banking firm or a brokerage firm. Their task is to sell the stock. They usually take a percentage of the stock as payment for their services. This percentage averages 8 percent for an IPO. If your venture shows high promise, they may purchase the stock outright from you, assuring the success and your offering. This is known as a "firm commitment" underwriting. Otherwise, they sell as much as they can– known as "best efforts"– and you get the proceeds (minus fees) after it is sold.

An IPO can be handled either by an investment banking firm or a brokerage firm

It can be very difficult to find an underwriter or broker-dealer who is interested in handling your public offering. Unless there has already been a high public interest in your company or your industry, most investment bankers or broker-dealers will not see sufficient return for their efforts to persuade them to make the time and effort investment to market your company's shares. You may find that you will have to do it yourself. This can be extremely difficult– perhaps not possible. Look at all possible avenues. For example, the idea of "affinity shareholders" has become popular in certain niche industries. These are people who have non-financial reasons for wanting to become shareholders in your company. Both Willamette Valley Vineyards in Oregon and Silver Lake Winery in Washington have targeted the wine-drinking segment of the public for their share offerings. A mail-order company specializing in "green" products marketed its stock to Sierra Club members. Other possibilities may be applicable to your company.

The accountant. SEC regulations require strict accounting compliance. Your underwriter will be quite hesitant for you to hire anyone but a major regional or national accounting firm experienced in SEC regulations. They fear that they may have trouble selling the stock if you have an unknown accounting firm doing the audit. Intimate knowledge of SEC Regulations and other laws and post-issue procedures by the accounting firm will be a source of comfort to both you and underwriter.

Conclusion on Stock Issues

Selling stock allows investors to own part of your company. You are not required to make set repayments to them, but they expect to share in profits and increases in stock value of the company. It is a means of raising substantial amounts of money. IPO's can result in dramatic increases in your equity in a company, and they allow you to get cash out of the business after a period of time. They are costly to undertake and require extensive reporting requirements to the SEC. Private placements are not regulated by federal regulations, but you may have difficulty in getting brokers to sell the stock. With either approach to issuing stock, you need an experienced attorney's assistance.

> **With either approach to issuing stock, you need an experienced attorney's assistance**

References

1.   Bernstein, Michael C./Wolosoff, Lester *Raising Capital: The Grant Thorton LLP Guide for Entrepreneurs* Chicago: Irwin Professional Publishing, 1996

2.   Bloomenthal, Harold S. Cannon Y. Harvey, and Samuel E. Wing. *Going Public Handbook 1992.* New York: Clark Boardman Co., 1993.

3. Ernst & Whinney. *Going Public.* New York: Ernst & Whinney, 1984.

4. Field, Drew *Take Your Company Public!* New York: New York Institute of Finance, 1991.

5. Pratt, Stanley E. *Pratt's Guide to Venture Capital Sources, 17th Edition,* Wellesley Hills, Mass.: Capital Publishing, 1993.

6. Bernstein, Michael and Wolosoff, Lester. *Raising Capital.* Irwin Profession Publishing, chicago, 1996.

7. Schilit, W. Keith. "How to Obtain Venture Capital." *Business Horizons.* May/June, 1987, pp. 76-81.

8. Timmons, Jeffry A. *New Venture Creation,* 3rd Edition. Homewood, Illinois: Irwin. 1990

8

Gathering Your Forces

*"It is better to have great people with a good idea
than to have good people with a great idea."*
General George Doriot

The people behind your venture will have a large impact on its success. Sizable companies have been built around one lead entrepreneur, but more often, several people comprise the driving force behind successful high-growth firms. But whether there is a single entrepreneur or several, all growing companies require the skills of a variety of people. Successful entrepreneurs realize the limitations of their own abilities and draw upon the talents of others. You can bring other people into your business in a variety of ways– as co-owners, employees, consultants, or as members of an advisory board such as a corporate board of directors. The first section of this chapter describes how you identify what skills are critical to your firm's success and also how you can obtain those skills; the second section of this chapter describes several of the most significant laws that govern the employer-employee relationship and how to comply with them.

The success of your venture will be determined, in large part, by the quality of your management team

Building Your Team

Determining What Skills Your Company Needs

You should assess which skills are the most important for the survival and success of your firm. The following lists will provide a starting point in your assessment. They contain skills in the general functional areas of marketing, production, finance/accounting, engineering, research and development, and general management. Go over the skills and write down which you think are essential for the success of your business. Once you have reviewed the lists, add any other skills you think are important in your particular competitive environment– such as exporting knowledge, legal

*The authors would like to thank Ms. Susan Peterson
of the Seattle law firm of Helsell Fetterman LLP for her
contributions to this chapter.*

expertise or connections with suppliers. Add those to your list of essential skills. Your list will change as the company grows, and a key to your success will be acquiring the necessary skills before the need for them becomes critical.

1. Marketing Skills

    a. Market research– able to identify and characterize markets
    b. Product management– able to develop sensible mix products
    c. Distribution management– understands marketing channels and which are appropriate for firm's products
    d. Product pricing– able to competitively price products, maintain profitable margin

> **"Every venture needs a founder who understands the need for supporting skills and knows where to find them, when needed."**

2. Production and Operations Skills

    a. Manufacturing– able to manage manufacturing process
    b. Quality control– able to define standards and meet them
    c. Scheduling– able to schedule people, materials, machinery for efficient production
    d. Inventory control– able to manage a system which determines what, when, and how much to buy
    e. Shop layout– able to design efficient shop layout

3. Finance/Accounting Skills

    a. Cash flow management– able to project cash requirements
    b. Raising capital– aware of different capital sources and how to approach each of them
    c. Financial analysis– able to perform break-even and ratio analysis and interpret them, able to interpret financial statements
    d. Accounting/bookkeeping– able to set up books and keep accurate financial records
    e. Credit and collections– able to develop and enforce credit policies

4. Engineering Skills

5. Research and Development Skills

6. General Management Skills

a. Strategic planning– able to analyze competitors, internal strengths and weaknesses, and external trends and able to develop competitive strategies
b. Organization– able to structure the organization in logical units, able to delegate responsibility, able to coordinate activities of people and divisions
c. Motivation– able to inspire managers and employees to high performance
d. Controlling– able to set goals and make sure goals are being met
e. Communication– able to communicate clearly with employees, media, customer, and others
f. Teamwork– able to get individuals to work as a team
g. Cheerleading– able to support and encourage employees

7. Other Possible Skill Areas

a. Legal expertise– knowledgeable in areas of taxes, real estate, contracts, patents, investments, etc.
b. Computer skills– able to use a computer to improve operations of firm
c. Any other skills which are critical to your particular industry

Every company requires a unique set of skills because of its competitive situation. However, many managers would support the following generalizations:

- Marketing expertise is paramount at startup. Companies need to develop new markets, enter new marketing channels, and decide on marketing strategies. If the originator of the company has strong technical skills but no marketing experience, someone should be brought in with marketing skills.

> **Marketing, financial, and production skills are critical to a company**

- Manufacturing companies need someone with production expertise. Building a successful prototype is far different from setting up an efficient production operation. If you manufacture a product, you need someone with production skills.

- Once sales begin to increase and the size of the company grows, financial and management expertise become critical. Without cash management and financial analytical skills a firm can quickly run out of money. Management skills become increasingly important as the number of workers increases.

Obtaining the Necessary Skills

Once you have decided what skills are the most important for your company's success, you have the task of finding the right people and deciding how they will be affiliated with your organization. Each of the following alternatives is discussed below:

1. Bringing in a co-owner
2. Engaging specialists as contractors
3. Hiring people as employees
4. Having people serve on your advisory board

Bringing in a Co-owner

Deciding to bring in a co-owner is a serious matter, since it means giving up some of your control over the business. Logistically speaking, bringing in a co-owner usually means forming a partnership, corporation or limited liability company and giving your co-owner an equity interest in the enterprise (see Chapters 6 and 7). Particularly if the co-owner is going to take an active role in operating and managing the company, you need to approach the relationship as carefully as you would a marriage. You'll probably be spending as much time with this person as you would a spouse. Incidentally, business divorce rates are higher than marriage divorce rates—*choose your co-owners carefully*!

It may not be easy to find a suitable co-owner. Your personalities should be compatible, and you must trust each other. Your skills should be complementary, as stated above. You shouldn't search for someone exactly like yourself, because you need different skills and ideas. However, your goals for the business should be consistent.

There are several good reasons to give up some of the ownership of your company and open yourself to the frustration of a co-owner. The first is financial. A co-owner almost always makes a financial investment in the company, increasing the business' resources. This may even permit the firm to avoid borrowing from commercial lenders, which reduces the risk of bankruptcy. The second reason involves your ability to attract the talent you need. At the outset, you may not be able to guarantee key individuals a salary equal to what they could get from an established enterprise. All you can

After you've decided on what skills are most important, you must find the right people

Choose your co-owners carefully

There are several good reasons to have a co-owner

offer is a piece of the pie. However, this can be a powerful draw for the top-notch people who have the skills you need. The third reason is commitment. You do not get the same commitment from a salaried employee that you get from a business owner. When a person's money is at stake, his perspective changes. If the skills you are seeking are essential to the success of the company, and you need a person's total commitment, sharing some of the ownership of the business makes sense.

Although there are good reasons for parting with some of the equity in your business, don't believe in a *leaderless democracy*. It will not work in the startup venture! You need to be the leader. To maintain your position, keep a majority interest in the company. When there are differences of opinion, someone needs to step forward and make a decision. Be sure that under the terms of the governing agreement, you have the authority (that is, the voting power) to do so.

> **A leaderless democracy will not work in an entrepreneurial company**

Contractors

Initially, certain types of skills are best acquired on an "as needed" basis– as contractors. For example, until your business grows substantially, you should engage the services of accountants and lawyers in this way. You will not need their services on a full-time basis, so use them (and pay them) only as needed. Other skills which you may need occasionally should be hired on a consulting basis– such as computer set-up, inventory design, etc.

Employees

Most of the people contributing to your organization will be employees. You hire people for skills that are essential to the organization on an ongoing basis and which you (and your co-owner(s), if any) aren't able to or don't have the time to do. To increase their commitment and motivation, you may offer profit-sharing as opposed to ownership. If you can demonstrate the possibility of significant profits, employees may be willing to work at very modest salaries.

Since employees comprise the largest segment of most businesses, the legal issues surrounding the employer-employee relationship are of key importance. The second section of this chapter describes several of the most important of these issues.

> **A board of directors can be invaluable to the startup company**

Advisory Boards

Companies that incorporate are required by law to have a board of directors, but any business can establish an advisory board. Boards can play invaluable roles for the startup company. They include:

Advisory. If your management team lacks certain skills that are important to the company, the board can provide them. The board members act as consultants, but board membership generally results in a greater level of commitment to the organization. Some board members may provide free consulting, but it is not something you should assume. They can also help resolve disputes in the company, set goals and objectives, and review financial statements.

Legitimacy. The people on your board can bring legitimacy to the company. Lenders may know board members and thus look more favorably upon a loan request. Suppliers may offer you credit based on board members' suggestions. You may be able to bypass certain local regulations, such as zoning requirements, if members speak on your behalf. A startup company does not have a track record, and prominent or powerful board members can open doors.

Powerful board members can open doors for your company

Monitoring. Since the board reviews management decisions, it provides discipline for management. Knowing that an objective group of professional people will be reviewing management decisions, you and your managers will tend to act in a professional and ethical fashion.

The role of the board changes over time

The role of the board changes over time. At startup, the advisory and legitimacy roles are critical. As the company grows, the monitoring role becomes increasingly important. Be aware that the composition of the board should change over time in response to these changing roles. As the company requires different skills, you should seek out new board members.

Who Should You Choose? First of all, you should choose individuals who you respect and with whom you can get along. Choose people who can effectively deal with present or future problems of the firm. Potential candidates include:

- Individuals whose skills complement those of the manager(s). If you are weak in financial matters, a person with a strong financial background could be a good candidate;

- Individuals who are involved with companies that are either customers of or suppliers to the industry—but not one of your company's customers or suppliers;

- Investment or commercial bankers who are not your company's investment or commercial banker and who realize that they never will be bankers for the company;

- Experts in some areas that are important to your company's continued growth and profitability; e.g. R&D, venture labor relations, community awareness, and the like;

You should choose people whom you respect and can get along with

- Individuals with a broad perspective who can look at problems from an insightful and objective point of view; and finally, most importantly,

- Experienced executives who have been where the company wishes to go and who can help anticipate potential problems.

You should strive to keep your board small, with either five or seven directors. A larger board becomes unwieldy, while a board smaller than this does not provide for sufficient interaction and breadth of experience. You should have a mixture of both internal and external directors. Internal directors would include people actively involved in managing the company. The people described in the paragraph above would be outside directors. This mixture balances the typically shorter-term, operational orientation of insiders against the longer-term, strategic orientation of outsiders.

Strive to keep a small board of directors

Getting People to Serve as Board Members. At start-up, you don't have much money to pay board members, so that should not be why they would want to serve. You want to sell them on the fact that yours is a growing, exciting venture of which they can be a part. They will be able to work with a group of people from which they can learn. Let them know that their opinions will be listened to and that they can help shape the destiny of your company.

However, you should not expect board members to go without compensation. Some small companies pay several hundred dollars to each board member at each meeting, which usually lasts an entire afternoon. Stock options are also used to compensate board members. Although some board members may be willing to provide free consulting services outside of board meetings, most companies pay them normal consulting fees.

You should not expect board members to go without compensation

Much of the success of the board depends on you. If you view your advisory board as interfering in decisions that are rightfully yours to make, you will have a totally ineffectual board. You need to seek out board members who are committed to the organization and who know that you are willing to listen to them.

The Rules of the (Employer-Employee) Game

Much of the success of the board depends upon you

While you may choose to share ownership of your business with a few carefully chosen individuals and you will periodically contract for the specialized services of others, the majority of people involved in your business on an ongoing basis will be your employees. One key to creating a productive workforce is careful selection of employees. Equally important to the smooth operation of your company and the avoidance of costly lawsuits is a basic knowledge of the laws governing the employer-employee relationship.

Employment "At Will"

In the state of Washington, in general, an employment relationship may be terminated by either the employer or the employee at any time, with or without cause. In other words, in general, your employee may quit, or you may fire her, at any time, for any reason. This general rule is referred to as employment "at will." However, there are a number of exceptions to this general rule. These exceptions are discussed in the following subsections. If you improperly terminate a worker's employment, or otherwise discriminate against an employee, you could find yourself in court.

Employment Contracts

The general rule of employment "at will" does not apply if you enter into an employment contract with your employee that provides otherwise. For example, you and your employee may sign a written agreement that states that she will work for a specified period of time. Generally, such agreements permit the employer to terminate the employee prior to the expiration of the stated term only "for cause." "Cause" can be defined to mean failing to adequately do the job, exhibiting dishonest behavior, etc.

Even if you don't have a written agreement with your employee, an employment contract may exist. For example, you and your employee may have discussed the issue and come to an oral agreement that he would not be terminated except for cause. An oral agreement such as this is just as much an employment contract as a written one. Similarly, if your employee manual sets out specific situations that will cause termination, you may find yourself facing an argument that you agreed not to terminate employees *except* in those situations. Be very careful to make no such promises unless you intend to be bound by them.

> You should have a basic knowledge of laws governing employer-employee relationships

Discrimination

There are several laws which prohibit discrimination in employment. At the federal level, Title VII prohibits an employer from discrimination based on an employee's race, color, religion, sex or national origin. In addition, other federal statutes prohibit discrimination based on age (if an employee is over 40 and under 70), or based on the fact that the employee has a disability or is pregnant. The Washington Law Against Discrimination prohibits discrimination based on all of the Title VII characteristics, and adds marital status to the list. Retaliation against a person who files a complaint or assists in the investigation of a complaint is also prohibited. In addition, some municipalities, such as the City of Seattle, expand the list further to include political ideology and sexual orientation.

> An oral agreement with an employee is just as binding as a written one

The practical implication of these laws is that if you wish to terminate an employee who is a member of one of these protected classes, you must be able to articulate a legitimate, non-discriminatory reason for the termination.

Furthermore, you should be aware that "discrimination" relates to more than just your decision to terminate a worker's employment. It means treating an employee less favorably with regard to job application procedures, hiring, advancement, termination, compensation, job training and any other terms, conditions or privileges of employment.

> Several laws prohibit discrimination in employment

Sexual Harassment

As an employer, you can be held accountable if you engage in harassing conduct or if it takes place on the job and you knew about it

One type of discrimination in the workplace that has been the source of numerous lawsuits against employers in recent years is sexual harassment. As an employer, you can be held accountable if you personally engage in harassing conduct. You also can be held accountable for the harassment an employee suffers from co-workers or management staff, and by non-employees in the workplace such as venders and customers if you knew about the harassment (or if it is so pervasive that you should know about it) and did nothing to stop it.

There are two types of sexual harassment: "quid pro quo" and "hostile environment." Quid pro quo harassment occurs when a worker's advancement or continued employment is conditioned on her (or his) submitting to sexual advances or if a more qualified employee is denied a promotion because they did not submit to sexual harassment. Hostile environment harassment occurs when harassment is so severe or pervasive that the worker's entire work environment is found to be abusive.

Be aware of what is going on in your workplace

The best way to avoid sexual harassment claims is to institute policies that prohibit harassing conduct and provide a mechanism for investigating reported harassment, implement an appropriate training program, and be aware of what is going on in your workplace.

The Law and its Administration

The law against discrimination and sexual harassment is administered and enforced by the Washington State Human Rights Commission. The Commission processes complaints, makes regulations, conducts studies, and provides educational and consulting services. The Commission is an agency of State government, operated by a five member commission, appointed by the Governor, and it's staff. The Commission has offices throughout the state (see Business Resource Guide, Regulatory Assitance) and can assist any person who wishes advise, information, or assistance. For more information, contact:

Washington State Human Rights Commission
711 S. Capitol Way, Suite 402
P.O. Box 42490
Olympia, Washington 98504-2490
360-753-6770 (Voice/TTY)

Wage and Hour Laws

The federal Fair Labor Standards Act and the Washington Minimum Wage Act establish minimum standards for the wages and overtime pay that you must pay to all employees who are covered by the Acts. Generally, the law (federal or state) that provides the greater benefits to employees is the one that must be satisfied. In 1995, the Washington statute set the minimum hourly wage for employees over the age of 16 at $4.90 per hour, somewhat higher than the federal minimum of $4.75 per hour. In addition, both the Fair Labor Standards Act and the Washington law require most employers to pay non-exempt employees for time worked in excess of 40 hours per week at one and one-half times the regular hourly wage. However, neither the federal law nor the Washington law require you to pay overtime for hours worked in excess of eight hours per day; vacation, holiday, severance or sick pay; premium pay rates for weekend or holiday work; or pay raises or fringe benefits.

> **Generally, the law providing greater benefits to the employees is the one that must be satisfied**

Nearly all industries in the state, including agriculture, are covered under the Washington statute. However, certain categories of workers are exempt from both the minimum hourly wage requirements and the overtime pay requirements. For those of your employees that fall into one of the following categories (generally referred to as "exempt employees"), you do not have to comply with the minimum wage and overtime requirements summarized above: independent contractors; volunteers; executives; administrative personnel; and professionals. For more information about state and federal wage and hour requirements, contact:

> **Certain categories of workers are exempt from minimum wage and overtime pay requirements**

Washington Department of Labor and Industries
Employment Standards
P.O. Box 44510
Olympia, Washington 98504-4510
1 (800) 547-8367

U.S. Department of Labor
Employment Standards Administration
Wage and Hour Division
Washington D.C. 20210

Conclusion

The quality of people in your venture will greatly affect its success

The quality of people in your venture will greatly affect its success. Assess honestly your own capabilities, and try to fill in the gaps. Don't believe that you can do it all. If you want to grow, you must bring in other skilled people. And when you do, be aware of the laws that govern the relationships in the workplace.

References

1.   Churchill, Neil C. and Lewis, Virginia L., "A Board for All Seasons," *Harvard Business Review*, May-June 1983.

2.   Gumpert, David (ed)., "How Small Companies Can Best Choose and Involve Outside Directors," in "Growing Concerns," *Harvard Business Review*, July-August 1980.

3.   Timmons, Jeffray A., *New Venture Creation*, 3rd Edition. Homewood, Illinois: Irwin, 1990.

9

Strategic Planning

"In Korea, we work for the future.
You (Americans) work for the weekend."
Unknown

Two great tennis players– Ken Rosewall and Roscoe Tanner– had very different styles of play. Tanner's approach was simple and straightforward– raw power. He hit his serves well over 100 miles per hour and hit aggressively nearly every shot. Opponents feared the days when he was "on," because his power was so overwhelming it could tear the racket right out of an opponent's hand. Rosewall, on the other hand, varied his game based on whom he was playing and what type of court surface was underfoot. Sometimes aggressive, sometimes defensive, sometimes fast, sometimes deliberate, he was a master at adapting his game in order to win.

Both players had approaches that made them top players in the world. Rosewall, however, is the one who is a legend. Why? He was a master strategist. Strategy, in the long run, will win over raw power, and Rosewall demonstrated that fact. He was a formidable opponent, no matter what the court surface, no matter who the opponent, for nearly a twenty-year period.

Strategy, in the long run, will win over raw power

Although Tanner was a great player, he was not a great strategist. He was not good at adapting to different playing conditions, such as the court surface. He did not vary his game significantly depending on whom he was playing– every opponent just prepared for cannonballs. Lastly, his career was not a long one. When the speed began to fall on his serves and other shots, which it does as players age, he did not have much to fall back on.

There are business lessons to be learned in the approaches of these two players. When you have a definite advantage over competitors, whether it be superior products or services, design skills, or marketing abilities, rely on those strengths and don't be afraid to take full advantage of them. "When you've got it, flaunt it." That is what Tanner teaches us. What Rosewall teaches us is that you need to consider the environment in deciding what competitive

Rely on your strengths and take full advantage of them

approach to take. He would consider court surface, wind, sun, motivation level of an opponent, and many other factors. You, as the premier strategist in your company, need to consider the economy, industry trends, changes in customers, and other environmental factors. You need to know who your competitors are, what their strengths and weaknesses are, and how they are going to react to your competitive moves. You, like Rosewall, can have a long and successful business career if you are willing to adapt to changing conditions in order to put yourself in a stronger competitive position. The purpose of this chapter is to present a "strategic" approach to managing your growing company.

You need to adapt to changing conditions

Strategic Planning

There are many different definitions of strategic planning, and most of them are vague and difficult to apply. Planning is the process of thinking about future events and taking action so that those events occur as you want them to. Strategic means nothing more than concentrating on the most critical factors affecting your company. *Strategic planning* is, therefore, the process of analyzing what opportunities and threats face your company, of assessing your company's strengths and weaknesses, and lastly of finding a fit between your company and its environment that gives your company a competitive advantage.

There are many examples of good strategic planning. One is Compaq, which manufactures high quality IBM-compatible microcomputers. When IBM first entered the microcomputer market, Compaq was the first to make its equipment fully compatible to IBM's, and the firm committed itself to equaling or surpassing IBM's quality. The foresight of top management to see that IBM would create a microcomputing standard (most companies at that time did not think IBM would) has paid them royal dividends.

The process of planning doesn't stop with the initial design of the business plan

Wal-Mart has been extremely successful in taking advantage of economies of scale and being able to offer merchandise at discount prices. Underlying Wal-Mart's strategy is a constant emphasis on keeping costs down. Christiansen & Fritsch, Inc., an award-winning direct marketing ad agency in Seattle, has undergone an evolution of corporate strategy. Initially, the company served some sixty clients, but now has a strategy of serving fewer but larger accounts. Each of the above companies has a strategy different than the other two, but all have been successful. Each has chosen a particular strategy and attempted to make all of the operations of the company revolve around that strategy.

There are also many examples of companies that have done a poor job of strategic planning at different times. J.C. Penney was the world's leading retailer of "soft" goods after World War II. The company had built its success on a strategy of cash-and-carry and selling primarily clothing. A competitor of theirs, which was much smaller, decided to start offering credit and to also carry "hard" goods, including hardware and appliances. J.C. Penney did not react to this competitive move, thinking that since their old strategy had worked a long time, why change? Penney's smaller competitor was Sears Roebuck and Co., which is now much larger than J.C. Penney. It took J.C. Penney more than a decade to realize that the old strategy was no longer appropriate. Since that time, both companies have struggled with different strategic issues.

Another example is Osborne Computer, a company that fell prey to a classic strategic mistake– poor timing. The Osborne I was the first portable microcomputer, was very affordable, and came with a full set of free software programs. Osborne was so successful with the Osborne I that they immediately began developing the Osborne II, a "new and improved" model. The company announced the II six months in advance of the anticipated shipping date. It was to be a much improved model with only a slight increase in price. After the announcement, no one wanted to buy an Osborne I, and the company couldn't survive six months without sales. It went bankrupt.

> **Timing is an important strategic issue**

Problems in Planning

There are two types of problem planners: the over-planner and the under-planner. The over-planner has everything planned from the moment of awakening in the morning to the moment when he puts his head on the pillow at the end of the day. His days are filled with "to do" lists, appointment books, schedules, and a need for absolute order. The following line from Jackson Browne's *Reach For the Sky* illustrates the problem.

> **The over-planner and under-planner are both problem planners**

"Without dreaming of the perfect love, and holding it so high above, that if you stumbled onto somebody real, you'd never know."

An entrepreneur needs to react quickly to opportunities, many of which are difficult to foresee, and if a perfect plan blinds him to those opportunities, he'll let them pass right by. Over-planning, though a rare bird in entrepreneurial circles, will drag a company down.

Under-planning is a common visitor to entrepreneurial firms. The hero of this company is a pistol-toting lead entrepreneur who loves to "shoot from the hip". Most of her days are filled with pulling the trigger on a fire extinguisher, trying to put out all of the brush-fires that could have been avoided by some planning. She fails to realize that her "gut-feel," which usually is right, can lead her to disastrous decisions for the company.

Good strategic planning lies in between these two extremes. It is a formal framework of evaluating the company's position in relation to its environment on an on-going basis. However, it should not lead to "paralysis through analysis." Companies need to analyze their opportunities, gather a reasonable amount of information, and then *do something*.

The Strategic Planning Process

The strategic planning process includes six steps:

1. Define the business and develop a strategic mission
2. Formulate strategic goals
3. Analyze the external environment and company strengths and weaknesses
4. Formulate strategies
5. Implement strategies
6. Re-evaluate strategies

Generally, you should try to start with #1 and work towards #6. Be aware that in most cases you can't work straight through without going back and changing what you had previously decided. For example, after you set a strategic goal of growing by 25 percent a year, your analysis of the industry may reveal that is unlikely, so you have to go back and change your goals. Or perhaps you decide that an appropriate strategy for your company is to be an industry market share leader, producing at high volume. After assessing your production capabilities, however, you may conclude that you can't really implement that strategy, even though it is a good one. These examples illustrate the *cyclical* nature of strategic planning– you have to keep going back and reassessing previous decisions. As J.C.

Penney demonstrated, you can't expect what was once a good strategy to continue being one.

Strategic Mission

Strategic mission is a basic statement of what type of business a firm is in. You need to consider what it really is that you provide to customers. For example, some companies have had to redefine what businesses they are in. AT&T decided that they were in the communication business, and not just the telephone business. Many railroad companies have redefined their business as the transportation business, since railroad was too restrictive. Many accounting firms are no longer "accounting" firms, they offer management consulting, financial analysis, and computer systems assistance. Your mission should accurately describe what it is that you provide to customers.

A mission statement will unify people in an organization

There are two primary advantages in having a concise, written mission statement. The first is to give direction to your company. Consider the following example:

A newly-elected president of a corporation stood before the board of directors to make an initial presentation. He had brought a board with metal arrows on it, and it appeared as below.

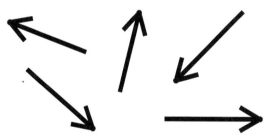

He said, "This is what the company looks like now. There are hard-working and productive people in this firm, but they're not pulling in the same direction. My intention is this," he said as he pulled a magnet from his pocket and slammed it against the top of the board. All of the arrows immediately pointed towards the magnet. "I will bring strategic purpose to this company. As a group, we will know where we are headed and we will all pull in the same direction."

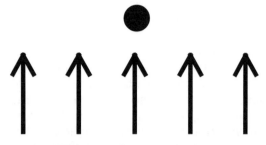

A mission statement will unify people in an organization. The second primary advantage of a mission statement is that it reminds everyone of what the company is trying to achieve. Day-to-day pressures require managers' and employees' attention alike. A common complaint of managers is, "I'm too busy running a company to worry about where it's going." A mission statement serves as a "guiding light" that helps people rise above the many details of running a company and keeps them centered on strategic direction of the company. Phrases portraying missions from reports of some successful Washington companies include:

> **A mission statement serves as a "guiding light" that helps people rise above details**

Immunex. To become a fully-integrated pharmaceutical company by taking products from inception of research to point of sale.

Procyte. Building a fully-integrated biopharmaceutical company.

Microsoft. The idea that someday we'll see a computer on every desk in every home.

Aldus. To create software that helps people throughout the world effectively communicate information and ideas.

MCI. To maintain profitable growth, MCI will: provide a full range of high-value services for customers who must communicate or move information electronically throughout the United States and the world; manage our business so as to be the low-cost provider of services; make quality synonymous with MCI to our growing customer base; set the pace in identifying and implementing cost-effective technologies and services as we expand our state-of-the-art communications network; continue to be an entrepreneurial company, built of people who can make things happen in a competitive marketplace.

Strategic Goals

Strategic goals are the most important goals in your company. They bring definition and measurability to your mission statement. Listed below are typical strategic goals for companies:

- Profitability
- Market Share
- Growth in Sales
- Quality of products or services
- Employee relations/growth
- Social responsibility

Strategic goals are the primary objectives in your organization

Each company will typically have some strategic goals different from these. McDonald's probably has a goal of opening a certain number of restaurants. Toyota's goal may be to attain a certain ranking on the consumer polls that evaluate quality. You should probably have no more than five to eight strategic goals. Strategic goals are the *primary* objectives in your organization. If you have too many of them, you can't concentrate on them.

Analyzing the External Environment

If you are like Roscoe Tanner and have overwhelming competitive strengths, you may not have to pay much attention to the environment. Just make sure your opponent is on the court and start blasting. Most businesses do not enjoy such recognizable competitive advantages; therefore, they must pay attention to what is happening in the world around them. There are three primary external areas for you to analyze:

You must pay attention to what is happening in the world around you

- The general economic, legal, political, and social environment
- The industry(s) you are in
- Your specific competitors

Each of these is described below, along with suggestions on where to obtain information.

The Economic, Legal/Political, and Social Environment. Although smaller businesses are usually affected less by these "macro" variables than are large companies, they cannot afford to ignore them. Economic factors such as gross national product, interest rates, money supply, and exchange rates can have an impact on the success of a small, entrepreneurial firm. If you sell to a local or regional market, you need to pay attention to the economy in your particular area. If you sell nationally or internationally, you

You cannot afford to ignore "macro" variables

should seek out broad economic information. The United States government publishes an incredible amount of economic statistics— check your local libraries to see if any are certified "depositories" of U.S. government publications. The Business Assistance Center has an office that assists businesses in finding economic statistics. The phone number is (800) 273-1233. The Northwest Policy Center at the University of Washington collects and publishes data on the Northwest economy. Call (206) 543-7900. Daily newspapers publish many of the above economic variables on a regular basis. You need to pay attention to the economy in the areas in which you are selling.

The legal and political environment also affects the way you run your business. There are new laws on such issues as firing an employee. Tariffs may affect how much competition you will face. Local zoning laws may restrict what you can do at your business site. New tax laws may affect your business decisions. It is wise to stay as current as possible on those legal and political changes which affect your business. Local newspapers, trade journals, and general business publications such as *Business Week* and *The Wall Street Journal* can provide valuable information.

Pay attention to national and local social changes

Social changes are occurring constantly in this country and in your specific market area– pay attention to them. The nation is becoming a more aged population, and in fifteen years the percentage of the population over fifty years old will be dramatically higher. While this change poses threats to some businesses, such as diaper manufacturers, it presents opportunities to others, such as nursing care facilities. In the last ten years, the number of two-income households has increased dramatically. This has spawned increased demand for day-care, fast food, and home cleaning services. If your company emits pollution, community attitudes will affect how you operate. The prevailing sentiments in your community towards unionization may dictate whether you can operate a non-union shop or not.

No business operates in a vacuum

No business operates in a vacuum. Economic, political, and social trends do affect most businesses and you cannot ignore them. Try to stay as well informed as possible about these issues and the way they might affect your company.

Industry Analysis. An *industry* is a group of firms whose products are so similar that they are brought into close competition. The industry is the most important environmental factor to analyze when formulating your strategic plan. Structure of the industry determines the intensity of competition and affects which strategies work well and which don't. Analysis of the industry helps you to make two major strategic decisions:

The industry is the most important environmental factor to analyze

1. Should you even be in an industry?
2. Which strategies have the best chance of success in the industry?

An assessment of the following industry structural characteristics helps to answer these two questions.

Market Size. You need to first establish that the market you are pursuing contains enough customers for you to make a profit. The greater the market size, the greater sales potential.

Market Growth Rate. A quickly growing market allows for entry of new firms, whereas stagnant markets tend to "shake out" companies. If you can establish a sizable market share in a growing industry, all you need do to grow is preserve your market share. You don't have to take away other competitors' customers.

Gross Margin. Gross margin for a firm is total sales minus direct costs (raw materials, direct labor, etc.) Although margins will differ between firms in an industry, the average margin in an industry is significant. A large gross margin allows a company to have some breathing room– to make a significant profit on individual units or to drop prices to increase sales. Industries with small margins tend to be very competitive.

A large gross margin allows a company to have some breathing room

Industry Profitability. Some companies do better than others, but still in many industries you find companies with profits near an industry average. Some industries have traditionally been quite profitable, while others have struggled.

Entry Barriers. Entry barriers are factors which inhibit newcomers entering an industry. Example of entry barriers include:

- High start-up costs
- Proprietary information (patents)
- Economies of scale
- Learning curve effects
- Brand loyalty
- Access to distribution channels

- Government regulation

High capital costs allow only companies that have been able to raise significant capital to enter the market. Most manufacturers who need a sizable plant and expensive equipment have high start-up costs. Patents can afford protection from potential competitors.

Entry barriers make it difficult to enter an industry

Polaroid has been the only camera maker to have self-developing film because of a patent. You need a lot of money to enforce patents, however, and as many entrepreneurs state, "A patent is only a license to sue. If you can't afford to sue, it won't do you any good." Economies of scale allow the cost per unit to drop when larger volumes are produced. For example, the cost per unit for machinery drops as more units are produced. Large companies such as McDonald's can spend heavily on advertising and keep the cost down at individual restaurants because there are so many outlets.

Learning curve effects are quite strong in some industries. A learning curve is simply the fact that you get more efficient at doing something the longer you do it. A strong learning curve exists in high quality furniture manufacturing. The companies that have been doing it for many years have advantages over newcomers because it is a skill that is not easily nor quickly learned.

Brand loyalty makes it difficult for companies to enter an industry. Some sporting goods companies develop high levels of brand loyalty, such as Rossignol in ski equipment. That loyalty makes it difficult for newcomers because they have to persuade customers to switch.

One or several firms can control access to distribution channels. A new potato chip manufacturer will have a rough time getting its products on grocery store shelves because there is a limited amount of shelving space, and that space is already taken by a proven brand.

Resist the temptation to think that entry barriers are bad

Government regulations can inhibit the entry of new competitors into an industry. Utility companies are highly controlled, as is access to that industry. There are only a limited number of commercial fishing licenses available in Washington, thus limiting newcomers.

Resist the temptation to think that entry barriers are bad. Ideally, you would like barriers to be as high as possible, but low enough for you to get in. Industries with low entry barriers, such as video rental stores, experience intense competition and usually suffer price wars.

Once you get into an industry, you would like to maintain the highest barrier possible to keep newcomers out.

Power of Suppliers. If the suppliers to your industry are few, they can wield considerable power over you. Computer manufacturers recently have had problems receiving microcomputer chips from the few large manufacturers of chips. The small computer producers have been hit especially hard because they have very little leverage when dealing with the large chips producers. Ideally, you would have a large number of suppliers, none of which could wield much power over you.

Power of Customers. Selling to only a few large customers can be risky. If they stop buying your products or choose to buy them from someone else, you lose a large chunk of your sales. Granted, some companies do very well selling primarily to the government and have done it for a long time, but even that puts you in a precarious position. Ideally, you would have a large base of customers who couldn't exert much control over you.

Try to have a large customer base

Amount of Product Differentiation. Some industries have standard, generic-type products, such as the paper industry. Companies have a difficult time making themselves unique in the marketplace. Other industries contain products which are quite differentiated. For example, there is a multitude of shoe manufacturers who have products that vary greatly.

Overall Intensity of Competition. Some industries are extremely competitive. A variety of factors can cause intense competition. Factors already mentioned– low entry barriers, little product differentiation, low margins, low industry growth– often lead to high competition. If the main players in an industry are committed to remaining in the industry, no matter what the cost, they can make life miserable for everyone else. For example, suppose you open a hardware store in a town with two other such stores. Both of your competitors have been in business for more than fifty years, are family owned, have paid off their land and building, and have no intention of doing anything except selling hardware. Do you think they are going to welcome you into the hardware community and make life easy for you? Entrenched competitors tend to be intense competitors.

A variety of factors can cause intense competition

Driving Forces

Driving forces are changes in industry structure or forces that affect the structure. They can pose threats to your company or provide opportunity. The sooner you detect these changes the easier it will be to deal with them as opportunities instead of threats. You should analyze all of the industry structural characteristics described in the previous paragraphs to determine whether changes are occurring or not. Described below are typical driving forces in many industries.

Changes in the long-term growth rate. If an industry is about to take off, you want to garner as much market share as you can before the growth occurs. An example of this is McCaw Communication Cos., Kirkland, Washington. Sensing upcoming growth in the cellular communications industry, the company began bidding for cellular franchises before others. McCaw now controls a large share of the licenses for these systems and is well on its way to establishing a national communications network. It is also working on networks in other places such as Hong Kong. If you sense early that industry growth is leveling off, options include selling out, acquiring competitors, diversifying, or changing strategy. The decline in the U.S. steel industry has forced surviving companies to change strategies. Seattle Steel has decided to operate a smaller version of the traditional steel mill (mini-mill), using state-of-the-art continuous caster technology used in Japan.

Entrenched competitors tend to be intense competitors

Changes in who buys the product or how they use it. Are there new customer groups who are now beginning to use your products? The home cleaning business used to depend on high-income customers for the bulk of their work. The increase in two-income families has changed that, and now the service is purchased by a much larger group of people. Perhaps a product of yours is being used in a different fashion than it had been previously. Spintech Corp., of Redmond, Washington, manufactures desalination equipment. Although originally used primarily to provide fresh water supplies for people near salt-water environments, the company's product is now being modified and used to produce "ultrapure" water for specialized industry applications (i.e. computer manufacturing).

Driving forces are changes in industry structure or forces that affect the structure

Product innovation. Are new products or product features being developed in the industry? Innovation can affect the competitive position of firms in the industry. Apple was on a downward slide relative to IBM until they introduced the Macintosh computer, which provided a fresh, visual approach to computing. CD-ROM disks are also shaking up the market for mass-storage devices in the microcomputer industry. The traditional hard disk storage system may become obsolete. Innovation occurs in almost all industries, and you need to stay on top of new developments and decide which have the potential to alter the strategic position of firms in your industry.

Process innovation. Process innovations are breakthroughs in the way products are made. Henry Ford's assembly line for cars was a process innovation. Robot usage in car factories is a process innovation. If dramatic changes are occurring in the way your industry is making products, you need to be aware of them.

Marketing Innovation. Mail order companies now sell the majority of computer software. The product lends itself very well to this distribution method because buyers are knowledgeable and know what they are purchasing. The software retailers who first sensed the increasing sophistication of customers and saw the trend toward increased mail-order shopping are the companies that established themselves early in that business and have reaped the benefits.

You need to be aware of changes occurring in the way your industry is making products

Entry or exit of major firms. Sometimes big players enter or exit an industry and change the way the game is played. IBM turned the microcomputer world around when it entered that market. Seattle-based Pizza Haven faced such a challenge when national chains like ShowBiz Pizza Place and Pizza Time Theatre entered the market, combining pizza with electronic entertainment. As chief strategist of your organization, you need to foresee entry and exit of major firms and position yourself accordingly.

Diffusion of proprietary knowledge. When patents run out or trade secrets are leaked, competition is usually affected. Sun Products of Kirkland, Washington, is an example of a company plagued by patent infringement problems. Its main product, the "headchair," a small headrest used by beach goers and sunbathers, was copied by others and sold at steep discounts. Even though it won settlements in court, the companies owing it money have gone out of business, leaving collection of amounts owed a difficult matter.

You need to see exit and entry of major firms and position yourself accordingly

Change from a differentiated to standardized product, or vice versa. In the last ten years, video cassette recorders have moved from being an unusual, expensive product to one that is in a majority of American households. Companies must change their strategies as this change occurs. Some products have gone in the opposite direction. Ten years ago, ice cream was basically ice cream. Now you can buy "super premium" ice cream which has more butterfat, costs twice as much, and is guaranteed to harden your arteries. The increased differentiation in the ice cream business has changed manufacturers' approaches.

Regulatory influences and government policy changes. Deregulation has turned the airline industry upside down. Removing limits on exporting logs has shaken the logging and wood mill industries. Government legislation can affect competition in an industry and should not be ignored.

Competitor Analysis

America's capitalistic system is based on the theory of free competition. Without competition, the system would collapse. From an individual company's perspective, however, the major strategic goal should be to reduce or to control the competition the firm has to face. This goal is not un-American; it strictly makes good business sense. To deal with competitors, you must know who they are, what their strengths and weaknesses are, and what their strategies are.

You should try to reduce or control the amount of competition you face

Determining Who Your Competitors Are. For a company new to an industry, the competitors are not always obvious. Go to a major trade show and you will probably discover most of them. Some companies will not feel threatened by you and will tell you about themselves and other firms in the industry. If you are aware of customers who have purchased the type of product you have, ask them who the major producers are. Talk to suppliers to your industry. Since they sell to similar firms, they can tell you about them. Customers, suppliers, and non-threatened competitors to your industry can provide you a wealth of information.

You must seek to understand your competitors' basic strategies

Analyzing Your Competitors' Strengths and Weaknesses. Your success will be determined in large part by your company's strengths and weaknesses relative to competitors. There are many factors to consider. On the next page is a grid which allows you to compare your company to competitors. Some of the factors may not be relevant to your industry and can be overlooked.

Understanding Your Competitors' Strategies. You must look beyond strengths and weaknesses of competitors and seek to understand their basic strategies and assumptions about the industry. Try to answer the following questions about your major competitors:

- How long have they been in the industry and how committed are they to staying in it?
- What is their basic approach to competing? Have they changed that approach much over the years?
- How do they react to strategic moves of other firms? Do they react strongly, or do they ignore what other companies do?

Assessing Your Company's Strengths and Weaknesses

Your strengths and weaknesses are relative to your competitors'. Therefore, you should analyze your capabilities at the same time you assess your competitors. Figure 9-1 allows you to make the comparisons. You may want to develop some type of scoring system, such as on a scale of one to ten. Be aware that some of the factors will not be relevant in your industry.

Figure 9-1. Evaluation of Companies' Strengths and Weaknesses

                              Company #1   Company #2

1. Products or Services
    Quality
    Reputation
    Breadth & depth of product line
    Warranty

2. Distribution
    Channel coverage
    Distributors' loyalty to firm

3. Marketing & Selling
    Market share
    Marketing skills
    Training and skills of sales force

4. Operations
    Quality of plant & equipment
    Quality control
    Labor force climate; unionization situation
    Access to raw materials
    Ability to manufacture efficiently

5. Research & Development
    Patents and trade secrets
    Quality of research equipment

> **Your strengths and weaknesses are relative to your competitors'**

Quality of research staff

6. Overall Costs
   Overall efficiency
   Ability to keep costs down

7. Financial Strength
   Cash flow
   Borrowing capacity
   Ability to raise equity capital

8. General Management Skills
   Leadership of top management
   Experience of top management
   Entrepreneurial savvy

A distinctive competence is a skill or activity that you do especially well compared to your competitors

Distinctive Competencies. A distinctive competence is a skill or activity that you do especially well compared to your competitors. Having completed the strengths and weaknesses above, you should be able to determine your distinctive competencies. You usually build your strategy around these, so this assessment is important. Described below are some common distinctive competencies along with Washington companies that reflect them.

Quality. 3-G Graphics, Inc., of Bothell, Washington, produces electronic clip-art (stock imaged arranged thematically). The company quickly acquired a reputation for high quality.

Service. Pacific Fish Co., a Seattle distributor of fresh fish to restaurants and grocery stores, uses "delivering on promises" to set itself apart from its competition. The company's focus is on personal service, even to its small accounts.

Location. The Herbfarm began as a roadside herb stand on a back road in Snoqualmie Valley, Washington. The tranquil country location is now home to a restaurant as well as a retail store. Combined sales are now $1 million per year, and the business employs forty-five. Many weary city folks are drawn to its relaxing pastoral setting.

Filling a Special Niche. Electronic Transaction Corp., in Seattle, developed a computer system to enable retail stores to detect bad checks at the point of sale. The company steered clear of traditional credit history services and created a special niche for itself. Revenues in 1990 were about $5 million, and the system (SCAN) processed some 338 million checks. The company was acquired in December of 1990 by the Deluxe Corp.

> **Find a distinctive competence that will work for your business**

Flexibility and Adaptability. Flexibility played a big part in Precor USA's ability to generate as much as $60 million in annual sales from selling rowing machines for health-conscious consumers, but market forces have resulted in the elimination of these machines in favor of stair-climbers, exercise bikes, and other types of exercise equipment. To survive, companies have to be able to change rapidly.

Reputation and Image. Icos Corp., a biotech company in Bothell, Washington, raised $33 million from private investors partly on the credentials of its founders.

Personnel. Immunex in Seattle has scientists who are leaders in their fields in bio-technology.

Value. Regardless of the quality of products, some companies are known for giving exceptional value. R.E. I., a recreation equipment co-op, was started after outdoor enthusiasts were unhappy with prices of equipment. Members receive state-of-the-art equipment plus a rebate on purchases at the end of the year.

Evaluating Your Own Personal Desires. One last factor has to be evaluated before you launch into setting your company's strategy– what are *your* desires for the company? Up until this point, you have done your analysis in an objective fashion, as if your personal motivations made no difference. In a small, privately-held company, strategy *cannot* be separated from the lead entrepreneur's personal motivations. Where do you want the company to go? What type of products do you think you should have? Where do *you* want to be in five years? Ten years? An objective analysis may point to a certain strategy making sense; however, if that strategy does not fit with your aspirations, it obviously won't work. Before formulating the firm's strategies, write down your personal goals for the company.

> **Strategy cannot be separated from your personal desires**

Formulating Strategy

Once you have analyzed the economy, the industry, your competitors, your firm's strengths and weaknesses, and your personal motivations, you need to look at strategic alternatives. The first decision you need to make is *what business to be in*. This may sound silly to you if you have already made that decision, but if you are not heavily committed at this point in your business you should question if this is a good one to be in. The industry analysis will help you decide if this line of business is a good one to be in. Each industry usually has some attractive and some unattractive features. Consider both and evaluate the overall attractiveness. Ideally, you would like to see industry characteristics as described below.

The first decision you need to make is *what business to be in*

Size of the market. Bigger is not always better, but you want to ensure there are enough customers to allow you to have substantial growth.

Growth of the market. A growing market allows you to grow without taking away from other companies' market shares, which helps to avoid fierce competition. Typically there is more opportunity in an industry that is earlier in its life cycle.

There are characteristics you should look for in an industry

Gross margin. A large gross margin allows you to generate a considerable gross profit with low sales. Since you will probably not have high sales for a period of time, this reduces your risk. Granted, Wal-Mart makes a lot of money selling low-margin items, but small companies cannot generate the sales volume that Wal-Mart does.

Overall profitability. Don't try to fight the current. Get into an industry that has shown profits. You may, through product differentiation, be able to enjoy higher profits than the industry average.

Entry barriers. You would like to have entry barriers as high as possible, but low enough for you to enter, if you are not already in the industry. You want to be able to protect your competitive position once you have chosen a particular strategy, and entry barriers make it difficult for newcomers to copy you. Look over the list of entry barriers described previously and consider how you can protect your position.

Power of customers. The broader the customer base, the better. There is danger is relying on only a few customers, who then are in strong bargaining positions against you.

Power of suppliers. The same principle applies to suppliers. If you are small and there are only a few suppliers, they will almost always favor your larger competitors. A diversity of suppliers is an advantage.

Amount of product differentiation. In general, smaller companies can prosper more easily in an industry that has differentiated products. For example, there are many styles of ladies clothing. This allows companies to focus on selective types and carve out niches. Contrast that to the manufacture of pencils, which is a standardized, non-differentiated industry. To succeed in that setting, firms usually need large market share. New companies can start off small more easily in differentiated markets.

> **To succeed in industries with little differentiation, companies usually need to achieve high market share**

Overall intensity of competition. Some industries are less hostile than others. Competitors have learned to live with each other or perhaps tend to ignore each other. Other industries are competitive blood-baths. The pizza restaurant/delivery business has been saturated with competitors, resulting in price wars and low profitability for most companies.

Driving forces affect the attractiveness of an industry. Change is a threat to those companies which are prospering under current conditions, but change also provides opportunity to newcomers. Young, entrepreneurial firms should look at change as a potential blessing. Look over the list of potential driving forces below. Are any of the following changes occurring?

> **Change in an industry provides opportunity to newcomers**

- Is the industry growth rate increasing?
- Are new customers entering the market? Are current customers beginning to use the products in new and different ways?
- Are new products being developed?
- Are new ways of manufacturing products being developed?
- Are new ways of marketing products being used?
- Are some major players leaving the industry?
- Have some patents run out? Are new patents being filed?
- Are products becoming more differentiated? The interest in premium ice creams opened the door for small companies such as Seattle's own local brand, Fratelli's, which was originated by John and Peter Morse.

- Have regulations changed? Airline deregulation opened the door for People's Express. Changes in banking laws allowed banks to become quite entrepreneurial.

Look for changes in the industry and analyze how they affect the attractiveness of that type of business.

You need to assess your capabilities of competing in the industry. The microcomputer industry is a thriving one, but not everyone should try to enter it. Try to determine what the *critical success factors* are in the industry. They are capabilities that firms must have in order to compete in the industry. Is it quality? Service? Unique products? Low prices? Look over the strengths and weaknesses for your company and see how well they match up with the critical success factors.

Competitive Strategy

Having looked at industry structural characteristics, driving forces, and internal strengths and weaknesses, you should be able to decide if you are in or are about to enter an attractive industry. These factors can do more than help you decide if you are in a good industry; they can give you clues about how to compete against other companies. There are three primary competitive strategies— cost leadership, differentiation, and focus— and each is described below.

Cost Leadership. Cost leadership is at the opposite end of the spectrum to differentiation. Cost leadership emphasizes keeping the costs down in making a product. The advantages of such a strategy are that you have higher margins than competitors and you are better able to compete on price. To have a cost advantage, you usually need high market share. High market share allows you to have economies of scale— you buy raw materials for less, you spread equipment costs over more units, you spread advertising costs over more units, among other savings. This strategy leaves you with lower unit costs than competitors.

A cost leadership strategy is usually characterized by several of the following features:

- High volume and market share
- Competitive or discount pricing
- An emphasis on cost reduction, i.e. tight budgets, low overhead, etc.

- Little money spent on research and development (if any is spent, it is to make the production process more efficient)
- No-frills products

In most industries, you can pick out one or several firms which stand out as cost leaders. Wal-Mart is an obvious cost leader in the general department store industry. PayLess Shoe Source has a definite cost advantage in the retail shoe industry. Bonanza restaurants compete with a few-frills, low price strategy. Recognize the difference between *cost* and *price*. Cost is the cost to you of making a product, whereas price is what you charge. Having a low price alone will not bring you success– competitors can match the price and you have a very thin gross margin. Having a lower cost is the basis of the strategy. If you have it, you can drop below competitors' prices and still have a decent margin, or else you can match their prices and have a larger margin than them.

Cost leadership emphasizes keeping the costs down in making a product

Differentiation.   Differentiation is a much different means of competing.   You make your product better or unique in some fashion so that customers purchase your product because of its superiority.   There is a great variety of ways of differentiating a product, and Chapter 2 describes quite a few of them. Design and engineering is one means. BMW takes this approach in making "driving machines." Superior technology is another, which Sun Computers employs in making high performance computer workstations. Unique features can differentiate a product, such as goretex fabric. It keeps rain off a hiker, but allows the fabric to breathe so that sweat evaporates. A unique means of distribution can differentiate companies, as Mary Kay and Avon have done with cosmetics.   A differentiation strategy is usually characterized by some of the following factors:

Cost is not the same as price

- Large emphasis on superior quality and/or service;
- Significant R&D expenditures;
- Premium pricing;
- Lower market share (than cost leaders); and
- An emphasis on creativity and being different.

A differentiation strategy allows you to maintain high margins because people are willing to pay premium prices for high quality. Typically, you also develop a strong reputation and brand loyalty, thus erecting entry barriers to other companies.

A differentiation strategy allows you to maintain high margins

Focus. A focus strategy is based on choosing a product line or target market which is more narrow than competitors'. In concentrating on fewer products, you can usually differentiate yourself because you are not spread so thinly. Consider a golf pro shop. It carries exclusively golf equipment and apparel, and if you have questions about either, a golf pro is happy to help you. Compare the pro shop to a sporting goods store, which carries baseball, basketball, football, tennis, weight-lifting, a multitude of other sports, and of course, golf equipment and apparel. If you ask the salesperson about what length club you should have, he'll say he doesn't know but he'll ask his weight-lifting buddy. By being more narrowly focused, you are better able to understand and meet customers' needs.

> **A focus strategy is based on choosing a product line or target market which is more narrow than the competitors'**

In certain cases, a focus strategy can provide cost advantages. Consider the oil drilling business. A certain segment of this market needs portable drilling equipment. The large drill manufacturers produce the portable drills using their standard production facility, which is large and capital intensive. The portable drill can be produced, however, in a small warehouse using relatively inexpensive equipment. A company that focuses on the portable line of drills is able to forego large capital expenditures, and therefore has a lower cost.

Different means of focusing exist. The first is by product or target market. Delorean concentrated on a type of automobile– the sports car. If the company had received a chance to get its feet on the ground and had its president stayed out of drug trafficking, it may have done well. Another type of focus is by geographic area. If you can offer products which are better suited to people in your particular area, you have an advantage over more widespread competitors. D.A. Davidson offers securities of regional companies that the nationally-based investment houses do not carry, for example. You can also focus by size of order. You may have large competitors who do not consider small, custom orders because they don't feel that they are worth the time. Small companies can capitalize on such niches. The key is to find a niche that is large enough to satisfy your growth expectation, but small enough to remain uninteresting to your large competitors.

> **Different means of focusing exist**

To be focused, you must be more narrowly oriented than your competitors. For example, a restaurant owner stated, "I am quite focused in my business. I am in the restaurant business, and that's it. We don't try to get into anything else." Interestingly enough, 90 percent of his competitors were involved only in the restaurant business. Focus is *relative to competitors*. You must be in a more narrow market segment or serve a smaller geographic area than competitors to be truly focused.

Focus *alone* is not a strategic advantage. Once you have chosen a particular segment, you must either have a better product or else be able to produce more cheaply than competitors. Focusing often allows you to do this because of your concentration on a particular market or geographical area. But if you can't excel in either quality or cost, focusing won't do you any good.

To be focused, you must be more narrowly oriented than your competitors

Be aware that most companies don't have strategies that drop cleanly into one of these strategic slots. In retail clothing, K-Mart has positioned itself pretty much as a cost leader. Recently the company has begun carrying many more brand name items, such as Nike and Converse in shoes. They discount them also, but they are definitely departing from a "no-frills" posture. Penney's and Sears seem to be somewhere in the middle ground between differentiation and cost leadership. They carry medium quality products at medium prices. The strategy is no accident– that segment purchases more clothing than either the high end or the low end. Therefore, variations in between cost leadership and differentiation are possibilities.

There can be a danger in this middle ground, however. It is called "stuck in the middle." Being "stuck" means that customers view you neither as a place to go to purchase quality items, nor as a place to go to get a good deal. If the market is such that one segment insists on quality, and the other is concerned with price, companies in the middle ground do not do well. Analyze the industry and determine if there seems to be this polarization of the market. Avoid middle ground in this case.

A focus strategy is usually differentiated

Determining Which Generic Strategy to Pursue. Unfortunately, there are no unbreakable principles in choosing the best strategy. The choice depends on the analysis that you have done up to this point. One of the best approaches is to apply the principles of industry and competitor analysis to *strategic groups* within the industry. In any industry, there tend to be clusters of companies that have strategies similar to each other, but differing with other clusters. Each of these clusters is considered a strategic group. Looking again at retail clothing, the cost leadership end is comprised of K-Marts, Fred Meyers, Targets, and others which are

There are no unbreakable principles in choosing the best strategy

generally viewed as discounters. The differentiated end is comprised of specialty shops such as Jeffrey-Michael, Ann Taylor, and Helen's of Course. In the middle area are the Penneys, the Sears, and the Lamonts, among others. There are quite a few focused segments: big and tall, petite, maternity, and others. List all of the strategic groups that you see and the firms in them. The strategies you assign to each group may or may not be variations of the three generic strategies described above.

Assess the attractiveness of each strategic group through industry and competitive analysis. Assume that you intend to open a single discount clothing store in Olympia. First consider the cost leadership group. The market is large and is growing, although not as fast as several years ago. The gross margins are relatively thin, since discounting is prevalent. Industry profitability is high– K-Mart and Wal-Mart do extremely well. Large entry barriers exist.

Assess the attractiveness of each strategic group in your industry

K-Mart experiences large economies of scale by being able to purchase in quantity and spread many costs over their large number of stores. They have a strong reputation that newcomers would have to overcome (which can be an advantage if you are able to overcome the barriers yourself). The power of suppliers is significant. Many of the suppliers are companies such as Osh Kosh and Nike. They will definitely give preference in order-filling and pricing to the larger companies. The customer group is broad-based, and therefore the risk of one or a few customers wielding much power is small. Product differentiation is not great. You tend to see a lot of the same merchandise in all of the discount stores. This typically leads to competitive pricing. Overall intensity of competition is great. Some of the large discounters will accept advertised prices of any of their competitors, which lets you know that competition is *intense* in this industry.

Try to avoid direct competition with large competitors

Some of the industry features are attractive and some unattractive. Two of them are probably overriding. The entry barriers to this strategic group are enormous. If you hope to be able to compete on a large-scale basis with the likes of K-Mart, you will have to enter the market in a big way. Small companies don't have such resources. Competing with K-Mart would tax the resources of even the largest competitors. The other striking industry feature is the intensity of competition. This industry is cut-throat. If you pose a threat to these companies, they will retaliate.

If you try to compete with K-Mart head-on, you will lose. But what about a focused approach to the cost leadership strategy? You see occasional "warehouse liquidation" sales by local, smaller companies. They buy quantities of goods at bankruptcy auctions, rent an abandoned retail spot, and advertise it as "below cost" prices. By focusing on this one approach, the companies are able to compete on price. They must do all right, because you continue to see them. The key to their success is to avoid direct competition and find a few niches where they can compete on price.

The differentiated end of the competitive spectrum is occupied by Pacific Big & Tall and the Size 5-7-9 shops among others. The market is not nearly as large as the cost leadership market, but that is almost always the case. Market growth is small. Gross margins are usually better in this segment since discounting is not normally used extensively. Some entry barriers exist, but not near the size in the cost leadership segment. Reputations for quality of the other stores pose perhaps the largest barrier. There are not large economies of scale. Power of suppliers is not great, since there are a large number of high-quality clothing manufacturers who can sell to you. Power of customers is not great, either, since you still will have a fairly large base of customers to sell to. There is a large amount of product differentiation, since many types of quality clothing are produced. Lastly, competition is moderate to high. Although many premium stores have closed, competition is still high for the now smaller number of customers. It still is probably not as fierce as in the cost leadership segment.

> **In general, a differentiation strategy is better suited to the entrepreneurial company than is a cost leadership approach**

The differentiation segment has its pros and cons. Although the industry is not growing and competition is stiff, margins are good and the entry barriers are not so formidable. This strategic group probably offers more opportunity than does cost leadership for the start-up company. A key strategic issue here is timing. Companies that can survive the hard economic times and the inevitable wash-out of companies will be in a good position when better economic times return. In general, a differentiation strategy is better suited to the entrepreneurial company than is a cost leadership approach.

A focus strategy often makes sense for the start-up company. The "big & tall" segment is a focus example in the retail clothing market. It is not an exceptionally large market, but it has been growing. Entry barriers are not great, although reputation and store location may provide some protection from new competitors. Gross margins are good– definitely higher than in the discount stores. Industry profitability has been good on a national basis. Power of suppliers and customers is small, since there is a large

> **A focus strategy often makes sense for the start-up company**

number of each and no one or few wield much power. The overall intensity of competition is moderate. There are only a couple of big & tall stores in town, and the discounters and premium retailers do not compete much in this market. The local big & tall market is not affected by the local recession as much as is the premium segment. The market is fairly differentiated, with a wide variety of products that allow firms to differentiate themselves.

You need to assess whether you have the skills and resources to compete in each of the strategic groups that you have identified. To compete with K-Mart in the cost leadership group, you need to match their buying power, which is enormous. It appears that nothing other than a huge company with large financial resources could successfully compete in this segment (other than the focused "warehouse liquidation" approach described previously).

Assess whether you have the skills and resources to compete in the strategic groups that you have identified

To compete in the differentiated or focused segment, you need to be better or unusual in some fashion. Can you get apparel that is truly unique? Do you have buying skills that surpass your competitors? Do you have ideas for merchandising that are unique? Do you have enough money to stock a premium line of clothing? Do you have quality salespeople that know how to sell the clothing you have? Is your location better than competitors'? The point is this:

> *"Having a good strategy is one thing.*
> *Being able to make it work is another."*

You need to be sure that you can implement a strategy before you charge ahead.

Find a strategy that you can *personally* be committed to

If you have found a strategy that seems sound and you feel that you can make it work, you have one last question to consider: "Is this a strategy that I *personally* can be committed to?" There can be a mismatch between the personality of the lead entrepreneur and the strategy she has chosen. The strategy won't work if she isn't personally committed to it. A cost leadership strategy requires strict attention to cost reductions, budgets, and few frills. The basic "spirit" of the strategy is get the product out to as many customers as possible, and don't worry about selling them something "special." The differentiation strategy requires creativity and ingenuity on your part. You need to have the desire to be the best, and a touch of perfectionism might be helpful. You have to be committed to quality.

With a focus strategy, you need to be absolutely committed to meeting the needs of whatever niche you have chosen. The CEO of the most prosperous waste management firm in San Francisco explained his success quite simply, "I love garbage." If you have a big & tall store, you need to know your customers inside out to be able to meet their needs. With a focus strategy, you need to be driven to be a "big fish in a small pond." By focusing, you are choosing to be in a smaller pond.

The Strategic Plan

Once you have gone through the steps in formulating strategy, you are ready to write a strategic plan. Having the plan in your head is not sufficient. Until you get it on paper, review it, and have others review it, it will not be organized. The following outline shows the typical elements in a strategic plan.

Your strategy needs to be well organized

A. Analysis of the Business and Its Environment

- The economic, regulatory, and social environment
- Industry structure
- Industry driving forces
- Competitors
- Internal strengths and weaknesses

B. The Strategic Plan

- Mission statement
- Strategic goals
- Corporate level strategy
- Business level strategy

C. Implementing the Plan

- Marketing strategy
- Financial strategy
- Personnel strategy

The elements in (C) are each discussed in other chapters of this book. The marketing strategy is covered in Chapters 4 and 10, the financial strategy is covered in chapters 7, 11, and 12, and personnel strategy is covered is Chapter 8.

Conclusion

You must continually scan the environment and assess your own strengths and weaknesses

Strategic planning is critical to your business. Don't expect that "shooting from the hip" is going to get you by. You need to continually scan the environment and assess your own strengths and weaknesses. Follow the outline in this chapter, write down your strategic plan, and then get after it.

References

1. Porter, Michael. *Competitive Strategy: Techniques for Analyzing Industries and Competitors*. New York: Free Press, 1980.

2. Thompson, Arthur A. and Strickland, A. J. *Strategic Management*, Eighth Edition. Plano, Texas: Business Publications, Inc., 1995.

═══════ 10 ═══════

The Marketing Plan

"Doing business without advertising is like winking at a girl in the dark. You know what you are doing, but nobody else does."
Steuart Henderson Britt

The purpose of marketing is to *produce long-term, profitable sales.* You do this by meeting the needs of your customers. Too many businesses are run with an internal orientation, focusing on what is good for the company. Such an orientation is dangerous. You tend to forget that customers ultimately pay the bills for your company. Don't assume that you know what your customers want because you're an expert. Take the time to listen to them and understand what they are looking for in the type of product or service that you offer. Tom Peters, in *A Passion for Excellence*, states, "If you concentrate on the customer and meeting his needs, the other stuff, like market share, profits, etc., will take care of itself."

There are two themes that you must incorporate to develop a good marketing strategy— *commitment* and *consistency*. No matter what strategy you decide on, you must be willing to "stay the course." Marketing efforts rarely produce instant results; only hyped-up sales promotions do that. Don't become discouraged if you spend money on a promotional campaign and sales only increase slightly. If you *commit* yourself to a sound marketing strategy, it will eventually bear fruit. Moreover, you must remain *consistent* in your message. Sears has suffered over the years from a lack of a consistent theme. The company has wavered back and forth from being a discounter, to a quality retailer, to somewhere in between. As a consequence, no one is quite sure what the company is now. Try to choose a solid strategy and stay with it.

Commitment and consistency are critical to a marketing plan

Choosing a Marketing Strategy

The process of formulating a marketing strategy is depicted in Figure 10-1. The goal of this process is to decide what product features and services to offer, how to distribute products, how to price, and how to promote products for each target market. The illustration makes the process look well-defined and sequential. *It is not.* Very often you will get to one stage of the process, decide that a previous decision was incorrect, and skip back to that stage. For example, assume that you own a ski resort and have chosen as a target market families just beginning to ski. As you research this market (see "2. Characterize Markets" below) you find that they spend a lot of time in the lodge drying off and trying to warm up. You only have a small lodge and don't have the money to expand it. Having done the customer characterization, you realize that you chose the wrong target market and must go back to that step and redefine your market. Or perhaps you had defined your market as intermediate skiers. After analyzing competitors, however, you realize that the competing ski resorts in your area all cater to this group and you would have no real advantage over them. You need to abandon that ship and again go back to choosing a new target market. You usually change your marketing strategy several times before you get through the whole process. This process allows you to refine and focus your marketing strategy. Each of the steps in the process is described below.

The process of setting a marketing strategy requires continuous revision

Figure 10-1. The Process of Setting a Marketing Strategy

1. Select Target Markets
2. Characterize Markets
3. Evaluate Competition
4. Formulate Marketing Strategy

Select Target Market(s)

You will be tempted to try to sell your products to a wide variety of customers. Resist that temptation. Most successful smaller businesses focus on a few *market segments* and try to meet the specific needs of those customer groups. Every market usually has several distinct segments whose needs differ somewhat from each other. Those which you choose to appeal to are called your *target markets*. The first step in the marketing process is to decide what target market(s) you will pursue. Each of them requires a distinct marketing strategy.

A quick way to fail is to try to sell to everyone

The landscaping business has several distinct market segments. One includes general contractors who build new homes, another includes homeowners, and another includes commercial establishments. Each one of these has needs different from the others' and requires a distinct marketing strategy. Each of these target markets could be further segmented. For example, you could divide homeowners into

Most small businesses are not focused enough

two groups: one that wants major landscaping work done and another that needs only grass mowing and tree trimming. The more narrowly you define markets, the better you will understand and be able to appeal to their specific needs. Of course you can carry this process too far. You could define markets so narrowly that there are only a few customers in each one. However, most small businesses suffer the opposite problem: they are not focused enough.

Characterize Markets
After you have selected a target market(s), you seek to thoroughly understand the needs of those customers. This is termed *characterizing the market*. Marketing research, described in Chapter 4, provides this information. Expert interviews, focus groups, secondary data, surveys, and experiments are all possible means of gathering information about customers. You want to know who buys products like yours, what motivates them to buy, what features they are looking for, what they are willing to pay, and what type of promotions they pay attention to. Analyze the customers in each of your target markets.

Analyze Competition
Customers can buy from you or from your competitors. If you do not know what your competitors are doing, you may be losing sales without a clue as to why. Many startup business owners claim that they have "the best product on the market." And yet they have not looked closely at competitors' products to make a valid judgment. You need to put consistent efforts into assessing what your competitors are selling and what they are charging. Chapter 4, Marketing Research, and Chapter 9, Strategic Planning, describe the process of analyzing competitors. Since each of your target markets may have different competitors, be sure to evaluate competitors in all market segments.

Look at what your competitors are doing to attract customers

Formulate Marketing Strategy
Once you have selected target markets and evaluated customers and competitors in each, you need to develop a marketing strategy for each. This is the fun part! This is why you have knocked yourself out doing all of the research described above. In fact, you need to keep reminding yourself of this goal. Otherwise, it is easy to get wrapped up in the research and lose track of what you really want to accomplish. The purpose of this whole process is to develop a good marketing strategy, not to conduct good research. There are four primary elements of a marketing strategy:

You need to develop a good marketing strategy

- Products, product features, and services offered.
- Type(s) of distribution.
- Pricing.
- Promotion.

These elements together comprise your *marketing mix*. Each of them should be consistent with the others. For example, if you are selling a no-frills product, you typically have discount pricing, mass distribution, and widespread promotion. On the other hand, if you are selling premium quality products, you usually need to charge premium prices and use select distribution channels. Your promotions should be high class. A *consistent theme* is important.

Products, Product Features, and Services Offered

Your choice of target market together with the products and services you choose to meet customers' needs is called *positioning*. David Ogilvy, who has placed several billion dollars worth of advertising through his ad agency and who is considered one of America's marketing authorities, states that positioning is the most critical marketing decision to be made. He says that the quality of advertising is much less important than the basic positioning of the product or service in the first place. If you can select the best market niches, and offer products and services that meet customers' needs better than competitors, you are well on your way to a solid marketing strategy.

Product positioning is more important than quality of advertising

Customers buy benefits, not products. People don't want shampoo— they want silky hair that smells nice. They don't want an old used car— they want cheap, reliable transportation. A Kirby vacuum cleaner salesman can't convince you to spend $1000 on a vacuum cleaner. However, he can convince you to spend that kind of money because you won't have to replace your $5000 carpet. Or, you won't have to live in a house with the awful dirt your old vacuum leaves behind (he'll show it to you). You must be able to clearly identify what benefits your products offer to customers. If you consistently think in terms of customer benefits and not product features, you will sell a whole lot more.

Anything can be differentiated

Most smaller businesses need to *differentiate* their products. You typically will not win a cost game with larger companies. Your products or services have to be better in some way. Chapter 2, Developing Business Ideas, discusses a variety of ways of differentiating products and services. Tom Peters, in *A Passion for*

Excellence, states, "Nothing is a commodity. *Anything* can be differentiated." The following are only a few means of differentiating products.

1. Higher quality product;
2. Quicker response to customers;
3. Less maintenance to customers;
4. Better warranty;
5. Better service;
6. Better trade-in policy;
7. Better compatibility with other products;
8. More flexible product usage;
9. Safer product;
10. Healthier product;
11. More compact or portable product;
12. More attractive product;
13. More status appeal;
14. Better service to dealers;
15. More convenient hours;
16. More fun for the customer; or a
17. Friendlier environment.

Try to differentiate your products or services in more than one way. Also try to differentiate in a way that is not easily copied. For example, Domino's Pizza was the original "fast delivery" pizza outlet— thirty minutes or less. They built their reputation on quick delivery. Unfortunately, the new high-speed pizza ovens allow just about anyone to meet that deadline. Domino's no longer enjoys that advantage, and about the only competitive tool they have left is discount pricing. That hurts them. You *may not* be able to differentiate in ways that are enduring. In that case, you have to be a constant innovator. You have to always be searching for a new way to stay ahead of the pack. Don't be a stationary target, keep moving.

Don't be a stationary target

You may be selling a product, but the service you offer may be what closes the deal. This is true of car dealerships. Many customers stay loyal to one dealership, regardless of the brands of cars offered. People trust that any car they buy will be well serviced and that the salespeople are giving them a fair deal. A copy shop is a copy shop, but certain ones develop a reputation for quick, error-free work and a willingness to bend over backwards to meet customers' needs. These are the ones that stay busy. One of the best marketing weapons a small business has is *good service*. You can beat most

One of the best marketing weapons a small business has is good service

larger companies on customer service. This may be the most important feature of the products that you sell.

Distribution Channels

Distribution channels are the means by which products get from the manufacturer to the customer. In every industry, there are usually several different channels that are possibilities. For many manufacturers, the standard distribution channel is to sell to retailers who sell products to the public. There is a variety of alternatives, however. Some industries have distributors who buy, warehouse, and resell products from many different manufacturers and resell to retailers. The automobile parts industry has such distributors. Some manufacturers use independent sales representatives, who promote their products to retailers. Although they neither own nor take possession of merchandise, they are the selling arm for many companies and thus can be considered part of the distribution channel. A few companies sell their products directly to consumers through a mail catalog. Some manufacturers sell products through catalog companies, which promote a large number of companies' products, usually under a central theme. These catalog companies, such as Eddie Bauer of Redmond, Washington, are direct mail retailers. The channels described are not the only means of distributing, but they are the most common. Each of them is depicted in Figure 10-2.

In every industry, several distribution channels may exist

Figure 10-2. Common Distribution Channels

- Mfger — Retailer — Consumer
- Mfger — Distributor — Retailer — Consumer
- Mfger — Sales Rep — Retailer — Consumer
- Mfger — Consumer
- Mfger — Catalog Co. — Consumer

You need to understand which distribution channels exist in your industry. In many cases, the manufacturer's dilemma is not to convince the consumer that a product is worth purchasing, it is gaining access to the distribution channels so that the product can be presented to the customer. Find out from whom retailers purchase in your industry. Do they buy from manufacturers, from independent sales reps, from distributors, or from a combination of sources? Once you have established what the channels are, talk to businesses at every step of the way. Find out what products they are willing to carry and what type of companies they want to deal with.

You will be tempted to "skirt around" established distribution channels because of the margins that they cost you. Of your final selling price, retailers may take up to 40 percent, sales reps 5-20 percent, and distributors another 10-15 percent. Compared to direct marketing, you may receive only 25-50 percent of the selling price of the product. It's hard to give up that kind of margin.

In spite of the fact they lose margins, there are several good reasons to consider going through established channels instead of attempting direct marketing. Direct marketing may not be easy for a startup company, plus sales may develop only very slowly. Established distribution channels allow you to get your products to a large number of retail establishments quickly. And although you may have to do a fair amount of marketing to get your products into channels, once they are in you are relieved of a lot of the marketing pressure. *Others* sell your products, while you can concentrate on meeting orders. Players in the channels also buy in quantity, relieving you of processing and filling small orders. If, in spite of these compelling reasons to go through established marketing channels, you are still tempted to market directly, refer to the subsection below on direct marketing.

There are good reasons to go through established distribution channels

Tradeshows and Consumer Shows. Tradeshows are a form of promotion (which is discussed in a separate section later in this chapter). Yet they are so valuable in getting into distribution channels that they need to be discussed here. Tradeshows bring players from all stages of distribution channels in an industry together under one roof and thus are helpful in penetrating those channels. Other advantages include your being able to show products to many buyers in a short period of time. They also relieve you of having to travel all over to meet with potential buyers. Compared to sending a salesperson out on the road to make individual visits to buyers, tradeshows are much cheaper. You can also contact distributors, sales reps, and catalog companies and check out your competition in just a few days.

Trade shows are valuable in getting into distribution channels

One of the largest tradeshows in the world is the annual COMDEX (Computer Dealers' Exposition) show. Approximately 2,000 manufacturers of computer products display their wares to approximately 80,000 resellers (mostly retail stores, but also distributors and sales reps). Each of the manufacturers has a booth with one or more salespeople who tell resellers about their products and try to get them to place orders for their products. The tradeshow benefits both the people who display and the buyers. The companies displaying get exposure to a large number of buyers in a short period of time. For the buyers, they get to evaluate a large number of competitive products under one roof. Most tradeshows are nowhere near this large. However, the activities in most tradeshows are about the same.

A *consumer show* is different from a tradeshow. In a tradeshow, the buyers are not buying for their own usage. Instead they resell products that they purchase. At a consumer show, individual customers are shopping for themselves. There are consumer shows in each of the major cities in Washington each year. Some examples include the Puyallup and Central Washington state fairs, the Seattle boat show, home improvement shows, auto shows, and numerous fishing and hunting shows.

A consumer show is different from a tradeshow

The advantage of this type of show is that you can sell at full retail and receive cash on the spot. The disadvantages are that there is not a regular circuit of shows to attend in the area, sales may not be significant, there are few follow-up sales after the shows, and you have to keep traveling to keep selling. The consumer shows provide a means of showing your product to consumers and gaining some sales. They will *not provide significant growth to you as a manufacturer*.

Consumer shows will not provide significant growth to you as a manufacturer

For a list of various Washington consumer shows, contact:

1) The Seattle-King County Conventions & Visitor's Bureau
   520 Pike Street, Suite 1300
   Seattle, WA 98101
   (206) 461-4411
   for a list entitled "Calendar of Events of Searrle-King County"

2) The Washington State Convention and Trade Center
   800 Convention Place
   Seattle, WA 98101
   (206) 447-5000
   for a "Schedule of Events"

3) Washington State International Trade Fair
   999 3rd Avenue, Suite 1080
   Seattle, WA 98104
   (206) 682-6900

4) Wenatchee Convention Center
   201 North Wenatchee Avenue
   Wenatchee, Washington 98801
   (509) 662-4411

Finding Out About Tradeshows. How do you find out about tradeshows that would be suitable for you? First, talk to people. Visit or call retail stores that carry the types of products that you make. Ask them if they attend tradeshows, and which ones. Seek information from competitors who are not threatened by you, perhaps in other locales. Talk to people in the same general industry who make different types of products than yours. For example, if you sell trout flies, talk to someone who makes lures. You would probably be attending the same tradeshows.

The best way to find out about tradeshows is to talk to people

There are other sources of information on tradeshows. Industry associations almost always announce major tradeshows. If you don't know which associations represent your industry, consult *The Encyclopedia of Associations*, which is in the reference sections in many libraries in the state. *The Tradeshow Week Data Book*, is the most complete listing of tradeshows in America. It is published annually and describes major national shows broken down in seven different ways, including industry and geographical area. It provides information such as exhibit space cost, number of exhibitors and attendees at the previous show, profiles of exhibitors and attendees, number of years in existence, and the show manager's address and phone number. Both of these can be good sources of information on tradeshows in specific industries.

Deciding Which Shows to Attend. The people you contact to find out about shows can tell you how good they are. If retailers, other manufacturers, and industry associations tell you which tradeshows exist, they will probably also tell which ones are the best. In most industries, as you talk to more and more people, the names of certain shows will tend to be mentioned over and over. Listen to people who have attended certain shows and find out how they view them.

Research the tradeshow before you attend to make sure it fits your needs

You should contact tradeshow managers and have them send you a packet about their shows. They will usually give you information such as how many people attend, what type of people attend, the price of a booth, and how many years the show has been put on. You want to find a show which caters to resellers of the type of product that you make. Therefore, a smaller show may be better for you than a larger show, if the smaller one has a higher percentage of the type of buyers you are trying to reach. For example, a ski manufacturer has the choice of attending a ski show or an outdoor sports show. Although more people may attend the outdoor sports show, there may be more *qualified* buyers for her product at the ski show.

Be aware that you don't want to attend a show that may generate more orders than you can fill. Although the order-taking will feel wonderful, you will have very unhappy customers if they cannot receive your products quickly. As a small manufacturer, you may want to exhibit in a smaller, regional show to test the waters before attending the larger shows.

You must prepare carefully for a tradeshow. Once you are there and the doors open, you must be ready for the onslaught of people. Several sources are listed in the reference section at the end of this chapter on preparing for tradeshows.

Independent Sales Representatives. Independent sales representatives, commonly referred to as "sales reps," can help a startup business penetrate markets. A sales rep is a business person who makes commissions by selling products of two or more different manufacturers. They sell primarily to retailers. They are not employees of the manufacturers, rather they work under contract. Independent sales reps are also called manufacturers' agents or manufacturers' reps. An agent oversees an office with multiple reps working in it. Therefore, if a company works with a manufacturer's agency a group of people will be promoting the product, whereas a rep is an individual salesperson. In most cases the rep is restricted contractually to a certain geographic area. She does not take title to the goods, is paid on a straight commission basis, and has little or no control over prices, credit, or other terms of sale. Although the rep is not a collection agent, manufacturers sometimes ask him to remind buyers of overdue accounts. Very importantly, the rep is an *independent* business person and is not an employee of a manufacturer.

There is a significant number of agents in the outdoor equipment industry, representing a large number of relatively small producers. These agents visit retail stores in their region, attempting to sell a variety of outdoor products, such as tents, backpacks, snowshoes, etc. The agent seeks to carry a broad enough line to generate satisfactory sales at each retail store. They are inhibited from

You don't want to take more orders than you can fill

You must prepare carefully for a tradeshow

carrying too many lines because they may not be able to adequately promote too large of a variety. Industries that have a large number of smaller producers tend to foster the use of independent sales reps. The outdoor equipment industry is only one of many industries that incorporates independent reps.

There are some good reasons to use sales reps, including:

- Your sales volume is not sufficient to attract full-time salespeople. For smaller manufacturers, this is often the case. By using an independent salesperson, however, you can contract with a rep who is already in targeted retail establishments selling other manufacturers' products. The rep draws a portion of her sales commission from each manufacturer, and therefore need not rely on only one for her income.

- You want to concentrate on manufacturing, not marketing. Many manufacturers have a strong production focus and have either no background or no desire to be involved in marketing. The independent agent can alleviate some, but not all, of the marketing pressure on your firm.

A sales rep is an independent business person

- You want to penetrate a market quickly. An established independent rep already has contacts and is selling to retail establishments. She knows the buyers, knows their preferences, and has already established a relationship of trust with them. These reps are in a better position to introduce your product than someone who does not know the buyers.

- You want to gain significant market share in a certain area. An independent rep in many cases can have a smaller geographic territory than a hired salesperson because of the variety of lines that she carries. She sells more per store, therefore she can concentrate on fewer stores. This concentration allows her to visit stores more often in a certain territory and gain greater market penetration for the products that she is selling.

The advantages of using sales reps are significant, but there are some disadvantages

- You want to reduce marketing costs. You pay an independent rep nothing if no product is sold. This reduces the financial risk to you by not requiring up front training and salary costs to salespeople. Reps also pay their own expenses.

- You want to gather information about competitors and customers. Independent sales reps are excellent sources of competitor information, since they are exposed to them often. They are not associated as closely with individual companies, and therefore can obtain information more easily. They are also in constant contact with buyers, and can get more objective information about customers than a person representing a particular company.

- You don't want to worry about hiring and training new salespeople. If an agency is hired, it hires salespeople and oversees training, removing that burden from you.

Problems Associated with Sales Reps. The list of potential problems is shorter than the list of reasons to work with reps, but almost every manufacturer who has used reps has had problems. They include:

1. Inability to find and work with good reps. The list of advantages of using reps is long, but there is one overriding challenge: *it is hard to find good people.* Manufacturers will tell you war stories about the difficulties of finding good reps and how difficult it is to tell in advance how well a rep will sell their products.

2. Inability to closely control reps' activities. Reps are their own bosses, and therefore are difficult to control. Since they carry a variety of products, you cannot ensure how much they are going to push yours. Their knowledge of your product and expertise in promoting it may not be as great as you would like. What controls independent reps more than anything else is that their goal is the same as the manufacturer: to sell product.

3. Reps under contract who are not selling up to expectations. A contract can make it difficult for a manufacturer to quickly drop one rep and pick up another.

It is not easy to find a good sales rep

How to Find Sales Reps. Finding good reps is not an easy task, and there is no one best way to look for them. Listed below are different means of searching for reps.

1. Talk to retailers. Since reps are selling to retailers, you should contact retailers and ask them from which reps they buy and with which they are impressed. Contact retailers not only in your immediate area, but also ones in larger metropolitan areas

where there is higher sales potential. Once you have the names of reps with a good reputation, then you must sell them on your products. Even if they are not willing to take your lines, they can probably give you names of other reps to contact.

2. Talk to manufacturers who make similar products. If they don't view you as a direct competitor, they may be very willing to give you names of people whom they feel are good. For example, if you produce computer forms, you may want to talk to producers of computer furniture, whose reps would also be selling to office supply stores.

3. Tradeshows often are good places to contact reps. If you have a booth in the show, put up a sign that you are looking for reps. In the show guide, you can place a want ad for reps, or look at the listings of reps seeking lines. In large tradeshows, there is frequently a booth set up by the industry rep organization to facilitate reps and manufacturers meeting each other. Retailers and producers of similar products are in large attendance at shows, so if you have the time to get away from your booth to talk to these people they can give you leads on good reps.

4. Manufacturers' Agents National Association (MANA) is the largest trade association of manufacturers' agents and reps, with membership of approximately 8,000. Manufacturers can join the organization as associate members for a fee of about $200 and have access to the *Directory of Manufacturers' Sales Agencies* and also receive a monthly magazine entitled *Agency Sales*. Pages from both the directory and the magazine show listings of agents looking for lines and manufacturers looking for agents.

Finding good sales reps can be a trial-and-error process

5. Industry associations exist in just about every industry, and they are an excellent source of information. You may have to join the association to get access to their information, but membership fees are usually under $200 per year. Membership usually entitles you to a directory of all members, an industry publication, and access to back issues of their publication. One often finds classified ads in the publications for reps looking for lines, and vice versa. The section of this chapter that deals with tradeshows discusses how to find out about industry associations. The primary source is *The Encyclopedia of Associations*.

6. Trade publications are published both by industry associations and other private groups. For example, in the log home industry there is no strong industry association but there are two trade journals that are widely read. They usually have want ads with listings of reps seeking lines and vice versa. *The Encyclopedia of Business Information Sources* is a good source of information about trade publications.

7. Yellow Page Directories in larger cities carry fairly large listings of reps under the heading *Manufacturers' Agents and Reps*. Most libraries carry phone books of major U.S. cities, or you can contact your local telephone company to obtain directories.

8. Want ads can be placed in major cities' newspapers, usually under "Help Wanted, Sales Positions."

How to Screen and Select Sales Reps. Manufacturers who use reps will attest to the difficulty in foreseeing which reps will work out well. Producers will humbly admit that reps that they thought would be tremendous have fizzled, and ones they had little confidence in sometimes ended up being winners. You try to screen as thoroughly as possible, but you are going to have to expect some turnover of people who just don't perform. Realize also that the nature of recruiting reps changes as you grow in sales and reputation. At first, you have to do all of the pursuing because no one knows about you. As you become more established, reps usually seek you out because they have heard that you have products that move.

At first, you need to pursue sales reps

Catalog Companies. The catalog industry has experienced a period of explosive growth in recent years, and the success of the industry is based primarily on the fact that people enjoy the convenience of shopping at home. "Independent" cataloguers produce no products themselves; rather, they market different manufacturers' merchandise through direct mail. The cataloguers purchase certain amounts of goods from the manufacturers and try to sell it all. There is a large number of mailing lists that the cataloguers have access to.

Orders with catalog companies tend to be large

For you, the manufacturer, the opportunity to sell to catalog companies can have advantages. First, order sizes tend to be large. If you sign a contract with a cataloguer, you usually sell at least several hundred units of a product. Secondly, you are able to order inventory and produce the goods knowing that they are already sold. This reduces the risk you typically have of overproducing and not being able to sell all of the finished goods. Thirdly, if you have a contract with one or more cataloguers, the amount of marketing work can be reduced in your firm. The contracts are usually substantial, and if they can be maintained, there is less of a need for brochures, sales calls, etc.

There can be disadvantages in trying to get cataloguers to carry your products. First, for most manufacturers it is not easy to find a *quality* cataloguer interested in carrying their products. There is an overabundance of catalog companies, with many going out of business every year. You should strive to get your products in reputable, established catalogs. Second, catalog companies will typically carry only one or a few of your products. If you have a broad product line, you will not be able to push them all through catalogs. Another drawback of selling to catalog companies is that they usually expect a price that is 5-10 percent below your normal wholesale price. Lastly, a disadvantage of catalog selling is that so many of your eggs are lumped in one or a few baskets. If a major portion of your business is through catalogs and only one catalog drops your product, your sales may plummet. The large catalog accounts are wonderful, but don't be lulled to sleep and forget about all marketing efforts.

> **There can be disadvantages in trying to get cataloguers to carry your products**

How to Find Out About Catalog Companies. As mentioned above, finding good independent catalog companies is not easy and requires research. The first step is to talk to people, including:

1. Consumers who like your type of product. For example, if you manufacture reproduction antique furniture, people who have antiques could probably tell you if they receive any catalogs with that type of product.

2. Trade associations. They can be good sources of information on cataloguers. Find out which associations represent your industry and ask them if they are aware which cataloguers carry merchandise from your industry.

3. Retailers. They may tell you which catalogs carry products in their industries. Be aware that the cataloguers are direct competitors to the retailers, hence the retailers may not want to tell you about them. In other words, if the retailers tell you that there are no cataloguers, don't be too quick to believe them.

4. Tradeshows. They often are attended by cataloguers. Typically, the catalog buyers would be attending the larger shows in the industry. Your presence in these tradeshows may provide you with contacts with them. Put up a sign in your booth or place an ad in the tradeshow program. Many of the other people selling at the tradeshow may be willing to give you their advice on catalogs. Don't be afraid to approach other merchants and talk to them about what works for them.

There are several directories of catalog companies. The most comprehensive is *The Directory of Mail Order Catalogs*, which is in the reference section of the several Washington libraries. This book provides information on not only catalog companies, but on companies that publish their own catalogs. A recent edition of the book contains 6,800 entries, which are indexed by product and by company name. The following information is provided for each entry: name, address, and phone number; a brief description of the types of products it carries; the credit cards it accepts; names of the marketing or sales manager, buyers, production manager, and list manager; frequency of publication; catalog price; whether a mailing list is available; size of its mailing list; length of its catalog; its sales volume; and, whether it sells books related to its area of specialty. Another book entitled *The Great Book of Catalogs* contains only 2,000 catalog listings.

To locate potential cataloguers, you search by product section for companies that catalog the type of products you make. Phone numbers and addresses are given for the companies in the directory. Distinctions are not made between those cataloguers that carry other people's products and those that market only their own. A mailing list of catalog companies can be obtained from the publisher of the directory at the rate of $85 for 1000 names. They will also print the labels.

Another source for contacting cataloguers is through the *Catalog Product News*. This quarterly publication that began in March of 1988 shows pictures of and describes a variety of products. You pay to have your products listed in the publication. The magazine is mailed to 23,000 buyers at over 6,000 catalog companies and showrooms, direct marketing firms, and home television shopping companies. In other words, it is a catalog for direct-order merchandisers.

Direct Marketing. The American public has grown to trust direct marketers. More than 90 percent of all Americans have purchased some product as a result of direct marketing. Its use is continuing to grow at over 10 percent per year, in spite of the fact that over 50 billion direct marketing pieces are already mailed each year. A variety of directing marketing means exist, including:

1. Direct mail
2. Telemarketing
3. Direct response television
4. Direct response radio
5. Inserts
6. Want ads
7. Coupons in newspapers and magazines
8. Catalogs
9. Postcard decks
10. Bulletin boards

> **90 percent of all Americans have purchased some product as a result of direct marketing**

In 1982, telemarketing surpassed direct mail in dollar expenditures. The fastest growing segment is postcard decks, wherein a marketer mails a stack of approximately fifty promotional postcards. The customer flips through the deck and either calls or mails in the postcards for products that interest her.

Advantages of Direct Marketing. The dramatic increase in direct marketing is no fluke. There are compelling reasons to use it, including:

1. You sell at retail price and don't give up margins to "middlemen".
2. You can easily track the success of your marketing program. When you run other ad campaigns, it is difficult to know what effect advertising has. With direct mail, you know immediately.
3. Your costs can be kept low. Many companies using exclusively direct marketing operate out of a garage or warehouse. As long as your promotional piece looks nice and the person answering the phone is polite, the customer doesn't know the difference. You can direct your campaign to small segments and keep your promotional costs down also.
4. Society is moving in a direction of relying more on direct marketing. People are rushed these days. They enjoy being able to shop from their home or office and not have to "go out shopping".

> **There are compelling reasons to use direct marketing**

5. You can be selective in choosing the group to which you will market. Mailing lists are becoming more and more refined and you are able to concentrate on specific market segments. Because of this selectivity, you can personalize your approach to different groups, even to different customers.
6. You can test your approach on a small sample of potential customers and refine or abandon it without spending a large amount of money.

Direct marketing does have some drawbacks

Disadvantages of Direct Marketing. If, after reading the list of advantages of direct marketing, you have begun to believe it is a panacea, understand that it is not. It does have disadvantages, including:

1. People are being bombarded with more and more direct marketing promotions. Your approach has to stand out to be noticed in the barrage.
2. Some products do not lend themselves well to direct marketing (see below).
3. You may not be able to reach nearly as many customers compared to other distribution channels.
4. It may be slower in producing sales than other channels.

Who Should Use Direct Marketing. Direct marketing works better in certain situations. Some of them include:

There are certain situations where direct marketing works best

1. When products are standardized and customers are educated about what they are getting. Customers feel that they don't need explanations of product features, they just want to know which are offered. Office supply products are sold directly through catalogs, and customers feel comfortable that they know what they are getting.
2. When you are having difficulty getting into established distribution channels. You may have no choice but to try direct marketing.
3. When you are selling products that people are embarrassed to buy in public. A significant portion of society has bladder problems. These people would probably appreciate being able to purchase "diapers" through the mail.
4. When your target market is small and focused. More conventional approaches, such as newspaper or television advertising, would be wasteful since your buying group is so small.

5. When your potential customers have difficulty shopping for the products that you sell, including elderly people or people living in remote areas.

6. When your industry is more mature. When an industry is young, customers are not very knowledgeable nor have they developed a "trust" for it. When it matures and people are used to buying products, they are more willing to order without seeing the product in person.

Who Should Be Cautious in Using Direct Marketing. Companies who are in the situations described below should carefully analyze whether they should attempt direct marketing.

1. Companies in young, emerging industries. Customers are not knowledgeable nor have they grown to "trust" the industry.

2. Firms with customized, highly-differentiated products. When people are shopping for highly-customized products, they usually want to see directly what they will be getting and want to deal face-to-face with someone.

3. Firms with large and/or heavy products. Freight charges may make these products non-competitive.

4. Businesses whose customers are more service-oriented than price-conscious.

5. Companies whose products are often purchased on an impulse basis. If you are selling blank audio cassette tapes, you may have a tough time direct marketing them. People usually buy them when they need them, and they can purchase them in a grocery store.

6. Companies selling products for which customers are not willing to wait. If a customer runs out of toilet paper, he's not going to wait a week for his order to arrive.

> **Companies in some situations should carefully analyze whether they should attempt direct marketing**

A variety of quality books on direct marketing is available. Some are listed in the reference section at the end of the chapter. They teach you how to implement direct marketing programs for each of the approaches mentioned in this section.

Strategy for Marketing Channels. If you can get your products into established marketing channels, your sales should increase dramatically. However, it usually takes time. In the interim, you need to make *some* sales to survive. Direct marketing to customers and retailers is usually a necessity in the early stages of product distribution. If there are any consumer shows in your area, they can produce good sales for you. Visit retailers in your region and try to

> **It takes time to get your products into established marketing channels**

get them to carry your products. Tradeshows will allow you to sell directly to retailers outside of your local area. Through these means, you will gradually build up a group of retailers carrying your products.

Once you are selling enough to prove the saleability of your products, you can concentrate on expanding your distribution. You need to be patient and persistent in seeking to break into distribution channels. If sales reps service your industry, you are better off in early stages to use them than to try to hire your own salespeople. If distributors serve your industry, find out who are the best ones and work on getting them to carry your products. Reps and distributors can gain *widespread* distribution for your products. As they grow in importance, you will probably rely less on selling directly to retailers and stop selling in consumer shows.

Reps and distributors can gain widespread distribution for your products

Some companies who become solidly established in distribution channels and whose products become well known consider drawing back somewhat from the channels and doing more of the marketing themselves. The firms grow large enough to afford their own salespeople and they drop their independent reps. Retailers want their products enough that they will purchase directly from the manufacturer instead of through distributors. The manufacturer, therefore, retains the margin that the distributor used to take. The company often times can pay more attention to individual accounts than could a distributor. In certain cases, product recognition becomes high enough that consumers will buy directly from the manufacturer. Once you are established in marketing channels, you might consider drawing back somewhat and doing more of the marketing yourself.

In general, the strategy for market channels is:

1. In early stages, do some direct marketing and sell directly to retailers to generate initial sales.
2. Work persistently to get into established channels, through sales reps and distributors.
3. Once you are established, you can increase your margins and your control of the marketing process by selling directly to retailers with your own sales force.

Promoting through Channels. To gain access to any distribution channel, you must first have a product that customers want and are willing to pay for. But there are other factors that can help you to get your products into channels.

Some factors can help you get your products into channels

1. Provide display cases or racks to resellers.
2. Offer good payment terms to resellers.
3. Provide prompt, reliable delivery of products.
4. Offer a good return policy.
5. *Service* resellers. Listen to their problems. Work with them.
6. Price products at prices that will sell but allow distributors and resellers good margins.
7. Package products appropriately.
8. Offer "co-op" advertising to resellers, wherein you pay part of the costs they incur in promoting your products.

Generally, you need to meet personally with distributors or sales reps to get them to carry your products. You can meet either at your or their place of business or else at a tradeshow. You need to have some type of printed material about your products, whether it be a flier, a brochure, or a catalog. You will need to decide which is most appropriate (and what you can afford). You should also have product samples available for them to look at. In many cases, it may take several visits and phone calls before any type of agreement is reached. Advertisements in industry journals and newsletters may put you in touch with interested distributors.

Eventually, you might consider drawing back somewhat and doing more of the marketing yourself

Most manufacturers use the promotion methods mentioned above in a "push" strategy. They put their efforts into "pushing" products into marketing channels and allowing the retailers to promote the products to the buying public. If you are a retailer, you need to use another approach— a "pull" promotion strategy. You promote products so as to "pull" customers in to buy them. Some manufacturers have well established products and also use a "pull" strategy to increase demand for products. Oshkosh B'Gosh products are pushed through distribution channels, but the company also does a fair amount of promotion directly to the buying public. You usually need considerable financial resources as a manufacturer to undertake a large-scale "pull" strategy.

Pricing
Price according to the market and not according to what a product costs you. Some businesses under price their products because they base it on their costs. For example, a manufacturer may be able to

produce a new chemical formulation for dog deodorant. The direct chemical and filling costs are only $1.50. The owner believes that a 50 percent gross margin on retail sales is fair, so he charges $3. His competitors charge $5. If he stays at $3, he may be making a mistake. He needs to analyze his positioning of the product. Does he want to be a discounter? Is that the image he wants? Will competitors drop their prices right down to his level if he sells for $3? He should base his decision on the market, and not on his costs. If he wants to be a discounter, he should analyze the market and determine how much he should drop his price below the industry standard $5 to be considered "a bargain." Perhaps his product is good enough to be considered "premium," and he could charge $7 for it. A healthy margin never hurt anyone. And besides, his formula may be copied and then he may have to start dropping his price.

Most manufacturers use a "push" strategy

Sometimes a small manufacturer's costs are high relative to the industry. You can't charge a higher price just because your costs are higher. You have to have a better product to do it. The only point at which your costs become a factor in pricing is when you decide whether you can afford to make a product at all. If your product is not highly differentiated and the market price leaves you with a thin margin, you may have to decide not to produce it at all. Once again, *price according to the market*. If you find you can't survive at the price you have to charge, consider getting out of it.

Price according to the market

Price your products in a manner consistent with your product positioning. If you have premium products, you should be able to charge premium prices. Part of your entry strategy with a product may be to offer a lower price than competitive products in the premium segment, and that is fine. Or, to reinforce the image that your product is better than others', you may consistently need to be priced above the competition. The important point is that your pricing strategy should be consistent with the rest of your marketing strategy.

There is a variety of unique pricing strategies. For new products being introduced, a short-term deep price discount strategy sometimes works. That is what Bernstein's did with its salad dressings. When they first came out, they priced it well below the industry average. People bought them because they were cheap. Once they tried them, they said, "this stuff is great." And they continued buying because it "tastes great, less costly." Several months later, those faithful customers were shocked to see that

There is a variety of unique pricing strategies

Bernstein's salad dressing was no longer less expensive than the market, but was considerably higher. They bought it anyway, though, because they liked it so much. Their strategy was a good one. Get people to try the product by discounting it, and once they realize how good it is, raise the price. You have to have a very good quality product to make this strategy work.

Another unique pricing strategy is to charge a low, competitive price for the main product, but keep a healthy margin on accessories or replacement parts. This is done with electric razors. You can buy a good quality electric razor for less than $40, and pricing is competitive between the major manufacturers. If you tear a hole in the thin metal screen, which you will in a short period of time, you find that the screen alone costs nearly $10. That is where they make their money. You're not going to purchase another new razor just because the replacement screen is expensive. Automobile dealers make much better margins on replacement parts than they do on new cars. For this strategy to work, you obviously must sell accessories or replacement parts besides your primary product.

> **Some companies make money on accessories and not on the main product**

Most smaller businesses should try to keep a decent margin on their products. Product differentiation and high customer service should allow you to gain sales without slashing prices. Again, the basic marketing strategy for most small businesses should be:

- Focus on a few markets
- Differentiate your products to those markets

If you do this, you should be able to maintain healthy margins.

Promotion

Promotion is the fourth and final component of your marketing mix. Its purpose is to educate customers about your products, create in them an interest in your products, and prompt them to buy. Promotion is also used to create an image of your company in customers' minds. With these critical goals, promotion is obviously very important. Four elements make up your promotional strategy– personal selling, publicity, sales promotion, and advertising. Each is briefly described below. You need to learn more about each of them, however, and references are listed at the end of the chapter.

> **Promotion is used to create an image of your company is customers' minds**

Personal Selling. Personal selling is asking customers for business, eye-to-eye. It is the oldest form of promotion. There are three critical steps to personal selling. The first is *contact*. Those first few moments that you have with a potential customers are incredibly important. Try to *establish a relationship*. Make sure that you are dressed appropriately. Be warm and honest with people. The best approach is to talk to customers *about themselves*.

There are three critical steps to personal selling

The second step is *presentation*. You are describing the features of your offering and the benefits to the customer. Remember, *people buy benefits and not products*. Therefore, focus on how your product will meet a customer's needs. Describe what is *unique* about your product. Try to *show them something*, rather than just talking to them.

The third step is *closing*, which is when the sale is made. In some cases you may present your products and close at a later date. But in many cases you must close while the customer is present or else lose them. Remember one overriding principle— *people like to buy*. They may be choosy and terribly tight with their money, but they still enjoy buying something new. Therefore, don't be afraid of closing. You're *doing your customers a service*! And besides, if they don't buy from you they will buy from someone else. You need to develop a sixth sense about when a customer is ready to purchase, and then you need to ask for the sale.

Four elements make up your promotional strategy– personal selling, publicity, sales promotion, and advertising

Publicity. Publicity can be the cheapest, and possibly the best, form of promotion. You can't control it precisely, but you can certainly take steps to affect it. One winery in Washington state spends almost nothing on promotion, yet it consistently receives articles in magazines such as *The Wine Spectator,* and other widely-read magazines. Ads of such length would cost hundreds of thousands of dollars. Those articles do not just "happen." The company relentlessly works with editors of magazines and critics, providing samples, conducting elaborate dinners and wine tastings. Publicity works well because someone else makes a testimony on your part. This carries weight. Think about new products, new employees, new markets, or anything interesting about your company that media might consider worthy of an article.

Sales Promotions. Sales promotions catch customers' attention and encourage immediate sales. They include such items as coupons, samplings, rebates, contests and sweepstakes, and point of purchase displays. They include whacky approaches such as camping on top of your business until a certain amount of sales occurs. The purpose is to draw attention to your products and encourage a prompt sale.

Advertising. Advertising is the most frequently used form of promotion. There are many ways to advertise your products. Listed below are the most common forms. Read books on advertising and learn the relative advantages and disadvantages of one medium compared to the others. Some companies hire ad agencies to put together all of their advertising and public relations, while others do a very respectable job in-house. Whichever way you go, it is still important for you to know as much about advertising as possible. Consider each of the following forms of advertising and how cost effectively it will reach your customers:

Advertising is the most frequently used form of promotion

1. Newspaper
2. Television
3. Radio
4. Magazine layout ads
5. Want ads
6. Yellow pages
7. Billboards
8. Transit (such as busses)
9. Personal letters
10. Handbills/flyers
11. Posters
12. Newsletters
13. Postcard decks
14. Gimmicks, including calendars, bags, notepads, matchbooks, pens, buttons, T-shirts, hats, actors, etc.

Conclusion

Marketing is the key to success for most businesses. Finance, accounting, and management are all important, but they take a backseat to marketing. Why? Because marketing is *your contact with customers*. And meeting their needs is why your business exists. A good marketing strategy needs to be top priority in your venture.

Marketing is the key to success for most businesses

Learn as much as you can about marketing. This chapter covers only general strategy issues. You need to learn the details. Don't assume that an ad agency can do it all for you. Read books and magazines and go to instructional seminars. The following reference section and Chapter 16, Business Resources, describe marketing resources. Make marketing a high priority.

Marketing is your contact with customers

References

1. Chapman, Edward A. *Exhibit Marketing*. New York: McGraw-Hill Book Company, 1995.

2. Gottlieb, Richard. *Directory of Mail Order Catalogs*, 1996 Edition. New York: Grey House Publishing, 1995.

3. Pinkerton, Betsy and Pinkerton, Steve. *The Great Book of Catalogs*, Fourth Edition. Pinkerton Marketing, 1988.

4. Porter, Michael. *Competitive Strategy: Techniques for Analyzing Industries and Competitors*. New York: Free Press, 1980.

5. Thompson, Arthur A. and Strickland, A. J. *Strategic Management*, Eighth Edition. Plano, Texas: Business Publications, Inc., 1995

6. *1996 Tradeshow Week Data Book*. New York: Tradeshow Week, 1995.

7. Rapp, Stan and Collins, Tom. *The Great Marketing Turnaround: The Age of the Individual and how to Profit from it*. Plume Publishing, 1990.

8. *Directory of Manufacturers' Sales Agencies*. Laguna Hills, California: Manufacturers' Agents National Association, 1991.

══ 11 ══

Cash Management

"Happiness Is a Positive Cash Flow." ©
Stan Rich

Cash flow is the *single most important* financial consideration of a business. In the short term, you need cash to pay your bills, purchase inventory, buy equipment, pay employees and yourself. You can't pay your employees with income off of your income statement; you must pay them with cash. A business doesn't go bankrupt because of a loss on an income statement; it goes bankrupt because it doesn't have the cash to pay the people to whom it owes money. Some people think that their bank and creditors will be lenient if they show them an encouraging income statement, even though they have no cash to pay their immediate bills. There are bankruptcy notices every week for people who believe that.

There can be some dramatic differences between net income and net cash flow in the short term. Accountants can calculate your financial statements by using different means, and your net income can vary greatly, depending on what means they use. Depreciation can be changed, inventory methods varied and other manipulations made, all of which change your income. An income statement can be manipulated to show just about anything you want to. You can't do that with a cash flow statement– you either have the cash or you don't.

In the long term, cash flow is also critical. Some business owners state, "Cash flow right now isn't important. We want to build the business up and sell down the road." Well, perhaps cash flow is not critical at this point in time, since they can pay their bills and have enough cash to live on. However, when they go to sell the business, cash flow will mean everything. It will make little difference at selling time how much profit they will have earned over the years– only the IRS is concerned with profits. What will make a difference to them is how much CASH they put in their pockets when they sell the business. They won't be able to buy a house, take a trip or buy a boat with profits, but they can with cash from the sale of it. Cash flow is *the* ultimate measure of the long term success of a business.

There can be dramatic differences between net income and net cash flow

In summary, put more emphasis on the cash flow statement than on the income statement, and take steps to manage the cash in your business. The cash in a business will not "take care of itself." You have to manage it.

Almost every business manager has experienced cash flow problems, and the symptoms are not pleasant ones. You can't pay bills on time, checks bounce, creditors call, you rob Peter to pay Paul, and spend large amounts of time with bankers trying to get money, all of which consume huge amounts of your time and your energy and force you to run the business in a very inefficient manner. There are a number of causes of cash flow problems:

The symptoms of cash flow problems are not pleasant ones

- Lack of profitability for an extended period of time;
- Seasonality of sales;
- A lack of planning; and surprisingly enough,
- Fast growth in sales.

The symptoms and possible solutions to each of these causes of cash flow problems are discussed below.

Breakeven Analysis

Many companies go through periods of losses and continue to pay their bills; however, a long-term lack of profits will cause cash flow problems. You can stay afloat by selling assets, borrowing to cover losses, or by other means, but they all tend to erode your equity in the business. A breakeven analysis allows you to predict what profits will be, based on a sales projection.

A long-term lack of profits will cause cash flow problems

The breakeven analysis tells you what level of sales you need in order to pay your expenses. At the breakeven point you are not showing any income, rather you are just covering your expenses. Be aware that a calculated breakeven point is *only an estimate*. It does, however, give you a ballpark estimate of whether or not the company will be profitable at a given sales level.

The first step of the analysis is to label all of your expenses as either fixed, variable, or a combination of the two. Fixed costs are those expenses that tend not to change with the level of sales of the firm. For example, rent and insurance costs do not generally fluctuate with sales. Whether you have a good month or a bad month, these areas are not affected. It doesn't mean they never change– your landlord can raise the rent, you can change locations and hence rent, or your insurance agent can certainly raise your premiums, but these are still considered fixed costs in the sense that sales levels do not affect them.

Variable costs are those expenses which fluctuate directly with sales. For example, sales commissions are variable costs, as is cost of goods sold. If you sell twice as much, your expense is twice as much. Some operating costs are a combination of fixed and variable expenses. Utilities can be a combination of the two expenses– you have to pay a certain amount to keep the lights on and the building heated, but if you have a good month, you spend more on electricity for your manufacturing process. Your payroll may be a combination of fixed and variable costs: if your salespeople are guaranteed a base, which is a fixed cost; plus commission, which is a variable cost.

Some expenses may be a combination of both fixed and variable costs

You can calculate the breakeven level of sales for either a month's or a year's time. If you are in a highly seasonal business, do a breakeven on an annual basis. If your business is not highly seasonal, a monthly breakeven is often easier to interpret than an annual one. If you are doing a monthly analysis, project costs for a "typical" month. Realize that a breakeven analysis is an *estimate*, and you need not be overly precise in your figures.

Figure 11-1 shows how one company classified all of their monthly expenses as either fixed or variable, or a combination of the two. For fixed costs, the total monthly amount is written in the "FIXED" column. The company shown pays $1000 per month in rent. Variable costs are written as a proportion of sales. Raw materials average 30 percent of sales, while direct labor averages 20 percent. The total fixed costs per month are $15,000, while variable costs add to .50.

A breakeven analysis in an estimate and need not be overly precise

The breakeven formula is:

BEP = FC / (1 - VC)

BEP is the breakeven point in dollars
FC is total fixed costs
VC is variable costs expressed in decimal form

Therefore, in order to cover expenses the firm must sell

$$BEP = 15,000 / (1 - .50) = \$30,000 \text{ per month.}$$

Figure 13-1. Sample Breakeven Analysis

COSTS	FIXED AMOUNT	VARIABLE %
Raw materials		0.30
Direct Labor		0.20
Merchandise		
Wages & Salaries	9000	
Payroll Expenses	1800	
Supplies	500	
Repairs & Maintenance	0	
Advertising	500	
Car, Delivery, Travel	300	
Accounting & Legal	200	
Rent/Lease	1000	
Telephone	150	
Insurance	100	
Utilities	150	
Taxes, Real Estate, Etc.	200	
Depreciation	400	
Other Expenses	700	
TOTALS	15,000	0.50

BREAKEVEN POINT =	30,000	
PRICE/UNIT =	75.00	
BREAKEVEN POINT IN UNITS =	400	

Realize that at this sales level, the company is only meeting expenses. Most people are in business to be able to take some money home. That amount can be added to fixed expenses. For example, if the owner wants to draw $3,000 a month, it is added to fixed expenses, which then total $18,000 per month. Plugging the numbers in the same formula yields a new breakeven point: $36,000 per month. This is how much the company will have to sell per month to pay all expenses and allow the owner to draw $3,000.

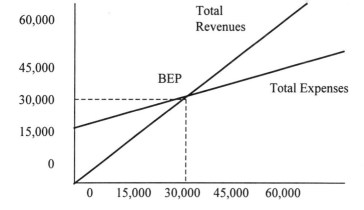

Figure 11-2 illustrates a breakeven graph based on the original calculated breakeven point of $30,000. Both axes are in terms of dollars. The breakeven point (BEP) is where the revenue and total expense lines cross. The vertical distance between these two lines is the amount of profit or loss that the company is experiencing. Naturally, at the breakeven point of $30,000 there is neither a profit nor a loss. At sales of $20,000, however, the company would have a $5000 loss, which is the vertical distance between the two lines at that point. If the company sold $40,000, it would earn a profit of $5000.

> **If a business is below the breakeven point, the main source of its cash problems is a lack of profits**

If a business is not above the breakeven point, the main source of its cash flow problems is simple—a lack of profits. The firm needs to increase revenues, cut expenses, or both before it will make much headway in solving its cash flow problems.

Cash Management Principles

If your business is profitable, but you still experience cash flow problems, you are not alone. In fact, it is a very common problem, especially in growing or seasonal businesses. There are three fundamentals to effectively manage the cash in a profitable business:

> **A profitable business may still experience cash flow problems**

- Planning
- Timing
- Frugality

Planning

The most important thing you can do to avoid cash shortages is plan

Probably the single most important thing you can do to avoid cash shortages is plan. Unfortunately, planning does not come naturally to many people. In fact, it is amazing the extent to which people go to avoid planning. Nevertheless, if you are going to control your cash, you must predict what your revenues and your expenses will be. Many people resist forecasting revenues and expenses because they are afraid the numbers will look bad, and that can be really depressing. In this case, ignorance is bliss. So what happens? A cash shortage occurs, which was foreseeable, but no one bothered to predict, and then the manager arranges a short notice meeting with the banker to see the business through the cash crunch.

Bankers do not like these kinds of meetings. Bankers do not like to be surprised, even on their birthdays. This business owner would have been much better off if three months previously he had taken a cash flow projection to the bank, showed the amount and timing of the cash shortage, showed how down the road the bank would be repaid, and made arrangements in advance. Bankers much prefer this type of setting for approving a loan– after all, they are in business of loaning money.

Figure 11-3 illustrates a cash flow planning sheet. The Small Business Administration has sheets such as this, as well as workbooks on preparing business plans for general types of enterprises such as retail, service, construction and manufacturing, and makes them available at low cost. General microcomputer spreadsheet programs, such as Microsoft Excel, are extremely helpful for allowing exploration of "what if" questions in such financial programs. More specialized (and expensive) programs, such as Ronstadt's Financials, provide extensive guidance for such forecasting and business planning. A spreadsheet template of this same worksheet is provided on the diskette included with this book. Here is how you use the sheet. In the "Estimate" column, forecast revenues and expenses for at least three months, and do it in pencil. Try to be as accurate as possible in the timing of your figures. For example, if you pay insurance every six months, get the figure in the correct month, and don't average it across all twelve months. If you can forecast for more than three months, that's all the better. If you can't project at least three months, this forecast will be of little value.

Figure 11-3. Projected Cash Flow Statement

	Jan Proj	Jan Act	Feb Proj	Feb Act
Beg Cash on Hand				
Cash Receipts				
(A)Collections				
(B)Int & Misc				
(C)Loan, Contrib				
Tot Cash Rcpts				
Tot Cash Avail				
Expenses				
Purchases				
Payroll				
Payroll Expenses				
Outside Expenses				
Supplies				
Repairs/Maintnce				
Advertising				
Auto & Travel				
Accounting, Legal				
Rent				
Telephone				
Utilities				
Insurance				
Taxes				
Interest				
Other Expenses				
Subtotal				
Loan Prin Payment				
Capital Purchase				
Start-up Costs				
Reserve/Escrow				
Owner Withdrawal				
Tot Cash Pd Out				
Cash Position				

The cash flow projection is the most critical step in avoiding cash flow problems

After a month has passed, write in the actual figures, compare them to your projection and if necessary, revise your ensuing projections (that's why they should be in pencil). You should then be able to forecast another month's figures. In this way, you make a "rolling" forecast as time passes, and you are constantly revising the forecast.

If you are going to implement only one portion of this whole cash management program, make sure it is this cash flow projection. It is absolutely the most critical step in avoiding cash flow problems, and that is to know in advance when a cash shortage is coming.

Timing
Many cash flow shortages are caused when "everything hits at once," in other words when timing is terrible. Some you can't avoid, many you can. Figure 11-4 shows a cash flow diagram. The basic strategy for resolving cash shortages is to speed up conversion of assets into cash and slow down the flow of cash out of the business.

Many cash flow shortages are caused when "everything hits at once"

Consider the circular part of the cash flow diagram. Cash is used to purchase inventory, which turns into sales, which turns into receivables, which turns back into cash. The strategy: slow down the flow of cash into inventory, but once you have bought merchandise, speed up the cycle of turning that into sales → receivables → back into cash.

You slow down cash outflows into inventory but speed inventory turns through good inventory control. The two primary types of inventory control systems are a bin and a perpetual inventory system. Either system tells you what, when, and how much to buy. Loose inventory control can be a terrible cash drain on a business. While you are scrapping to pay your bills, there may be a tremendous amount of cash tied up on your shelves that is either overstocked or is not moving. You must know what products are moving in your business, how much you will be selling, and how long it takes you to get those products once you have ordered them. Many Japanese companies are expert at timing the arrival of raw materials so that they don't end up being stored for any lengthy period of time, and hence they tie up very little cash.

If you've got old merchandise sitting on your shelves, mark it down and get rid of it. It's freezing your cash. If you don't know which merchandise moves and which doesn't, you must learn it. Purchase the products that move, and don't overbuy. Without risking stockouts, minimize how much merchandise you carry and try to time getting merchandise in with when you will be selling (and get good suppliers!).

Be very careful about paying bills late as a strategy to improve your cash flow (although it is probably the most commonly used). Very few people are foolish enough to pay bills early, unless discounts are given. The discounts, by the way, can be significant. A 2/10 net 30 discount is the same as putting the money away for twenty days in an account bearing 36 percent, which is tough to find these days. Unless you have an understanding supplier or other creditor, your paying late will upset them (and will probably cost you dearly in interest). If you are going to rely on them for prompt and consistent delivery so that you trim your inventory, you'd better be prompt in paying them. Do not pay late as a strategy to improve your cash flow. Pay when your bills are due.

Do not pay your bills late as a strategy to improve your cash flow

The next portion of the cash cycle is converting inventory into sales. Again, you are attempting to speed the flow of other assets into cash. You need good marketing to do this. Chapter 10 explains the steps in formulating a sound marketing strategy.

Accounts receivable are in many cases the cause of cash flow problems. Make sure that you are not offering credit to the wrong people. For a fee, credit bureaus will check on applicants' credit histories. Standard credit forms are available at office supply stores. For smaller firms, calls to other creditors are a less expensive way of checking credit. Don't believe everything on a credit application form. Check it out. It takes time and some money, but may really save you headaches in the long run. A clear, written credit policy must be adopted and adhered to. The policies will vary between industries, in some cases dictated by what is standard in the industry. Don't let your customers *ever* give you the excuse that you hadn't told them what your credit policy was.

Let your customers know up front what your credit terms are

Even the most careful credit checks will still result in accounts that are overdue. Careful attention to those accounts will help keep them to a minimum. The fairest assumption is that customers want to pay as agreed. The majority will, when reminded, pay in a timely manner. However, a customer's situation may change from that which existed when the agreement was made. Restructuring a debt is usually better than turning the account over to a collection agency.

Standard collection letters are available from a variety of sources. The key to good collections is *diligence*. Do you remember the parable Jesus told about the man who woke his neighbor in the middle of the night to borrow a loaf of bread? Well, the neighbor was very upset and didn't want to give him anything, and so told him to go away. The man kept knocking, and even though the neighbor didn't want to give him any bread, he did so just to be rid of him. The best bill collectors operate under the same principle. Don't bully the people who owe you money, just be persistent. They may not want to give you any bread either; but if they have any money, they'll pay you just to get you out of their hair. On the other hand, if you sit back and don't do or say anything, you'll go right to the bottom of their list to be paid.

The key to good collections is diligence

Figure 11-4. The Cash Flow Cycle

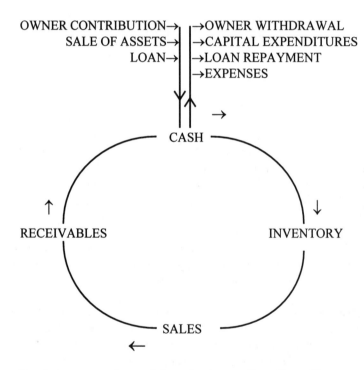

Consistency must be used in enforcing credit policy. If terms are "net thirty," customers must be notified immediately if they are overdue. If late payment interest charges are written in the policy, they must be enforced. Some business owners who pay after the discount date and still take the discount. Why? Because the company they buy from never clamps down on them. All you need do is let a customer slide once on a late payment or not paying interest, and chances are they will continue to do so. Even if it costs you more to send the notice than what you will collect, you need to do so. Good credit control requires diligence.

Other Cash Flow Timing Issues. For seasonal businesses, there are approaches you can take to spread your expenses to more cash-rich times. Look at all of your expense accounts: can you arrange to pay them when you have more cash available? Start with suppliers. Are they willing to extend longer credit terms so that you are able to pay once your heavy selling season is over? What about people from whom you purchase equipment? Can they wait also? Can you arrange to pay your insurance at different times? What about your accountant? Some of these may not be possibilities, but they are certainly worth a try, and you may be surprised how willing some of these people would be to accommodate you.

> **Good credit control requires diligence and consistency**

Non-cyclic Cash Considerations. Referring back to the cash flow diagram, you will see that there are cash inflows and outflows outside of the circular part of the diagram. These represent steps that you can take on an occasional basis to improve cash flow. You can obtain additional cash by selling assets. Many times you can sell non-productive assets when cash shortages are foreseen. Foresight is important, because rarely can you immediately liquidate assets. For example, Bill once owned a golf pro shop and taught golf. He owned a $3000 video camera system which helped him to analyze students' strokes. He loved the system, and that was the problem. The business it generated couldn't justify the expense, yet he had to have it. When cash got really tight, he sold the system and at quite a loss. The moral of that story is that the asset was not critical; it froze a lot of cash and he waited to try to sell it until he had to. Don't make the same mistake. Get rid of marginal assets when you can get a reasonable price, and don't wait until you absolutely need the cash.

> **Foresight is important to improve cash flow**

Many businesses are continually strapped for cash because they are undercapitalized and need further investment to provide a working capital cushion. You can obtain additional funds through loans or equity investment. To get either, you probably need to present a business plan to a banker or investor. An outline and description of a business plan is presented in Chapter 13. A line of credit is the "ultimate" bank loan, whereby the bank puts money into your account as needed, up to a certain limit. This takes enormous pressure off you as a cash manager, but bankers are hesitant to give this type of loan. Another possibility of easing cash pressures is to refinance current debt, borrowing a larger amount, and thereby providing an immediate chunk of cash to work with.

Many businesses are continually strapped for cash because they are undercapitalized

Other possibilities for improving cash flow are found on the right side of the cash flow diagram, and they involve slowing down the non-cyclic outflows of cash. Foremost is cutting expenses. Can you reduce your expenses without significantly reducing the quality of your product or service? Can you remove any "fat" that may exist in the firm? This will increase both profitability and cash flow.

Slowing capital expenditures is another means of improving cash flow. Are projected capital expenditures really needed? Have you thoroughly analyzed the purchase's impact? Will purchase of the equipment cause cash shortages in ensuing months? These are questions you should ask before every capital purchase. Avoid buying equipment on an "emotional" basis.

Increasing owners' contribution to the business or decreasing owners' withdrawals are often "last resorts" to resolving cash flow problems. Many owners take small withdrawals and have already invested most of what they have. In some cases, however, owners can postpone withdrawals during cash-tight periods, or else invest extra funds during those same periods, if they can see the crunch coming.

Frugality

When times are good, don't think they will last forever

Frugality is the last cash management principle, and the concept is simple: When times are good, don't think they will last forever. When there is cash in the till, don't run out and buy new equipment, give bonuses, or take that long-postponed trip until you have completed a cash flow projection and made sure that you will have enough cash to survive the tough times. Even if tough times are not on the horizon, why not put a chunk away just in case things don't go as expected? The Japanese save three times per capita as much as Americans do, and it provides them with a real advantage– they have something to fall back on. That cushion, even if never used, may provide you with a tremendous peace of mind.

Conclusion

In summary, these are the steps you should take in managing your cash:

- First, do a breakeven analysis and make sure you know how much in sales you need to meet expenses. If you are below that level consistently, you will not avoid cash flow problems. You need to increase revenues and/or decrease expenses.

- Next, if you are above the breakeven point but still experience cash flow problems, follow these guidelines:

- Project your cash inflows and outflows on a cash planning sheet. This will help you to foresee when you might have shortages.

- Work to speed up your cash inflows and slow down your cash outflows in the cyclic part of the cash flow diagram.

- Talk to people to whom you pay money, and try to arrange payment schedules that fit the cash flow pattern in your business. If approached *in advance*, most people are reasonable in working with you.

- If necessary, consider steps to increase cash flow in the non-cyclic portion of the cash flow diagram.

- When times are good, save some of the money, and don't believe that the good times will last forever.

There are specific things you can do to improve cash flow

The Washington Entrepreneur's Guide

12

Exporting

"The road to success is usually off the beaten path."
Frank Tyger

This chapter was written by Sam Kaplan, Communications Manager and Lise Sellier Fitzpatrick, Customer Service Coordinator, of the Trade Development Alliance of Greater Seattle. The authors of the Washington Entrepreneur's Guide appreciate their contribution to this book.

According to the U.S. Department of Commerce, 15 percent of U.S. exporters account for 85 percent of the value of U.S.-manufactured exports. One-half of all exporters sell in only one foreign market. However, the international market is more than four times larger than the U.S. market and growing– growth rates in international markets often exceed the U.S. growth rate.

Many companies do not realize it, but they are already engaged in the international economy. An international company may be competing with them by developing the same product overseas and planning to sell it in the U.S. for a better price. Not only that, but catastrophes overseas can also drive up the price of components in the product. So the question is not whether companies should engage in the global market (they already do), but whether there are markets to which the company should export and whether they are ready to export.

Many companies are already engaged in the international economy

---

Advantages of Exporting
- enhance domestic competitiveness
- increase sales and profits
- gain global market share
- reduce dependence on existing markets
- exploit corporate technology and know-how
- extend the sales potential of existing products
- stabilize seasonal market fluctuations
- enhance potential for corporate expansion
- sell excess production capacity
- gain information about foreign competition
  Source: Breaking Into the Trade Game

Disadvantages of Exporting
• incur costs of new promotional material
• subordinate short-term profits for long-term gains
• incur added administrative costs
• allocate personnel for travel
• wait longer for payments
• modify products or packaging
• apply for additional financing
• obtain special export licenses
Source: Breaking Into the Trade Game

Your product could be a service export rather than a product. Service exports often require a different approach than products. For example, while you may not need an overseas business partner in exporting a product, with services it is probably unavoidable. See the section "Service vs. Product Exports" near the end of this chapter for more information.

Export Marketing Plan

You should approach exporting just as you approached opening your business– you must develop a plan of action. When opening a business, you create a detailed business plan. To go international, you should develop an export marketing plan. Creating an export marketing plan is crucial to properly evaluating whether your company has the ability to sell its product or service internationally. As in creating a business plan, your export marketing plan will require you to look at your business and resources in their entirety. It will allow you to determine your firm's potential for exporting, better manage your international business operation, communicate your ideas for exporting to other businesses and financiers and give you the tools to act rather than react as you begin exporting.

An export marketing plan should answer the question of whether you are ready to export. It will also prepare you for exporting by examining and defining:

* export pricing strategy
* targeted markets for export
* methods of foreign market entry
* costs and revenues associated with exporting

- financing possibilities
- transportation method
- partnership and investment possibilities

**You can turn to these places for help on
creating an export marketing plan***

- *Breaking into the Trade Game: A Small Business Guide to Exporting*, published by the U.S. Small Business Administration and AT&T, available from SBA and the Government Printing Office. This publication provides a step-by-step process for developing your international marketing plan. You can get more information about the publication on the World Wide Web at: http://www.northern.edu/facts.html.

- *Your International Business Plan: A Workbook for your International Business Plan*, Small Business International Trade Program of Portland Community College.

- Local trade consulting companies; you can locate such companies through chambers of commerce, the Trade Development Alliance of Greater Seattle's international business cards directory on the Internet, through resource guides at your local library and through the good old yellow pages. In addition, your bank or law firm may also be helpful in providing advice and locating a consulting company.

**all sources' contact information can be found in the back of this
book in the Resource Directory.*

Your Product's/Service's Export Potential

Will a product that has been a great success in the U.S. sell overseas? Being successful in the domestic market is a good sign it can succeed in certain international markets. In other words, a product's best chance of success overseas may be in markets with similar needs and conditions as the U.S. market.

> **An export marketing plan should answer whether you are ready to export**

Other markets with considerable differences from the U.S. may still offer potential. You need to examine what makes your product successful in the U.S. and determine which markets would allow that same type of success. In markets dissimilar to the U.S., you can examine the factors differentiating the two and determine whether they will affect your product. For example, will the climate in southeast Asia affect durability? When examining other markets, you should ask whether there is there a large enough population with disposable income willing to purchase the pleasures of your product. Other factors to examine include environmental, social, cultural, local availability, raw materials or product alternatives, and government import controls.

Being successful in domestic markets is a good sign that your product can do well overseas

Assuring Quality and After-Sale Quality in Foreign Markets

What happens when something goes wrong with your product overseas? It may be easy to service your customers' needs locally and maybe even nationally, but how do you handle the problems of customers half-way around the world? When determining your company's ability to export, this will be a key question. The more complex your product, the more effort may be needed in after-sales service. You will need to ask a series of questions to determine the amount of service required for overseas sales. For example, what skills or special training are required to:

Service of your product will be a key question when determining whether you should export

- Install your product?
- Use your product?
- Maintain your product?
- Service your product?

Before offering the same warranties or service contracts you provide for your product in the U.S., make sure you can fulfill those promises in the foreign market. However, in some markets, if your company and product are unknown, a generous warranty may be essential to building trust in the market. Obviously, the necessary service varies by the product type, the quality of the product and the distribution channel employed. But it is an important factor to remember: the work of exporting doesn't end at the front door of your company.

Make sure you can fulfill your warranty promises before you make them

Can You Afford The Financial Risk Of Exporting?

Exporting can be more financially risky than domestic sales. The markets where you need to sell your product may be unstable–economically, politically or both. Because your business partners and customers are farther removed from your company, there is a greater risk of fraud, non-payment and other monetarily damaging events. In addition, in many markets you may find legal protections, well, less protective, or at least different, than in the United States. For example, the theft of intellectual property rights is a huge problem in certain parts of the world.

Exporting can be more financially risky than domestic sales

In addition, in exporting it may take longer to receive payment for your product or service than when you sell domestically. If your company's financial situation is weak, it may be unwise to begin selling internationally. In other words, do not look at exporting as the express train to profits; be prepared for the long-haul.

The Basics Of Exporting

Selecting Your Market(s)

Once you have determined that your product would do well in foreign markets, you need to decide what regions to target. A good theory to apply in choosing a market is the Willie Sutton/Wayne Gretzky theory of exporting. When asked why he robbed banks, Sutton replied, "That's where the money is." Gretzky's explanation for his success in hockey is that he skates not to where the puck is, but to where it will be. You should combine both strategies in looking at markets in which to export. A market, no matter how glamorous and intriguing, will do you no good unless there are people there with money willing to buy your product or service. At the same time, you don't want to enter markets already saturated, but instead find markets with great potential.

You need to decide which foreign markets to target

Market research is difficult and often speculative

Market research is difficult and often speculative. In general, there are two kinds of research methods: primary and secondary. In primary market research, a firm gathers information on various markets through interviews, surveys and other means of direct contact. In secondary market research, a company collects data from already compiled sources, such as government trade statistics. The former is expensive and time-consuming, the latter is prone to being out-of-date, in error and too general for use. Many companies specialize in market assessment. The organizations on the next page may be able to help you find such companies and help you in your research. In addition, the booklet *Tools of the Trade* lists international organizations in Washington state and is available from the three organizations listed under the state category below.

It would be helpful in research to determine the proper code of your product

If you cannot afford to do primary research, secondary research is an option. First, you need to classify your product. The *Standard Industrial Classification (SIC)* code is the U.S. system for classifying goods and services. By identifying the proper code for your product, you can more precisely collect and analyze data associated with the product. However, data originating from outside the U.S. is organized under the *Standard International Trade Classification (SITC)*. Your product could be assigned a different code under this system.

Completing the classifying trilogy is the *Harmonized System (HS)* which assigns codes to products for export. In doing your research, it is helpful to know the SIC, SITC and HS codes for your product or service. The U.S. Department of Commerce can assist you in determining the correct code for your product.

Market Research Help

Federal

- **The U.S. Export Assistance Center (EAC)** is designed as a one-stop shop for questions on federal export promotion and finance programs. The EAC can deliver services directly or refer you to appropriate public and private sector partners. The EAC integrates representatives of the Small Business Administration (SBA), the U.S. Department of Commerce (DOC), the Export Finance Assistance Center of Washington and other federal agencies.

- **The U.S. Small Business Administration (SBA)** provides programs for small businesses through research assistance and on a wide range of management challenges, including finding the best foreign markets for particular products or services.

- **The U.S. Department of Commerce** with its worldwide network of international trade specialists in major international markets and throughout the U.S. provides counseling, marketing research, customized representative searches, international background checks and other assistance.

- **The Export Finance Assistance Center of Washington** provides payment structuring guidance and credit risk evaluation for export transactions as well as access to both public and private export financing resources including Export-Import Bank's programs.

State

- **Washington State Department of Community, Trade, and Economic Development** helps to locate potential buyers and representatives for Washington state companies and has a wealth of market research and statistical information.

- **The Trade Development Alliance of Greater Seattle** publishes an *International Market Report* every two years detailing the Greater Seattle area's current and future markets.

- **The Washington Council on International Trade** publishes annually an overview of Washington state's trade statistics called the *Washington State Trade Picture*. Addresses and phone numbers included in Business Resource Guide.

You should have a feel for the basic trade statistics of your region. A good place to start is finding out who are Washington state's current largest customers.

Washington's Top Export Customers

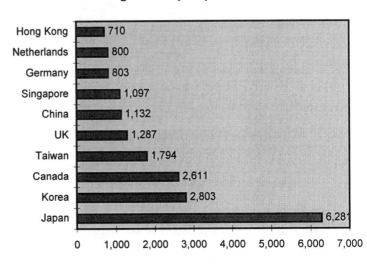

Hong Kong	710
Netherlands	800
Germany	803
Singapore	1,097
China	1,132
UK	1,287
Taiwan	1,794
Canada	2,611
Korea	2,803
Japan	6,28

You do need to dig deeper into trade statistics

You still need to dig deeper into trade statistics. Suppose you are exporting a product dependent on a good telecommunications network. It would be useful to know how many lines per capita a country has.

Telephone Mainlines (per 1000 persons) World Bank - 1992

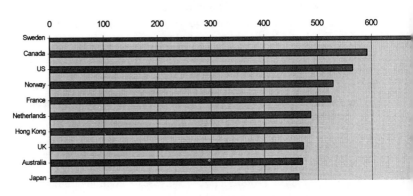

Or, if you sell software, it would be useful to know where computer sales are growing the fastest and which markets have the most computers.

Computers and Peripherals: 1994 Market Size and 1994-96 US Export Growth (US$ millions)

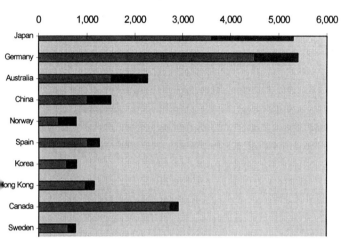

Statistics are only useful to you if you know where to find them. The *World Development Report* is published by the World Bank, which is where the telecommunications statistic is from. Other entities, such as your local library and those listed in the market research box, can help you find resources also. In addition, you need to know about the National Trade Data Bank (NTDB).

Statistics are only useful if you know where to find them

Tips for conducting market research

- Compare the quality of your product with those in the markets you are researching.
- Compare prices with similar products in markets.
- Determine who are your major customers.
- Determine who are your major competitors.

In addition to using the NTDB, there are a number of other easy steps a company can take to conduct market research. Talk to your local U.S. Department of Commerce office and to the Washington State Department of Community, Trade, and Economic Development. They are there to help you and are a great resource for information and advice. Your local chamber of commerce will also have helpful information and is a good place to network for

---

National Trade Data Base (NTDB)

The NTDB is a trade library of more than 190,000 documents on export promotion and international economic information from more than 20 federal sources, which is updated monthly. With the NTDB you can conduct databank searches on markets, tariffs and non-tariff barriers, importers, logistics and product information. The NTDB contains the latest census data on U.S. imports and exports by commodity and country; the complete Central Intelligence Agency (CIA) World Factbook, current market research reports compiled by the U.S. & Foreign Commercial Service, the complete Foreign Traders Index, which contains more than 50,000 names and addresses of individuals and firms abroad interested in importing U.S. products and a multitude of other data sources.

The more you learn about the NTDB, the more you can use the data for specific searches useful to your market research. For example, the telecommunications statistic used above was derived from the NTDB.

You can subscribe to the NTDB on CD-ROM or on the Internet. However, you can also access this information at the Export Assistance Center or at many public libraries.

When used with knowledge and foresight, it can be a great tool for marketing research and for other parts of your export planning.

---

export business partners. In addition, there are a number of country- and region-specific organizations in Washington state which can be helpful to you. Examples of such organizations include: the Washington State China Relations Council, the Foundation for Russian-American Economic Cooperation and the Japan-America Society of the State of Washington.

How to Enter a Market

There are two types of exporting: direct and indirect

Once you have chosen your markets, how will you sell your product in far-off places? There are two basic methods of exporting: direct and indirect. To export directly may require more expertise, time, and money than your company possesses. It will mean you handle all aspects of exporting, from market research and planning to

---

The Washington Entrepreneur's Guide

foreign distribution to collection of money. You need not despair if you feel you are not ready to tackle such a large task; there are a number of ways to indirectly export your product.

Indirect Exporting

- **Commissioned agents** find customers for your product or service. They will pass on the request for your product or service to you and occasionally help with logistical functions such as shipping and export documentation.

- **Export Management Companies (EMC)** act as the export department for your company (or sometimes for several producers) by representing your product to possible international customers. EMCs will actively seek out customers for you and handle the logistics of transactions.

> **Exporting directly may require more expertise, time, and money**

- **Export Trading Companies (ETC),** similar to EMCs, facilitate the export of your company's product. The terms EMC and ETC are often used interchangeably.

- **Export agents, merchants, remarketers** purchase the products from your company, repackage the product and market and resell the product at their own risk.

- In **Piggyback marketing**, an arrangement is made with another company already exporting to a market to export your product as well.

All of these methods have their advantages and disadvantages, and all of them require giving up some control of your product— either its marketing, packaging or some other aspect. This means you will want to be careful which method you choose, and just as importantly, which company or agent you select. In other words, be as careful in the selection of your export partner as you would in choosing any business partner.

> **Each method has advantages and disadvantages**

Using The Internet To Help You Export

The Internet is a useful way to find information and make contacts for exporting your product or service. It also provides a convenient way to communicate with your international business partners and customers. Washington state organizations such as the Trade Development Alliance of Greater Seattle, the Office of the Special Trade Representative and the Washington Council on International Trade (WCIT) (see Chapter 16) maintain home pages on the Internet which contain useful information. The Trade Alliance home page, for example, contains links to other useful web sites around the world and to such international organizations as the World Bank. WCIT keeps Washington state trade statistics on their home page. The National Trade Data Bank is on the Internet and many international chambers of commerce also maintain web sites on the Internet.

Time differences and the cost of phoning can make phone calls a difficult way to communicate with your customers overseas. However, Email through the Internet can be a cheap, practical method of communicating with your customers, business partners and others essential to your export operations.

The Internet is increasingly a way to market your product or service. You can create your own web site advertising your product or service. Customers can even order your product via your web site. In addition, there are now services and organizations which allow you to place trade leads through the Internet. For example, the Hong Kong Trade Development Council allows you to post a trade lead directly through their web site.

The Logistics Of Exporting

An international freight forwarder acts as your agent in moving cargo

You have identified markets for exporting. The question you have now is– how do you get your product from here to there? Most exporters, either new-to-the-game or experienced, choose to rely on an international freight forwarder to assist with documentation, shipping and logistics.

An international freight forwarder acts as your agent in moving cargo to the overseas destination, and is knowledgeable about the rules and regulations of importing and exporting to your chosen

Trade Missions, Trade Fairs, and ATA CARNET

Various organizations in Washington state organize trade and business missions to international markets. These can be great ways to travel to these markets and receive help in business matchmaking, market research, and making contacts. The Trade Development Alliance of Greater Seattle, the Washington State Department of Community, Trade and Economic Development and other groups organize these missions.

International trade fairs taking place here in Washington state and overseas are another way of making contacts and selling your product. In fact, for some products trade fairs are *the* way of marketing and selling your product. The Washington State International Trade Fair is one organization which can provide information and assistance on trade shows.

ATA CARNET: You may not want to leave home without it
An ATA Carnet is an international customs document which acts like a passport for your merchandise and allows temporary, duty-free imports. A multiple use document valid for one year from issue, the ATA Carnet can simplify the customs process when taking your products on business calls or exhibiting at international trade shows.

It reduces the cost of exporting by eliminating the value-added taxes (VAT) and duties or the posting of security normally required at the time of importation. The ATA Carnet is accepted by nearly 50 countries, including Canada and Japan, as well as many nations in Europe (including Eastern Europe), the Pacific Rim and Africa.

An ATA Carnet application form can be obtained through the U.S. Council for International Business (sole issuer and guarantor of the ATA Carnet) by calling 1-800-5-DUTY FREE or writing to the U.S.I.B at 1212 Avenue of the Americas, New York, NY 10036.

market, as well as various methods of shipping, U.S. government regulations, and the documents connected with trading overseas. As your exporting agent, freight forwarders can:

- Assist in preparing price quotations by advising on freight costs, port charges, consular fees, costs of special documentation, insurance costs and other export-related expenses.

- Recommend packing materials to protect your merchandise in transit.

A freight forwarder can be an exporter's best friend, or a worst enemy

- Prepare and review crucial documents such as letters of credit, commercial invoices, and packing lists to ensure that everything is in order.

- Facilitate the shipping of your product by reserving space on a transport vessel, ensuring that the product is delivered to the carrier for loading.

Finding An International Freight Forwarder

- Let your fingers do the walking: The Yellow Pages, Washingt State International Trade Directory and other directories have pag of listings for freight forwarders.

- Ask your banker or other business associates for referrals

- Check with your local chamber of commerce or other busin organizations for members who are freight forwarders

- Go surfing (on the net): some freight forwarders advertise us home pages on the Internet or can be found in on-line members listings for the Greater Seattle Chamber of Commerce, Tr Development Alliance of Greater Seattle and other organizations

REMEMBER: A freight forwarder can be an exporter's best friend, c a worst enemy. A good forwarder is essential to an exporter, so select one as you would any other business partner. Conduct a background check to make sure they are reliable, have a good track record and wil best suit your business' particular needs.

Shipping

One of the first logistical steps to getting your product to international customers is determining a method of shipping. There are three modes of transportation: land, sea and air. Analyze your needs, and evaluate the advantages and disadvantages of each transportation option. For example, although an electrical product won't spoil during an ocean voyage, if it is paid on delivery, shipping it by air means getting paid more quickly even though the air freight may cost more. A freight forwarder can assist you in selecting the correct transportation mode for your needs.

You need to develop a method of shipping

Documentation

Once you have selected how you will get your product to the market, you should go about compiling the necessary documentation. Exporting differs from domestic sales largely in the amount of documentation required. Proper completion of forms is critical to smoothing the transportation process and ensuring that your shipment arrives safely and on time. In addition, slight discrepancies or omissions in documentation may result in merchandise not being exported, non-payment or even the seizure of your goods by U.S. or foreign customs. While a freight forwarder can help prepare the necessary documentation, you are ultimately responsible for the accuracy of the information.

You will need to compile the necessary documentation

In the shipment of your product, you are likely to need the following documents:

Commercial Invoice. You will use the commercial invoice as a bill for the buyer of your product, outlining basic information about the transaction. Since some governments use the commercial invoice to assess customs duties, it is sometimes useful to prepare the invoice in English *and* the language of the country of destination. In some cases, it may be necessary to list a *destination control statement* on the invoice, notifying the carrier and all foreign parties that the item may be exported only to certain destinations.

You will need to have certain documents

Consular Invoice. Certain nations require a consular invoice, which must be completed in the language of the destination country. You can obtain this document from the destination country's consulate. There is often a fee involved for the consular invoice.

Export License. The U.S. exercises export controls based on the type of goods being shipped and their ultimate destination. Most exports do not require a license or are shipped under a "general" license which does not require an application. Should your particular export be subject to controls, you will need to obtain a "validated" license.

Shipper's Export Declaration (Form 7525-V). The most common document used by exporters, the Shipper's Export Declaration (SED), enables the Bureau of Census to compile statistics on U.S. exports. The SED is necessary for mail shipments valued at over $500; other shipments valued at more than $2,500; or for all shipments covered by an Individually Validated Export License, regardless of their value. In some cases, it may be necessary to list a *destination control statement* on the SED, notifying the carrier and all foreign parties that the item may be exported only to certain destinations.

> The most common document used by exporters is the SED

Certificate of Origin. Although a commercial invoice may contain a statement of origin, some countries (particularly those subject to certain free trade treaties) require a Certificate of Origin. This document qualifies the product for preferential duty rates if the U.S. has an agreement with the country of destination to allow entry of certain products at lower tariffs. You can purchase the form at local stationery stores and have it signed and authorized by the local chamber of commerce.

***Export Packing List*:** This is an itemized list of the material in each individual package and it indicates the type of package (box, crate, drum, etc.) and the individual net, legal, tare and gross weights and measurements (in U.S. and metric systems). Attached to the outside of a package in a waterproof envelope marked "Packing List Enclosed", it is used by shippers and forwarding agents to determine the total shipment weight and volume, as well as whether or not the correct cargo is being shipped. The list may also be used by customs officials to check the cargo.

> **An export packing list is an itemized list of the material in each package**

***Insurance Certificate*.** Necessary if you are providing insurance, this document confirms the type and amount of coverage for merchandise being shipped. The certificate should be made in negotiable form and must be endorsed before submitting to the bank.

Inspection Certificate. Foreign purchasers may request that you certify that goods being shipped meet certain specifications. Usually this process is performed by an independent third party, which will supply the certificate.

The greater the detail you give, the greater chance your goods will move quickly

Shipper's Instructions. This provides your freight forwarder with detailed, necessary information. The greater the detail, the greater the chance your goods will move free of problems. A freight forwarder can supply a commonly used form.

> Much of export documentation is routine for freight forwarders or customs brokers acting on your behalf, but *you* are ultimately responsible for the accuracy of the documentation.

Bill of Lading. This provides evidence to title of the goods and sets forth the international carrier's responsibility to transfer your goods to their named destination. A bill of lading can be either non-negotiable or negotiable. In some cases, it may be necessary to list a *destination control statement* on the bill, notifying the carrier and all foreign parties that the item may be exported only to certain destinations.

A bill of lading can be either non-negotiable or negotiable

Air Waybill. When using air freight, air waybills take the place of bills of lading. Air waybills are only issued in non-negotiable form, therefore both you and the bank lose title to the goods once the shipment commences. The air waybill usually contains a customs declaration form. In some cases, it may be necessary to list a *destination control statement* on the waybill, notifying the carrier and all foreign parties that the item may be exported only to certain destinations.

Inland Bill of Lading. Documents the transportation of goods between inland points and the port from where the export will emanate. Rail shipments use a *waybills on rail*, while pro-forma bills of lading are used in truck shipments.

Delivery Instructions. This is prepared by a freight forwarder giving instructions to the trucking or railroad company where the goods for export are to be delivered.

Dock Receipts. This transfers shipping obligations from the domestic to the international carrier as the shipment reaches the terminal.

Help for the Logistics of Exporting

Breaking Into the Trade Game, A Small Business Guide to Exporting
National Trade Data Bank: A Basic Guide to Exporting
The U.S. Department of Commerce Bureau of Exporting (BXA) holds training seminars on its regulations in various cities around the U.S. every year. Check with the U.S. Export Assistance Center for dates and locations.

Preparing a Product for Export
Your product may need to be adapted for each market, as well as the supporting marketing information. Your product may need modifications to conform to government regulations, geographic and climactic conditions, buyer preferences or standard of living. To obtain information about government regulations in your targeted markets, you can contact the nearest Department of Commerce office which can provide you information or sources for information.

Your product may need to be adapted for each market

Packaging and marketing
Marketing techniques used in America do not always work overseas. For one thing, people in your targeted market may not speak English. Translation can be expensive but may be necessary. In addition, even the colors used in your brochure could be problematic. In some countries certain colors are associated with death, national flags or other cultural factors.

Marketing techniques used in America do not always work overseas

A classic example of not adapting a product for a market was the Chevy Nova. Chevrolet decided to sell the Nova in Mexico and launched a large marketing program. Despite the huge marketing campaign and all of Chevrolet's efforts, the Nova sold horribly in Mexico. What Chevrolet had not thought through was that nova means "no go" in Spanish. They wanted people to buy a car they were marketing as unable to run.

> ### Examine These Questions the DOC Asks When Considering Repackaging Your Product
>
> - Are international brand names important to promote and distinguish a product? Conversely, should local brands or private labels be employed to heighten local interest?
>
> - Are the colors used on labels and packages offensive or attractive to the foreign buyer?
>
> - Can labels be produced in official or customary languages if required by law or practice?
>
> - Does information on product content and country of origin have to be provided?
>
> - Are weights and measures stated in the local unit?
>
> - Must each item be labeled individually?
>
> - Are local tastes and knowledge considered? A dry cereal box picturing a U.S. athlete may not be as attractive to overseas consumers as the picture of a local sports hero.

A little research on language or culture can go a long way

Or take the example of an American executive misunderstanding a British company's use of the phrase "to table." During a meeting, a representative from the British company announced he wanted "to table" the discussion. The American assumed he meant to delay the discussion, not realizing that in Britain the phrase "to table" means to discuss something immediately. The American waited months to bring the discussion back up and offended the British company which wanted to discuss the subject immediately, leading to the breakup of their partnership.

Service vs. Product Exporting

Many services are exportable

Sure it may be possible to export your product, but what about services? Many services are exportable. Engineering, architectural design and other services are performed worldwide by many companies. Other services which are frequently exported include:

- banking and financial services
- insurance services
- legal and accounting services

- computer and data services
- teaching services
- management consulting services
- environmental services

Since services can often be less tangible than a product, more attention should be paid to translation issues. Services can also be more time-dependent than a product and often require more personal involvement than in selling products. This means gaining greater cultural awareness in your targeted markets and tailoring your service to the specific needs of the buyer. Partnering with an international business will be the key to your service exports. In exporting a product you may be able to get away with not understanding your target market. But because of the personal involvement required in exporting a service, you or someone on your staff will need to be knowledgeable about the target market. The U.S. Department of Commerce and the other organizations listed as helpful in product exporting can also help you in your service export.

> **More attention should be paid to translation issues when exporting a service**

Mistakes in Exporting
The top ten mistakes (as listed by the U.S. Department of Commerce) in exporting are:

Number 10: Failing to consider licensing or joint-venture agreements. Many reasons, such as import restrictions in some countries, insufficient personnel and financial resources, or a limited product line cause many companies to dismiss international marketing as a possible option.

Number 9: Failing to consider using an export management company.

Number 8: Failing to print services, sales and warranty messages in locally understood languages. Without a clear understanding of sales messages or service instructions, personnel will be less effective in performing their functions.

Number 7: Unwillingness to modify products to meet regulations or cultural preferences of other countries.

Number 6: Failing to treat international distributors on an equal basis with their domestic counterparts. Often companies carry out institutional advertising campaigns but fail to make similar assistance available to their international distributors. This is a mistake that can destroy the vitality of your overseas marketing efforts.

Number 5: Neglecting export business when the U.S. market booms. Such neglect can seriously harm the business and that of the overseas representatives.

Number 4: Chasing orders from around the world instead of establishing a basis for profitable operations and orderly growth. Exporters should concentrate their efforts in one or two geographical areas until there is sufficient business to support a company representative.

Number 3: Insufficient care in selecting overseas distributors. The complications involved in overseas communications and transportation require international distributors to act with greater independence than their domestic counterparts. Since a new exporter is usually unknown, your foreign customers will buy on the strength of your distributor's reputation.

Number 2: Insufficient commitment by top management to overcoming the initial difficulties and financial requirements of exporting. It may take more time and effort to establish yourself in a foreign market than in a domestic one. Although the early delays and costs may seem difficult to justify when compared to your established domestic trade, you must be patient! You should look to the long-term, and shepherd your international marketing efforts through any early difficulties.

Number 1: Failing to obtain qualified export counseling and to develop a master international marketing plan before starting an export business. Remember the drill: first, define goals and objectives; then, develop a definite plan.

══════ 13 ══════

The Business Plan

*"You're successful at hockey when you skate to where
the puck is going to be, not where it's at."*
Wayne Gretzky

The term *business plan* has become very popular in the last decade.
Bankers and venture capitalists want to see one before they make an
investment decision. Business schools are putting increased
emphasis on the need to write one for any business, whether new or
existing. Experienced business people encourage aspiring
entrepreneurs to "write the business plan." Their advice is sound.
Writing a business plan forces you to think about all aspects of
running your new venture. You may spend up to two hundred hours
researching and writing the plan at a time when you are already
incredibly busy. However, you must find the time. You need to
know what you are getting into before you forge ahead.

There are rewards for developing a business plan. If you are
seeking investors, it allows them to critically evaluate your venture.
Most of them will not even talk to you if you have not prepared it.
A written plan allows others to give you suggestions. The financial
section of the plan may open your eyes. You may discover that
there is little chance of a profitable business and stop your plans
before investing a lot of money. In certain cases, the information
uncovered in researching the market may steer you to change your
product or the way it is marketed.

> **You have to find
> the time to write
> the business
> plan**

You need to be involved in writing the plan *yourself*. If you hire
someone else to do all of it, it's not the same. You need to have a
solid understanding of your business and its environment. Granted,
hiring others to do some research or to edit the plan makes sense,
but you need to be intimately involved yourself.

A business plan is a comprehensive description of your business, the
environment in which it operates, and how you will run it. Most
plans describe three years into the future, although some project for
five or more years. Nearly every section of this book needs to be
incorporated into the plan. You can't write a business plan without

knowledge of a broad spectrum of business principles. The plan is larger in scope but includes all the sections of a strategic plan. The business plan adds information to the strategic plan and includes more detail. There are numerous outlines for business plans, but all are quite similar. The outline below describes the major sections of a typical business plan.

- Executive Summary
- The Company and Its Overall Strategy
- The Market and Competitors
- Marketing Strategy
- Design and Development Plans
- Manufacturing and Operations Plan
- Management Team
- Overall Schedule
- Critical Risks and Problems
- The Financial Plan
- Proposed Company Offering
- Financial Exhibits
- Appendices

You can't write a business plan without knowledge of a broad spectrum of business principles

Each of these sections is described below, along with the questions you should try to answer in each. Be aware that some questions will not be pertinent to your business and can be disregarded. Conversely, each business has certain unique operating circumstances that need to be described but cannot be included in a general outline like the one above. The outline presented is a general, well-accepted one. Don't be afraid to adapt it to convey any unique aspects of your business.

Don't be afraid to adapt the business plan outline

Generally, business plans are written in third person. They contain enough detail to allow an expert to assess the venture as well as enough explanation, possibly in an appendix, to let a non-expert clearly understand how the business is supposed to work. Pictures and diagrams are usually especially helpful. Books can be found in the library on how to write business plans that give more details and examples of what to include. General guidelines from *New Venture Mechanics* for some things to avoid include the following:

1. *Length for Its Own Sake.* The body of the plan should be no longer than twenty-five to thirty pages maximum. Appendices should be kept down to only those most needed. Inclusion of whole articles or brochures is usually less effective than including only highly selective excerpts or depictions and giving references to the rest.

2. *Irrelevant Information.* Unless the information is a direct part of the logic, it should be left out. General references usually are not helpful.

3. *Self-Adulation.* The writing style should avoid self-congratulatory words and phrases such as "our excellent," "the fine experience of the management team," "the great promise of this venture," and so forth. It is better instead to give facts and, if it exists, the evidence from which such judgments can be deduced by the reader.

4. *Bad Writing.* Having others review the plan to improve its clarity can be helpful.

5. *Professional Jobbing Out.* The entrepreneur should write the plan himself or herself as evidence that he or she truly understands it.

6. *Reliance on the written document alone.* Personal presentation will also be required if the plan is intended to persuade anyone to contribute importantly to the venture.

Executive Summary
The executive summary, in one to two pages, should catch the reader's attention and give him an overview of the plan. Three elements are of critical interest to a potential investor– the market opportunity, the management team, and the financial returns. These need to be described in this section. If you are trying to raise money, you need to describe the terms of investments that you are seeking. Potential investors always read the summary first to determine if the plan merits a complete reading. If you don't make a good presentation up front, you will probably lose the investor. If you aren't seeking to raise capital, the summary is still important because you need to clarify the basics of your business.

The Company and Its Overall Strategy

You have to start the plan somewhere, and a short history of the company (or idea of the company) and backgrounds of the people involved make sense. Keep the backgrounds short, since you will be describing management in detail later on in the plan. The following questions are typically addressed:

- How and when did the company (or idea) get started?
- What has been the development process? What stage is the company at now– still working on prototype, patent approved, sales achieved, etc.?
- How did major players in the company get involved?
- Briefly, what are the firm's products and services?
- What is the current opportunity?

Next, you want to describe your company's general strategy. The analysis supporting your choice of strategy will be included in the following sections in the plan. Review Chapter 9, Strategic Planning, in writing this section. Answers to the following questions can be included:

- What growth stages do you foresee in the next three years? Will you be opening other branches, expanding sales to other areas, vertically integrating, adding people, etc.?
- What industry(s) will you compete in? Will that change over time?
- What are your primary advantages over competitors?
- Which of the following strategies will you follow– cost leadership, differentiation, focus, or a combination? How will you make that strategy work?
- If you need to raise money, how do you intend to do it?
- What are your (and any partners') personal goals for the business?

The Market and Competitors

In this section, you must establish that markets exist for your products and that you are able to enter those markets and successfully compete. There are three primary components of this section– industry analysis, competitor analysis, and customer analysis. Each is described below.

Industry Structure. The structure of an industry has a large impact on the success of firms in it. You should thoroughly understand this structure before deciding on your company's strategy. Industry structural analysis is described in detail in Chapter 9. Answers to the following questions may be important to convey in this section of the business plan:

- What are total sales in the industry?
- What is the growth in the industry?
- What are typical gross margins?
- What is the average profitability in the industry?
- What entry barriers exist?
- What industry driving forces exist?
- What strategic groups exist in the industry? What are the characteristics of the strategic groups? (answer the questions above for each group)
- What do firms have to do well to succeed in the industry?

Competitor Analysis. To survive and succeed, you must compete with other companies in the marketplace. Very few firms need not monitor nor react to competitors' moves. Chapter 9, Strategic Planning, discusses competitor analysis. Review that chapter before writing this section. First, decide what is important to do to be successful in your industry, then evaluate how other companies in your industry rate on those factors. What are the strengths and weaknesses of major competitors? A table is often the best way to present your evaluation. You need to evaluate companies against each other. Several firms in your industry may have high-quality products, but which one(s) is known as the quality leader? Which is (are) the most efficient and can keep costs below others? Answers to the following questions can be used in your Competitor Analysis section:

The structure of an industry has a large impact on the success of firms in it

For all major competitors, evaluate:

- What is the quality of their products and services?
- What is their reputation?
- Are their customers brand loyal?
- How wide is their product line?
- What type of warranty do they offer?
- How do they distribute their products?
- How large is their market share?
- How well do they market their products?
- How efficient is their manufacturing operation?
- Do they have good research and development skills?
- Do they have patents which give them an advantage?
- Do they have strong financial resources?

- Do they have good managers?

Again, what is important is comparison of competitors, not merely a description of each.

You need to understand customers and what motivates them to buy a product like yours

Customer Analysis. To be successful, you must sell to customers. If you understand customers and what motivates them to buy a product like yours, you will be better able to design your product and present it to them so that they will buy. In this section of the plan, you are trying to describe in detail who your customers are. If you are not able to answer most of the questions posed below, you need to do some marketing research. Chapter 4 describes means of obtaining information about customers.

A very important point made in Chapter 10 is that you may be selling to several different target markets. For example, an all-terrain-vehicle (ATV) manufacturer may be selling to farmers, recreationalists, the Forest Service, and other groups. Each of them has somewhat distinct needs, and each certainly needs to be approached in a different fashion. Each of these groups requires a different marketing strategy. Therefore, if you are selling to more than one target market, you must describe each in this Customer Analysis section. Answers to the following questions can be used in this section:

For each target market:

- What type of people purchase your products?
- What ages?
- Sex?
- Income groups?
- Married vs. single?
- Where do they live?
- How often do they usually buy?

Analyze customers in *each* of your target markets

- How much do they usually spend?
- How price sensitive are they?
- How quality conscious are they?
- What features do they want?
- How much service do they need (and are willing to pay for)?
- Where do they shop for this type of product?
- Do they do much comparison shopping?
- What types of promotion reach them?
- What TV programs do they watch?
- What radio stations do they listen to?

- Do they read a newspaper?
- What trade journals do they read?
- How brand loyal are they?
- How satisfied are they with current products?

There are many other questions that could be asked concerning customers. The key in this section is to relate who customers are and what their thought processes are when they buy products like yours.

Analysis of "middle people." Many businesses do not sell directly to customers. Rather, they sell products to distributors and/or retailers who in turn resell the products. It is just as critical to know what is important to these people in their buying decisions as what the final consumers want. A good example of this is the grocery business. Grocers have the ability to carry a large number of products that they can obtain from many distributors, but they have limited shelf space. The grocers evaluate more than just the products when deciding which ones to carry. They want to know what type of packaging will be used, how often products will be delivered, if display racks will be provided, what type of payment terms are offered, what type of return policy is provided, etc. Talk to the "middle people" that you will need to deal with and understand what motivations they have in choosing suppliers. The characterization of these people should be included in this Customer Analysis subsection.

> Talk to the "middle people" that you will need to deal with and understand what motivations they have in choosing suppliers

Marketing Strategy

Marketing is more than selling, it includes your decisions on target markets, product features, how you will service products, pricing, promotion, and distribution. Your marketing strategy should directly support your overall competitive strategy. If you have chosen a differentiation strategy, your marketing strategy should detail how you will implement that strategy in the marketing area. Consider Nordstrom's. It is differentiated by quality of clothing, customer service, and the ease and fun in shopping there. Its marketing plan supports that strategy. The store charges premium prices for its clothing and its promotion is targeted to people who can afford the prices. It promotes its products as very high quality and differentiates itself with a no-questions-asked return policy. Its promotional materials reflect this quality. Its compensation system is geared to individual performance of sales people, allowing them to earn incomes that are exceptionally high compared to sales clerks of most stores, thereby motivating them to work very hard at serving customers effectively. That is not to say Nordstrom's is the

> Your marketing strategy should directly support your overall competitive strategy

only "right system." Other stores succeed with different strategies. But the pieces of any system should fit together logically. You should seek consistency such as this in your marketing strategy.

You need a marketing strategy for each target market that you select. Nordstrom's probably targets several groups. One is the affluent person who wants quality products with the Nordstrom's name. Another is the customer who is willing to pay more for the personalized service and no hassle return policy. Each of these groups may require a different marketing strategy. You may not be able to attract both with one strategy. Review Chapter 10, Marketing Strategies, before writing this section of the business plan. For each of the markets that you target, try to answer the following questions:

> **You need a marketing strategy for each target market that you select**

- What features of your product make it better or unique?
- How will it be packaged?
- What type of warranty will be offered?
- What services will be offered along with the products?
- How will products be priced?
- Will prices be changed over time?
- Will quantity discounts be offered?
- How will products be advertised?
- Will you attend trade shows? Which ones?
- Will you print a catalog?
- If you use "middle people," how will you "sell" them on your products?
- Will you use direct marketing? Telemarketing?
- Will you need to offer an "800" number?
- What credit policies will you offer? Will you accept MasterCard and VISA for payment?
- Will you employ multi-level marketing?
- Will you use your own sales force? How will you train them?
- Will you use manufacturers' reps?
- Will you use distributors?
- If you sell overseas, how will you do it?
- Will you use any other means of distributing your products?

Design and Development Plans
If you have a product or service which needs further design work before it can be put on the market, those plans need to be described in this section. If you are looking to raise money, investors will want to know the state of product development and what needs to be completed. If product development is completed, but you foresee

continued product redesign in the next several years, describe those plans. If you have no further product development plans, this section can be omitted. If you do have them, answers to the following questions can be included in this section:

- What is the current status of product development?
- What remains to be finished, and when will it be completed? How much will it cost?
- What product improvements or further design work will be undertaken in the next three years?
- What patents are currently secured? Are there any others that will be pursued in the future?

Manufacturing and Operations Plan

If you are a manufacturer, this section should first describe how you make your products. Next, you describe how business is to be conducted on a day-to-day basis. If you are not a manufacturer, you will describe just the latter. You show that you know how to "run the business," and are not just theorizing on how the business should operate. Answers to the following questions can be included in this section:

> **The Operations section describes how your business is run on a more day-to-day basis**

- Where will your facility(ies) be located? What advantages does the location hold– labor availability, visibility, proximity to customers, proximity to suppliers, low cost, etc.?
- What type of plant or store facility will you have?
- What type of machinery and equipment will be used?
- Will equipment be purchased or leased?
- Is there room for expansion?
- How much manufacturing will be done on-site, and how much will be subcontracted?
- Will manufacturing be done on a continual, assembly-line process, or will it be a job shop?
- Will inventory be stocked? If so, what inventory control system will be used?
- How will the business be run on a day-to-day basis?

Management Team

The management team is critical to the success of your business. Be sure to read Chapter 8, Gathering Your Forces, before writing this section of the business plan. As mentioned in that chapter, make sure that your company has skills in the areas of marketing, finance, and production (if you are manufacturing), showing a blend of good technical and managerial skills. You would also like

> **Try to show a balance of skills in your venture**

to show that people are experienced in the roles they are filling. Answers to the following questions can be included in this section:

- What is the organizational structure (draw it) of the company?
- What are the general responsibilities of each of the major people in the firm?
- For key management personnel, what is each person's educational background, job experience, or other abilities that suit them for the position they have in the company?
- Which people will be owning partners, and which will be hired employees?
- Who will be on the board of directors? What are their backgrounds?
- Will outside consultants be hired? What are their skills?
- Will profit-sharing or employee stock ownership be offered?

Overall Schedule

In this section, you are writing a schedule of major events to launch your new enterprise. It is important that you project the order and timing of major events in your company's development. Each firm will have a unique set of events to schedule, but the following questions relate to what are major milestones for many businesses. If some of them have already occurred, list them and state when it took place.

The Overall Schedule projects the order and timing of major events

- When will the company be incorporated?
- When will design and development be completed?
- When will patents be secured?
- When will prototypes be completed?
- When will the plant/store be completed?
- When will sales first occur?
- What will be the trend in sales growth?
- When will additional people be brought in?
- When and where will sales be expanded geographically?

Critical Risks and Problems

Every business has its risks. The purpose of this section is to force you to think about the major risks in your undertaking and to plan how you will address those potential problems. If you are trying to raise money, you might wonder how wise it is to point out potential problems to investors. They are going to think of them, anyway, so you may as well come right out and show that you have thought about them and have some kind of game plan for dealing with them.

Describe how you would deal with potential problems

The following list of questions is by no means exhaustive of the types of risks that businesses face, but they are fairly common ones.

- What if competitors react by dropping prices?
- What happens if sales projections are not met?
- Can costs be substantially higher than projected?
- Is there a good chance that supplies will be hard to come by?
- Will it be difficult to get good people to join the organization?
- What if a patent is not obtained?

Describe the three or four most critical risks in your proposed venture, and state what you will do if each occurs. Try to state how you would deal with each potential problem and survive and succeed in spite of it.

The Financial Plan

You need to determine that your venture will be a profitable one and that cash flows are sufficient to pay all bills. This section of the business plan needs to describe the major conclusions from four financial statements– breakeven analysis, cash flow statement, income statement, and balance sheet. Review Chapter 11, Cash Management, before writing this section. This section should be the *description* of the financial worksheets. The worksheets themselves are included in the section entitled Financial Exhibits. You want to write this section without overwhelming readers with numbers; rather, you want to describe your *general conclusions* of what all the numbers in the financial exhibits mean. A one to two paragraph analysis of each of the four financial statements is appropriate. Your underlying assumptions for generating the worksheets belong with the worksheets themselves, and not in this section.

> **You need to describe your financial projections and not just grind out pages of numbers**

Spreadsheet templates for each of these financial analyses are included on the diskette provided with this book. You can generate these financial statements by hand, but with only a beginner's understanding of a computer spreadsheet program you can do it on a computer and greatly speed your work. On the diskette, BUSPLAN.wk4 is a Lotus file; BUSPLAN.wb1 is a Quattro Pro file; and BUSPLAN.xls is an Excel file. A description of the financial templates and instruction in their usage is included on the first page when you open the spreadsheets.

Breakeven Analysis. Breakeven analysis lets you know how much you have to sell in order to pay your bills (see Chapter 11 for a detailed description of breakeven analysis). It also tells you what profit or loss you would have at different sales levels. It is only a general estimate. You want to show early in the financial section that you will have enough sales to reach breakeven in a reasonable period of time after startup. Most businesses are not immediately profitable. It may take several months, in some businesses several years. Your cash flow analysis will show how you will survive until your business reaches a breakeven point. State what the breakeven point in sales dollars is and how soon the firm will reach it. If your sales projections grow quite larger than breakeven volume, state how much profit would be generated at those sales levels. If it is very difficult for you to accurately predict sales levels for your company, relate how much profit or loss would occur at several different possible sales levels.

Use the computer financial templates on the diskette to generate your financial projections

Cashflow Analysis. Cash is the lifeblood of a business. You don't necessarily go broke by not making a profit. You go broke by not having enough cash to pay your bills. In the early years of a business, you should pay more attention to the cash flow statement than the income statement.

In this section of the plan, you are describing the cash position of the company for the next three years. The first year is usually broken down by months, and years two and three are broken down by quarter. You want to state the beginning cash position, the general trends in cash position, and causes of any major fluctuations in cash flow. These could include seasonal sales, capital purchases, taking out or paying off of a loan, owner withdrawal or cash infusion, or any major expenses. If the cash balance becomes low at some point, describe why it happens and how the company will address the problem.

In the Cashflow section of the plan, you describe the position of the company for the next three years

Income Statement. The income statement subtracts expenses from revenues, yielding net profit. Profits provide returns to investors and are a source of capital to build your company. In this section of the business plan, you want to describe the trend in profits over a three-year projected period and also the major determinants of profits. Describe trends in sales, gross margin, major expenses, and net profit. Explain any major fluctuations in profits over the three-year period. Several financial ratios are important to relate. Return on sales, return on equity, return on assets, and gross margin percentage should be stated.

Balance Sheet. The balance sheet shows what your company owns, what it owes, and the difference between them– which is called net worth. You should project a balance sheet at startup and after one, two, and three years. In this section of the plan, you should describe your major observations of trends in the balance sheets. Growth in assets, debt, and equity should be cited. A few financial ratios and their trends should be stated. The current ratio gives an indication of the liquidity of the firm. Debt/equity measures the amount of borrowing that supports the company. Inventory turnover and days receivable indicate how well those current assets are managed. You would like to be able to compare the ratios to industry standards and demonstrate the financial soundness of your company.

> **Pay more attention to the cash flow statement than the income statement**

Proposed Company Offering

This section is included only if you are trying to raise capital by borrowing or by getting people to invest on an equity basis. Chapter 7, Raising Capital, discusses strategies for raising money. If you want to borrow money, state how much you need, when it will be paid back, and what you will use it for. If you know what you intend to offer for collateral, state that.

If you are seeking equity investments, you need to describe what you are proposing. Be aware that investment terms are negotiable, hence your proposed offering is only a starting point. State how many shares you are selling, what the selling price is, and what owners' resultant percentage of ownership would be. Equity investors are typically looking to cash out of the investment in a three to ten year period, and you should describe how that will be a possibility for them. Chapter 14, Harvesting a Business, describes different means of getting cash out of an investment in a company.

> **Be aware that investment terms are usually negotiable**

Financial Exhibits

The financial exhibits in your business plan should include a breakeven analysis and graph, pro forma cash flow statements, pro forma income statements, and pro forma balance sheets. The breakeven analysis is usually done only for the first year. The cash flow and income statement projections are done on a monthly basis in the first year and by quarter in years two and three. Sample templates for all financial projections are included on the diskette with this book. The major assumptions you use to arrive at your projections should be included with the financial exhibits and *not* in the financial section of the plan.

Conclusion

If you write a thorough business plan, you know the business inside and out

Writing a business plan is a formidable task. You have noticed in this chapter references to almost every other chapter in the book. If you write a thorough business plan, you know the business inside and out. Take the time to research and write the business plan. Once you have done it, continue to update it and keep it current. There is a tendency to forego continued planning once your venture is started because you get too busy to keep up with it. Believe the experts— continue to refine your plan. Listed below are a list of "Do's and Don'ts" from Timmons' *New Venture Creation.* [2].

1. Do keep the business plan as short as you can without compromising the description of your venture and its potential. Cover the key issues that will interest an investor, and leave the details of secondary importance for a meeting with an investor. Remember, venture capitalists are not patient readers.

2. Don't overdiversify your venture. Focus your attention on one or two product lines and markets. A new or young venture does not have the management depth to pursue a number of opportunities.

3. Don't have unnamed, mysterious people on your management team, such as Mr. G., who is currently a financial vice president but will join you later. The investor will want to know early on exactly who Mr. G. is and what his commitment is to your venture.

4. Don't describe technical products or manufacturing processes in a way and with a jargon that only an expert can understand. A venture capitalist does not like to invest in what he doesn't understand or what he thinks you don't understand because you can't explain it to a smart fellow like himself.

5. Don't estimate your sales on the basis of what you can or would like to produce. Do estimate carefully your potential sales, and from these determine the production facility you need.

Continue to refine your business plan

6. Don't make ambiguous, vague, or unsubstantiated statements. They make you look like a shallow and fuzzy thinker. For example, don't merely say that your markets are growing rapidly. Determine and delineate past, present, and projected growth rates and market size.

7. Do disclose and discuss any current or potential problems in your venture. If you fail to do this and the venture capitalist discovers them, your credibility will be badly damaged.

8. Do involve all of your management team in the preparation of the business plan, as well as any special legal, accounting, or financial help that you may need.

9. Don't claim that you have no competition, or indicate that you expect to "get rich quick." Both are good ways to turn off investors and others who know better.

References

1. Rich, Stanley R. and Gumpert, David E. *Business Plans That Win $$*. New York: Harper and Row, 1985.

2. Timmons, Jeffry A. *New Venture Creation*, 3nd Edition. Homewood, Illinois: Irwin, 1990.

The Washington Entrepreneur's Guide

=14=

Harvesting a Business

"I don't care at all about the invention.
The dimes are what I'm after."
Isaac M. Singer

The sign of a true entrepreneur is his ability to plan how to get out of a business at some point with cash in his pocket. Any "exit plan" requires building value in the enterprise. In general, most entrepreneurs do not intend to run one business all of their lives. Their greatest thrill lies in undertaking new ventures. To have this liberty, you must be able to *harvest* the old business. Harvesting is simply drawing cash from the business and need not necessarily involve selling it. Six harvest strategies are described briefly in this chapter:

1. The outright sale of the business
2. The cash cow
3. The management buyout
4. The merger
5. The employee stock ownership plan (ESOP)
6. The public offering

> **Most entrepreneurs do not intend to run one business all of their lives**

The Outright Sale

This option leaves you the most freedom to pursue other ventures. Ideally, you would like the entire sales price in cash up front. Also, you would prefer to have no continuing obligations to the business, such as warranty or indemnity obligations. In many cases, the potential buyer will offer a package that is less attractive. It may include balloon payments, carrying a contract, stock ownership, and/or stock options for you. It is not unusual for a buyer who wants you to "carry paper" (that is, accept deferred payments reflected by a contract, promissory note or other documents) to employ a strategy best described as "your price, my terms; my price, your terms." Obviously, you would far prefer your price and your terms, especially if your terms include all cash at closing. But keep in mind the likelihood that you will encounter this strategy when you are setting your asking price. If you do receive an offer that includes deferred payments to you, then you need to decide how badly you want to sell the business. Each of these options means less liquidity for you and far greater risk. There are thousands of business owners in this country running firms that they had sold on contract and later received back because the new owners could not make it.

If you do agree to sell your business on terms, then be sure the deferred obligation is adequately secured. The most obvious security for a deferred purchase price is the business itself, in the form of security interests in the business's assets or its stock or both. Those thousands of business owners who are running firms they once sold were able to get their businesses back only because they had a right to through their security instruments. The business itself is not always the appropriate security for the debt. If your business is one of those that could very easily and quickly be run down by bad management or poor customer service, taking back the business after the buyer fails to make his payments to you may not do you much good. If the business becomes valueless, your security will be valueless as well. You may wish to investigate the possibility of obtaining security that is not connected to your business– real estate, for example. Whatever the form of the security you obtain, its documentation and "perfection" (the process of putting the rest of the world on notice of your continuing rights in the business or its assets) is a highly technical area for which you will require the services of an attorney.

The business itself is not always the appropriate security for the debt

You may also wish to consider insisting upon other controls on the manner in which the business is operated, to increase the likelihood that the buyer will actually make the deferred payments to you. Those controls may range from the relatively mild requirement of periodic financial reporting to you to enable you to monitor the business's continuing health, to more restrictive requirements preventing the business from incurring additional debt or making distributions of money above a set amount to its new owners until you have been paid in full. Remember, though, that you will have to strike an appropriate balance between controls that protect you, but allow the business to operate in an efficient and profitable way for the new owner.

You may want to insist on controls that encourage the buyer to make deferred payments to you

How much is your business worth? There are a variety of methods to quantitatively calculate the value of your business– but don't forget, *your business is worth what someone is willing to pay for it.*

You may have a great business selling caribou hides out of northern Alaska, but when it comes time to sell the business you may have trouble finding someone willing to live at 70 degrees North Latitude. Conversely, you may be able to sell a professional baseball team at a far higher price than its cash flow could justify because people find it glamorous to own such a business. Four commonly used methods of calculating the value of a business are described below.

The Net Worth of Your Business. The most straightforward means of calculating the value of your business is to subtract the amount of debt and other liabilities you have from the value of your assets, which results in your net worth. Calculating debt is easy. Calculating the amount of other liabilities and *accurate* asset values is not. For example, you may have product warranty obligations that cannot be calculated accurately until claims are made. On the asset side, for example, if you own a restaurant you will show kitchen equipment as assets on your balance sheet. If you tried to sell the equipment, you probably couldn't get much for used equipment. Therefore, the listed value on the balance sheet may be much different than its true value. The same principle applies to real estate. Accounting rules state that you must list it at its original purchase price. If you have owned the property for a few years, chances are that it has appreciated. When you use this method, try to list assets at their true value, instead of at their book value.

> Your business is worth what someone is willing to pay for it

Many business sellers will put "goodwill" as an asset on their balance sheet. Goodwill is the added value of a business beyond what assets are worth. Accountants shudder at the term, and in some cases the extra value does not exist, while in others it truly does. As an example, a software company may have value far beyond the worth of its assets if its software has significant sales potential. Yes, the company is worth more than its net worth, and goodwill definitely exists. Its value is difficult to calculate. Ironically, "badwill" has never been listed on a seller's balance sheet. Certainly it exists also.

> Valuations of your business are only estimates

Discounted Cash Flows. To determine the present value of a business, you discount its future cash flows. Review Chapter 11, Cash Management, on the differences between profits and cash flow. You may wonder how far into the future to project cash flows, since theoretically the business could exist infinitely. Discounting reduces to almost nothing the value of cash flows far in the future. Seven to ten years is reasonable. Included on the diskette provided with this book is a Lotus 1-2-3 template entitled NPV (for net present value). The template steps you through the process of calculating the net present value of future cash flows. This method of business valuation assumes that buying a business is no different than investing in other assets, such as stocks and bonds. You need to look at the stream of cash flows that the asset generates and then *discount* the amount of the cash to present day values. For example, the value of $1000 given to you five years from now is not nearly the value of $1000 given to you today. If you invested the $1000 today in a bond yielding 8 percent and let it sit for five years, it would be worth $1469 in five years. Clearly, you have to adjust for the timing of cash flows to make them comparable. What is the current value of receiving $1000 five years from now? If 8 percent is the rate you can earn, $681 today would be worth $1000 in five years. $681 is the *present value of* the future cash flow. It is calculated by discounting the future cash flow.

Projecting future cash flows is not easy, especially when you try to do it fifteen to twenty-five years into the future. If you look at current cash flow, project inflation and a growth rate, you will come up with a reasonable cash flow projection. You and your potential buyer will have to argue over how reasonable the numbers are. If you plug those numbers into the NPV program, it determines a net present value for you. For example, a business that shows a positive cash flow of $10,000 in each of the next ten years and then a positive cash flow of $15,000 in each of years 11 through 15 has a calculated net present value of approximately $105,000 if the discount rate is 8 percent. The *discount rate is* somewhere between what you can get if you invest your money in a fairly safe investment and what the bank lending rate is to you.

Calculate the worth of your business using both the net worth and net present value methods. The value of your business is *probably* in between the values each of these methods generates. Again, the *real value* of your business is the price that you and a buyer agree upon. Remember also that the *terms* of the deal are just as important as the selling price. If you are able to get cash up front, a lower price may be a far better deal than one which you have to finance a large part of and/or accept part ownership.

Multiple of Earnings. *A multiple of earnings approach* to business valuation, like discounted cash flows, assumes that the worth of a business should be based on its income, and not on its net worth. The approach is less sophisticated than is discounted cash flows, yet

> The final selling price of your business will probably be between the discounted cash flow value and the net worth of the business

> Remember also that the terms of the deal are just as important as the selling price

it is widely used. The value of the business is its current income times a certain multiplier. The multiplier varies by industry and by region. For example, a bakery in Spokane may sell at a multiple of three times earnings, while a software company in Silicon Valley may sell at twenty times earnings. Commercial real estate agents and business brokers in your area can give you an idea of what a reasonable multiplier for your business might be. This approach provides only a rough estimate of value and is not based on very objective data. It is an estimation of what a typical buyer might pay for a typical business in the same general industry. Is your business typical?

Multiple of Recast Net Earnings. A variation of the prior approach values the business at its "recast" net earnings times a multiplier of three to five. The premise of this valuation technique is that an entrepreneur should be willing to pay three to five times the "real" net earnings for the business, in theory providing the buyer with an approximate annual return on his investment of 20% to 33%, depending on the multiplier. While the use of this method is currently in vogue among some business brokers, it usually is an aggressive approach from the seller's perspective. The process of recasting the earnings of the business generally will reduce certain expenses to market value, particularly the expenses of the owner's compensation and related benefits, thus increasing earnings and inflating the purchase price. The recasting of earnings sometimes will result in the lowering of earnings, particularly in circumstances where revenues are adjusted to eliminate non-recurring income, but the usual result is to increase the earnings of the business. There is plenty of room for argument between you and the buyer as to how to recast the earnings and as to the multiplier you should employ. A sophisticated buyer will point out that under this approach, he would be buying the business based on future earnings forecast to be produced by an expense structure that is overly optimistic from an historical perspective. Moreover, it will be the buyer's labor and acumen that actually produce the forecast result. A buyer who uses this method could be said to be paying you for the fruits of his own labor.

> **A multiple of earnings approach assumes that the worth of a business should be based on its income, not on its net worth**

The Cash Cow

A *cash cow* is a business which generates cash flows beyond what it needs to operate and grow. This excess cash is at the owners' disposal to invest in other ventures (or vacation homes or whatever). Not a lot of businesses are in this enviable position. Usually the opposite is true. Even successful, growing businesses frequently run short of cash. Nonetheless, some firms can become cash cows and allow their owners to either use the cash or the borrowing capacity of the business to start other companies.

Cash cows are usually established high-margin businesses. Growth is not significant, and the firm usually has either high market share or a very strong reputation. The past efforts that went into designing products and/or creating markets can be curtailed and the rewards of previous hard work are reaped.

The Management Buyout

Many managers dream of owning the company where they work. They know the business. The problem in selling to them is that they usually do not have a lot of cash to purchase the business. As a result, most management buyouts are done with small amounts of cash down and a large note with the old owners. If you are selling to a manager or managers of your business, try to get as much cash down as possible. When settling on a selling price, use the methods outlined in the section above.

If you do sell the business on contract, at least you know the management skills of the new owners. Some management buyout contracts have provisions that pay a portion of profits to the former owners. These can be advantageous to you if the company prospers, but you need to be careful. As mentioned many times in this book, accountants can legally change the profits of a company by using different accounting conventions. Profits of the company can be manipulated to avoid having to pay you. Consult a good business attorney and write in the contract how profits are to be calculated. Some management buyouts are done gradually. For several years, managers buy in gradually to the business. You and the managers can see how it is working before deciding on a final buy-out contract.

The Merger or Acquisition

Being bought by or merging with another company is a special type of "outright sale." The biggest difference is that the other company is usually quite larger than you and operates the business as one of several enterprises in which they are involved. Several companies in Washington have been acquired by larger firms, including K2, a ski maker which was initially acquired by Cummins Diesel, and United Control, which was acquired by Sundstrand.

Buyouts usually have special terms. In many cases, the acquiring company will want you to stay on as a manager of the company and will expect you to sign non-competing clauses, making it illegal for you to start another company in the same industry. You usually retain some ownership in the company as an incentive to have the firm prosper. In some cases you may exchange stock with the larger company. In doing so, its more liquid stock is easier to sell and provides the "harvest."

Buyouts usually have special terms

The Employee Stock Ownership Plan (ESOP)

ESOPs have become increasingly popular in small and mid-size companies. They allow employees to purchase shares of the business. From a motivational standpoint, it gets employees committed to the long-term success of the firm. From a harvest standpoint, it allows owners to achieve liquidity through sales of stock to the plan and to employees. Although such a plan does not provide for a total sale of the business, it can provide some liquidity to current owners.

ESOPs get employees committed to the long-term success of the firm

Over the last eight years, Washington state has seen the use of employee ownership grow more quickly than almost anywhere else in the nation. There are now an estimated 200 firms in Washington in which non-managerial employees own a substantial amount of their company stock. Three of the five largest grocery store chains in Spokane (Rosauers Supermarkets, Tidyman's Warehouse Foods, and Yoke's Pak'N'Save) are majority owned by their employees. Several engineering firms in western Washington (Parametrix, Coffman Engineers Inc., Shannon & Wilson, W & H Pacific) aerospace suppliers (Flight Structures Inc., Stoddard Hamilton, Precision Machine Works), temp agencies (Humanix) and contractors (MacDonald-Miller Industries), are using employee ownership to provide incentives for higher productivity and as a means for their founding owner to "cash out" and retire while keeping the company competitive and in local ownership. Some employee ownership firms, like Baugh Construction and Starbucks, even tout their status as part of their commercial advertising and credit it publicly as part of their reason for success.

There are significant tax advantages for the business owner who sells to his employees, for the bank which lends to them, and for the company which has an employee ownership plan. But tax advantages alone do not make for good business. National and state studies show that companies which combine employee ownership with employee participation (in identifying new processes and markets) tend to grow more quickly and have greater productivity than their competitors. Those studies also show that participative employees outperform their non-participative competitors.

There are significant tax advantages for the business owner who sells to his employees

Washington also has a state program which focuses on employee ownership. Through the employee ownership program at the state Department of Community Trade and Economic Development, the state provides information, referrals, technical consultation, and, in distressed areas, assistance in accessing state and federal financing programs. The program has successfully assisted over 20 companies in becoming employee owned. The program staff may be reached at 360- 586-8984.

The Public Offering

Public stock offerings are complicated and expensive

Public stock offerings are complicated and expensive. Few companies do it. In 1983, the best year for small company new stock offerings, only 888 companies "went public." For a company that is able to do it, however, relatively large amounts of money can be raised and owners can achieve a high level of liquidity. Chapter 7, Raising Capital, discusses the public offering process in detail.

Preparing Your Business for Harvest

The existence of a serious problem may increase the time it takes to sell your business

Whatever your strategy for harvest, you will want to devote considerable energy to putting your business in its best possible condition before marketing it. Every business has at least a few problems that ought to be dealt with before a buyer begins his inspection of the company. You will be far better off dealing with those problems yourself now, before you enter into negotiations, for several reasons. First, you should anticipate that a sophisticated buyer and his advisors will unearth any lingering difficulties and use those problems against you in the negotiation over price. Your failure to deal with those problems now will cost you money. Second, a shrewd buyer will attempt to leave the problem with you to fix later at your expense. The purchaser may insist on an indemnification agreement from you that requires you to incur all of the unknown future expenses of a potential claim or other problem, including the attorneys' fees and other costs associated with actually solving the problem. You may want a clean break from the company, without lingering doubt as to your liabilities. Third, generally speaking, it is easiest to fix a problem and to control the costs of a solution while you control the business rather than after you no longer do. Finally, the existence of a serious problem may

The Washington Entrepreneur's Guide

increase the time it takes to sell your business, or even make it impossible to sell it at all.

Before you market the business, ask your advisors for their help in valuing the business in its present condition, identifying its faults and virtues. You should try to anticipate the arguments the buyer will use in his efforts to reduce the price. Then, strongly consider dealing now with all of the identified problems that can be dealt with now. Don't expect to be able to solve all of your problems in the week before you begin marketing. Preparing a business for sale is a time-consuming process that ought to be a part of your usual operations during the life of your business. You are likely both to increase the selling price of the business and the speed with which you can sell it.

> **You should anticipate the arguments the buyer will use in his efforts to reduce the price**

Conclusion

The most important aspect of a harvest strategy is to plan it in advance. Granted, in the early years of your venture you are too busy building it to worry about harvesting it. But after year three, if you are interested at all in eventually harvesting, you should begin to think about how it will be done. Nearly all of the six approaches to harvesting described above take considerable time to orchestrate. You might consider a plan that allows you to cash out of the business in years seven through ten.

Even though you may not be able to conceive getting out of the business after a few years, realize that your feelings may change over time. After many years in a business, people burn out or get bored and then want a change badly. You should *not want to sell badly* when you go to sell. Buyers sense this and will offer you less. Be patient. Industry and economic conditions greatly affect what price you can get for your company. If you are in a rush, you will probably make some foolish mistakes.

> **The most important aspect of a harvest strategy is to plan it in advance**

If you get an offer, try to evaluate it objectively. Your emotions are so tied up in your business that this may be difficult to do; however, realize that most people believe their businesses are worth far more than they truly are. Don't be greedy. Many entrepreneurs have turned down initial offers condescendingly and later accepted lower offers out of desperation.

Lastly, do a thorough job in seeking out advice on harvesting. Most business brokers, like real estate agents, are motivated by the commission on the sale. They would rather get a sale, at a lower price, than no sale at all. Plus, they are sometimes not involved in long-term planning for a harvest– they would like to see a sale in the next six months. This is not a criticism of brokers, but it is the reality of the system in which they work. Ask around about who might be able to give advice on harvesting. Be persistent and patient in finding them. Wise counsel is important.

If you are in a rush to sell, you will probably make some foolish mistakes

References

1.   Timmons, Jeffry, A. *New Venture Creation*, rdd Edition. Homewood, Illinois: Irwin, 1990

2.   *Growing Concerns*, ed. David Gumpert, New York: John Wiley & Sons, 1984

=====15=====

The 1990's and Beyond: Small Companies and the Washington Economy

As the new century approaches, Washington will continue to be a good place for small companies and the entrepreneurs that establish them to do business. The state's current extended period of significant annual economic growth cannot continue indefinitely. However, any economic downturn is likely to be temporary given the fundamental strengths of the State, its citizens and its enterprises.

In many respects, the challenging decade of the 1990's has strengthened economic prospects for the 21st century. The maturation of the natural resource economy (including forest products, agriculture, fisheries and mining) and the temporary decline of Boeing employment by mid-decade have forced the state to work even harder at economic diversification. The success of software and high technology companies has broadened the base from which the state can build its future.

Whether small businesses focus upon retail, manufacturing, information services or other sectors, several characteristics of the state's economy are having profound impact upon their prospects:

Washington's continued position as a premier exporter among states. Washington exports a higher percentage of its goods and services than any other state, and this level has grown during the 1990's to a per capita level more than three times the national average. The export focus has created enormous opportunities for smaller enterprises both as direct exporters and as suppliers to larger companies that have greater access to external markets.

> Several characteristics of the state's economy are having profound impact on small businesses

This chapter was written by Mr. David Harrison, chair of the Northwest Policy Center. The authors of the Washington Entrepreneur Guide appreciate his contribution to this book.

The extraordinary quality of life the citizens of the state enjoy. Quality of life continues to be a strong factor driving the Washington state economy. No small number of entrepreneurs have gravitated to the state or remain because of the access to its natural beauty, its clean air, water, and open space, and its vibrant cities.

The state's increased level of economic diversification. Small enterprises are well served both by the strength evident in the state's old economy (including such companies as Weyerhaeuser and Boeing) and in such relatively new information and technology companies as Microsoft, AT&T Cellular (formerly McCaw), and Immunex. The economic over-reliance problem of the past is best captured by the saying "If Boeing sneezes, Washington catches a cold." Those times are at least starting to change. Because of the economic strength of other sectors, the Seattle metropolitan area was been able to withstand significant Boeing layoffs in the mid 1990's without going into an economic tailspin. Boeing still provides tens of thousands good jobs for Washingtonians and hundreds of millions in sub-contracts for Washington companies.

Stronger local and domestic markets. As Washington's population has grown and its economy has diversified, local markets for Washington-made goods and services have continued to expand. With the advent of the North-American Free Trade Agreement (NAFTA) the Pacific Northwest economic region has emerged not only as a strong international force but as an area that grows market opportunities for its own companies at home. As trade barriers are removed, British Columbia has become very similar to a domestic trading partner.

> **Local markets for Washington-made goods and services have continued to expand**

A dependable, highly skilled workforce. Washington's workforce is very competitive with that of other states. A considerable investment in such sponsors of worker training as community colleges is intended to assure that small and large companies alike can keep up with technological change and with modification of manufacturing practices.

A place for small business. Even though Washington is known as the home of such international companies as Boeing and Microsoft, it is more dependent on small business than many other states. More than 60 percent of Washington workers work in companies of 100 employees or less, compared to a national average of 55 percent.

> **Washington state is still a place for small businesses**

A rich natural endowment. Many companies continue to gain reap economic rewards from the rich natural endowment of the state. As population growth and environmental standards constrain the total amount of trees that can be harvested or agricultural acres planted, such companies as Weyerhaeuser and Tree Top maximize the economic value gained from the limited resource. They secure profits and strengthen the economy through processing these commodities into value added products from doors to apple juice. The rich resource base also includes the water power which has been harnessed to provide low electricity rates to Washington enterprises and homeowners.

Strong, statewide economic health. The economic vitality that has been experienced since 1990 has been shared by most of the state rather than being restricted to the Seattle metropolitan area. Such medium sized cities as Yakima, Vancouver, Bellingham and Walla Walla have seen solid employment growth. Even communities like Port Angeles and Aberdeen/Hoquiam which have been impacted by the upheaval in the timber industry have seen recent economic upturns.

The economic circumstances that new and emerging enterprises face is ever-changing. Business leaders and policymakers continue to tackle such business climate issues as the nature and level of taxation and business regulation. Even as these discussions continue, and as national and international economic forces impact the state, Washington's economy (and the opportunities that economy provides for small business) can be expected to remain fundamentally sound.

> **Economic circumstances change often**

The Economic Transformation Proceeds

For the past decade, Washington has been in the throes of a fundamental, irreversible economic transformation. To be sure, the state has before faced economic change and cyclical downturns and upturns brought about by any number of forces. In natural resource dependent industries, the ebbs and flows had become so commonplace that either a boom or a crisis always seemed just around the corner. Jobs that had been lost would be regained when the mill started hiring again. The state's economy was especially susceptible to increases in borrowing rates, which would decrease the demand both for new home construction (made from Washington lumber) and airplanes. However, when rates went back down, the economy would find its footing yet again.

> **For the past decade, Washington has been in an economic transformation**

Times have changed. In all too many cases, the mill is closed and will never start hiring again. Such Washington's natural resource dependent sectors as wood products, agriculture, mining, and fisheries are facing an all new set of factors, including population growth encroaching on land previously used for production. Their options are constrained by environmental standards and their products are in a new level of competition with those produced worldwide.

Even in the face of these challenges, these sectors remain strong An increased emphasis on adding value to commodities is benefiting local economies, creating new natural resource dependent jobs, though not enough such jobs to make up for all of the job losses suffered in rural communities. These industries are here to stay and can be depended upon in Washington, but they can no longer be expected to significantly increase in size or to act as the primary driver for future economic gains, even in natural resource dependent small communities.

There is a similar story regarding the Boeing Company. The single most successful manufacturer of airplanes in the world today will occupy that same position a decade hence. What will permanently change in the upcoming decade is the number of employees needed in order for the company to maintain its preeminent role in the aerospace industry. At its employment peak, Boeing employed over 100,000 workers in the Seattle metropolitan area, providing the area high paying manufacturing jobs that were the envy of the nation. Boeing's employment has subsequently dropped to less than 75,000 as the company pursues the efficiency gains that will keep it strong. Its contribution to the state's economy will remain huge. In fact, Boeing, forest products and agriculture combined still play a role in generating every third job in Washington state when one considers the "multiplier effects" of their activity. Like forest products and agriculture, Boeing is unlikely to again become the driver of a new level of economic vitality.

Large companies will no longer dominate the Washington economy

New economic energy will come from smaller companies

Instead, the state of Washington has derived and will continue to gain much of its new economic energy from hundreds and even thousands of smaller companies. Perhaps this new wave of entrepreneurism for the 21st century is particularly appropriate given the economic contribution made in the 20th century by two companies started on a shoestring by risk-takers named Bill– Boeing started in a garage by William Boeing in 1916 and Microsoft established by Bill Gates nearly 70 years later.

In the 1990's, the success of such larger companies as Microsoft and AT&T Cellular has improved the prospects and accelerated the growth of many of the smaller companies that are loosely grouped together and designated "high technology" enterprises. These are companies involved in such markets as computers, software, medical instruments, biotechnology, and environmental technology. Many are critical to the economy not only as employers but as an impetus for the location or emergence of additional such companies. Some also help mainstream companies address technological change.

These "high technology" companies together represent an all new sector upon which Washington can rest at least a part of its future fortunes. By 1996, well over 80,000 Washingtonians held jobs in such companies. This growth trend is expected to continue not only in the Seattle metropolitan area but in the balance of the state as well. A sales tax exemption granted to manufacturing companies who invest in plant and equipment has helped spur future expansion plans, including location of a major Intel facility in Dupont (between Tacoma and Olympia), and the expansion of the Matsushita plant in Puyallup.

There is a growth trend in "high technology" companies

Analysts allocate many of the jobs generated in emerging technology companies to the "services" sector in economic data, which also includes retail activity. In the most recent year for which complete data is available, this category accounted for nearly 23,000 of the 57,000 new jobs created in Washington state. During that same year (1994), gains in other manufacturing jobs did not quite make up for 10,000 Boeing layoffs. The trade sector including shippers of goods was strengthened considerably, adding nearly 19,000 jobs. This sector will remain strong as the Northwest takes advantage of its position relative to the growing economies of the Pacific Rim.

Total employment has grown in Washington in every year since 1990. Through 1995, nearly 300,000 new jobs have been created. Through all of the good news, there is still at least one warning sign. Because many of the job losses have taken place in the higher wage manufacturing sector and many of the jobs gains have been in somewhat lower wage service industries, the state will have problems sustaining average wage rates and maintaining per capita income levels.

The trade sector has been strengthened considerably

During the period 1988-1993, the state's growth in population, employment, and per capita personal income exceeded the national average on a yearly basis. In 1994, growth in per capita income dipped below the national average for the first time in several years and was expected to do so again in 1996.

The State Seeks to Manage its Growth

High population growth has bolstered markets for goods and services

The state of Washington has grown faster than the national average in population in every year since 1985. The fact that over five and a half million people now call Washington their home has bolstered markets for the goods and services provided by Washington companies, and has boosted the technical skills of the state's workforce. In-migration has even influenced per capita income, as those arriving have greater assets on the average than those departing. However, that same population growth has also given rise to new concerns regarding how quality of life will be protected in the state.

New laws try to control congestion and keep open space with the population increase

This annual population increase is fueled not only by net in-migration in the range of 30,000-50,000 persons per year, but by the fact that birth rate is exceeding the rate of death among state residents. Concerns about congestion and the decrease in open space proximate to metropolitan areas stimulated the passage in 1993 of a state Growth Management Act. The law requires most Washington counties to prepare comprehensive plans providing for additional population growth and more clearly designating lands for residential and multi-family housing, open space, and lands for commercial and industrial use. It also requires capital facilities planning to prepare for the schools, roads and other "infrastructure" for growth that is emerging and to identify the source of the revenue which will cover the costs of these facilities.

Many of the cities and counties that have completed their comprehensive plans have prepared an element of the plan expressly focused upon economic development strategies. Like the other economic development efforts that are underway statewide, these plans reveal both the economic similarities and the differences between the regions of the state.

The economic growth of the mid-1990s has been fairly evenly spread throughout the state. This more even pattern is in sharp contrast to relatively recent periods in the early 1990's where the Seattle metropolitan area was receiving virtually all of the job growth while other areas were experiencing double digit unemployment, and earlier periods where less urbanized areas were growing strongly and the Seattle economy was mired in a "Boeing recession."

By the 1990's, most of the 39 counties were experiencing employment growth. Even the slowest growing counties were benefiting from the continued in-migration not of people but of small companies whose owners were seeking such Washington factors as a reliable workforce, enhanced quality of life, lower business costs for some sectors, and somewhat less regulation (at least in comparison to California, which was the original location for many of these companies.)

The *Spokane* area has succeeded in widely diversifying from its earlier position as a service center for a large agricultural and forest products area stretching from the Cascades to Western Montana. Spokane is home to dozens of technology companies and boasts a high powered civic effort which has been responsible for the rebuilding of much of downtown and for the ongoing promotion of the city.

Economic analysts expect Washington to have a healthy economy well into the future

The *Seattle–Tacoma* metropolitan area has seen economic growth not only in the two largest cities but in smaller cities like Kirkland and Auburn and through much of Snohomish County. Much of the economic activity is centered around technology companies and around the construction of regional shopping complexes. The region has yet to resolve major traffic congestion problems that affects the cost of shipping goods and services to market.

Such cities as *Yakima* and *Wenatchee*, heretofore focused almost entirely on agriculture and food processing, have also diversified. In-migration has contributed to housing problems in Yakima as out-of-staters make a lifestyle choice in selecting Washington communities. Communities along the I-5 corridor like *Bellingham* and *Olympia* also benefit economically from quality of life as well as from easy access to larger metropolitan areas.

Other communities are struggling to achieve economic stability in the face of external forces which have buffeted them. *Aberdeen* and *Port Angeles* both lost employment due to changes in the timber industry. *Bremerton*, whose numerous naval installations have been impacted by federal defense budget cuts, has gained some spillover economic impacts from activity in Seattle and Tacoma. The *Tri-Cities* are in a similar uncertain position due to federal cutbacks in

The state is not isolated from the national recession

spending at the Hanford Nuclear Reservation. These communities are taking economic advantage of the considerable expenditures of the federal government in cleaning up nuclear waste, and are using advances in waste management technology to spur new enterprises.

Facing the Future

Economic analysts expect Washington to have a healthy economy well into the future. The state is by no means insulated from a national recession. In fact, many of the elements of its economic success (including the sale of airplanes and other dimensions of the state's intensive trade focus) depend in part on interest rates remaining relatively low.

Still, the Washington future seems bright. The growing economies of the Pacific Rim will continue to generate economic activity. The state's assets remain plentiful, and its liabilities modest. As transportation systems and costs change, and some products of the information economy have no weight at all, there is a "declining disadvantage of distance" in the location of export-focused firms. As the cost of shipping their products to market diminishes, more and more owners of such enterprises can utilize quality of life as a prime element in their business location decisions. If Washingtonians maintain their treasured quality of life, their state will have continued economic advantage for some time to come.

The growing economies of the Pacific Rim will continue to generate economic activity

WASHINGTON BUSINESS RESOURCE DIRECTORY

How this directory is organized: This resource directory has been compiled from a number of sources. The resource directory lists federal, state, non-profit and private sector resources available to the entrepreneur in the State of Washington and is organized by category as follows:

BUSINESS & TECHNICAL ASSISTANCE	*SPECIALTY INDUSTRIES*
TAXES & TAX CREDITS	*DAYCARE*
EXPORT	*WORKFORCE*
FINANCE	*GENERAL*
LICENSES, REGISTRATION & PERMITS	*MANUFACTURING*
TRAINING & EDUCATION	*RECYCLE*
MINORITY & WOMEN BUSINESSES	*TOURISM*
PATENTS & COPYRIGHT	*SAFETY*
REGULATORY ASSISTANCE	*FILM & VIDEO*

The directory was too large to include a list of all the local revolving funds and other local programs by county in this book. The attached diskette does include files with *Programs Listed By County* (the filename is ***county.doc*** and it is in MS Word format. It is also in WordPerfect format in ***county.wpd***). This file lists primary resources available to the entrepreneur locally and is organized by county. Four county contact points are listed. The first, and most important, is the *Economic Development Council* which can provide information and referral about many of the other programs available throughout the state and act as an advocate for the entrepreneur. The listings by county also includes: *Community Development Finance*, *Small Business Development Center* and *Loan Programs* (local revolving & micro loan funds).

State, Federal, And Program Listings

Business & Technical Assistance

Bioenergy Technical Information
WSU Cooperative Extension Energy Program
925 Plum Street SE, Building 4
PO Box 43165
Olympia, WA 98504-3165
(360) 956-2069
This program provides technical assistance to manufacturing and commercial facilities interested in using biomass (wood, municipal waste and agricultural residues) fuels. Help is also provided to identify biomass sources and in selecting appropriate technologies and/or consultants.

Business Assistance Hotline
Department of Community, Trade & Economic Development
PO Box 48300
Olympia, WA 98504-8300
(360) 664-9501 Local & Outside Washington   (800) 237-1233 Washington (360) 586-4840 TDD
The Business Assistance Hotline is a one-stop service which provides new and existing small business owners with timely, accurate information regarding resources, rules, regulations, licenses, and business start-up and expansion. A business information counselor is available to answer business related questions and refer callers to appropriate contacts for additional assistance. The hotline is a statewide information and referral service.

Business Diagnostic Center
Business Diagnostic Center, School of Business Administration
University of Washington
Mackenzie Hall DJ-10
Seattle, Washington 98195
(206) 685-8785   Fax: (206) 685-9392
The Business Diagnostic Center is a management consulting organization developed in 1991 and operated entirely by graduate MBA students at the University of Washington's School of Business Administration. Their goals are twofold: first to provide local businesses and non-profit organizations with fresh insights into their operational and strategic decision making; and second, to enable MBA students to apply and develop skills in the local business community. The Business Diagnostic Center begins accepting project proposals in August for selection in December and completion the following spring. The project selection process includes an assessment of the business's commitment to the project and identification of projects with a reasonable scope for completion by full-time MBA students.

Business Enterprise Center (BEC)
Business Enterprise Center
1200 Sixth Avenue, Park Place Building, Suite 1700
Seattle, WA 98101-1128
(206) 553-7311   Fax: (206) 553-4155 (206) 553-7070 Recorded Information
The SBA Business Enterprise Center is a briefing and business center which helps entrepreneurs with business research and planning through cutting edge technology and computerization. This "one-stop" center provides more than 2000 small business planning tools, together with business information, free counseling and one-on-one service.

Using state-of-the-art computers, graphic workstations, CD-ROM technology and interactive videos, the entrepreneur can access market research databases, use planning and spreadsheet software, and browse thorough vast libraries of information. The library and software provides assistance to the entrepreneur in crafting their own business and marketing plans. Visitors are welcome to quickly access the Electronic Library to download helpful texts to manage their businesses, or to spend several weeks in the center polishing up their business plan. Since the Enterprise Center opened its doors in 1991, more than 50,000 small business owners and budding entrepreneurs have tapped into its rich resources.

Both the Business Enterprise Center and the Business Information Center below give entrepreneurs and aspiring entrepreneurs free access to hardware, software, books and publications that help them plan their business, expand an existing enterprise, or venture into new business arenas.

Business Information Center (BIC)
Business Information Center, Coralie Myers, Manager
1020 West Riverside Avenue
Spokane, Washington 99210
(509) 353-2800   Fax: (509) 353-2600   Internet http://www.spokane.org/bic
The Spokane Area Business Information Center (BIC) is a one-stop reference facility with computer workstations, video monitors and audio cassette players, and over 200 entrepreneurial guides to help you plan your business venture. BIC personnel can direct you to other resources and can also arrange free counseling sessions with a volunteer from the Service Corps or Retired Executives (SCORE).

The BIC is uniquely designed to guide the small business owner or manager in the research and preparation of a workable business plan, the key component to small business success. The BIC has books, workshops and business plan software to help both new and existing businesses chart a path for the future. The Business Information Center is open Monday through Friday, Business hours are 9:00 a.m. to 4:00 p.m.

Business & Job Retention Program
Department of Community, Trade & Economic Development
2001 6th Ave, Suite 2700
Seattle, WA 98121
(206) 464-6282
The Business and Job Retention Program works with at-risk manufacturing and processing firms to reduce the number of business closures, layoffs and failures. The program provides technical and problem solving assistance to retain existing businesses and jobs.

Commercial Education, Training and Technical Assistance
WSU Cooperative Extension Energy Program
1212 North Washington, Room 106
Spokane, WA 99201
(509) 324-7985
DESCRIPTION: Training, information and technical assistance for small business, schools, institutions, municipalities, utilities, trade associations, professional organizations and universities. Assistance with walk-through audits and identification of energy efficient practices and products to reduce energy consumption. OUTCOMES: Develop and deliver integrated energy and total resource management information, education and technical assistance services to a variety of clients. Training on use of computer bulletin board and Internet services to identify resources to aid in the efficient operation of commercial facilities.

Community Colleges
Washington has 28 community colleges that offer a wide variety of adult education programs, including entrepreneurial skills, management, marketing, computer, accounting, job training, college transfer, basic skills, adult literacy and many others. *See Workforce/Training for a list of community colleges and contact the one in your area.*

Consultation and Compliance Services Division- Consultation Services
Department of Labor and Industries
Consultation Section
(800) 547-8367 or contact the local L & I office (*See Regulatory Assistance Section- Department of Labor and Industries*)
The consultation section assists businesses by providing an apprenticeship program, labor management cooperation program and consultation services in the area of risk management and vocational employer. Specialists in safety and health are available to assist employers in understanding and complying with worker protection laws

The apprenticeship program coordinates the state's job training program operated in conjunction with the state's workers and employers. The Labor/Management Cooperation Program is an outreach effort aimed at returning injured workers to their jobs and reducing workers compensation expenses.

District Heating and Cooling
WSU Cooperative Extension Energy Program
925 Plum Street SE, Building 4
PO Box 43165
Olympia, WA 98504-3165
(360) 956-2030
Provides facilities (or public works) managers, owners, designers, planners, engineers and operators extensive technical, economical and air emission information about a District Heating or Cooling application for commercial, industrial, or public institutions. The computer program, HEATMAP (available in Windows and DOS platforms) may be used to plan new energy systems, evaluate existing system performance or model the effects of various potential alternative system strategies including upgrades and expansions. Assistance is also provided in obtaining project funding from multiple sources.

Economic Development Councils
Economic Development Councils across the state provide local business assistance resources, community profiles, business seminars, industrial site information, export assistance and finance assistance to small business wishing to expand their operation, and entrepreneurs who wish to start a business. Economic Development Councils also have access to many of the resources in this directory and can often provide written information on programs and provide referrals.

Adams County
John Taylor, Executive Director
Adams County EDC
455 E. Hemlock St.
Othello, WA 99344
(509) 488-5785
FAX: (509) 488-2034

Asotin County
Sally Ledgerwood, Executive Director
Lewis-Clark EDA
504 Bridge Street
Clarkston, WA 99403-1833
(509) 758-4790
FAX: (509) 758-1309
E-mail: sallylw@palouse.org

Benton/Franklin County
Richard Greenberg, President - CEO
TRIDEC
901 N. Colorado St.
Kennewick, WA 99336
(509) 735-1000
FAX: (509) 735-6609
E-mail: tridec@oneworld.owt.com
World Wide Web: http://www.owt.com

Chelan/Douglas County
Charles DeJong, President/CEO
Quest for Economic Development
327 E. Penny Road, Suite D
Wenatchee, WA 98801
(509) 662-8016
FAX: (509) 663-0455
E-mail: quest@televar.com

Clallam County
Bart Phillips, Executive Director
Clallam County EDC
102 East Front
P.O. Box 1085
Port Angeles, WA 98362
(360) 457-7793
FAX: (360) 452-9618
E-mail: ccedc@olympus.net

Clark County
Robert Levin, President
Columbia River EDC
100 E. Columbia Way
Vancouver, WA 98661
(360) 694-5006
FAX: (360) 694-9927
E-mail: info@credc.org
World Wide Web: http://www.credc.org

Columbia/Garfield/Whitman County
Jack Thompson, Executive Director
Palouse EDC/AgriTechnics
N.E. 1345 Terre View Drive
Pullman, WA 99163-5101
(509) 334-3579
FAX: (509) 332-6991
E-mail: info@palouse.org
World Wide Web: http://www.econd.org/

Cowlitz County
Clint Page, Executive Director
Cowlitz County EDC
U.S. Bank 1452 Hudson, Suite 208
P.O. Box 1278
Longview, WA 98632
(360) 423-9921
FAX: (360) 423-1923
E-mail: cedc@aol.com

Ferry/Stevens County
Brent Grening, Executive Director
TRICO
347 W. Second, Suite A
Colville, WA 99114
(509) 684-4571
FAX: (509) 684-4788
E-mail: trico@plix.com

Grant County
Thomas Wendt, Executive Director
Grant County EDC
Grant County Courthouse, Rm. 101
P.O. Box 369
Ephrata, WA 98823-0369

(509) 754-0978
FAX: (509) 754-2417

Grays Harbor County
Tami Garrow, Executive Director
Grays Harbor EDC
506 Duffy St.
Aberdeen, WA 98520
(360) 532-7888
FAX: (360) 532-7922
E-mail: ghedc@techline.com

Island County
John Hitt, Executive Director
Island County EDC
P.O. Box 1949
Oak Harbor, WA 98277
(360) 675-0684
FAX: (360) 240-0315
E-mail: icedc@whidbey.net

Jefferson County
Erik Andersson, Director
EDC of Jefferson County
734 Water Street
P.O. Box 877
Port Townsend, WA 98368
(360) 385-6767
FAX: (360) 385-6768
E-mail: edcjefco@olympus.net
World Wide Web:
http://www.econd.org/edcs/jefferso

King County
EDC of Seattle & King County
701 5th Ave, Ste. 2510
Seattle, WA 98104
(206) 386-5040
FAX: (206) 386-7821
E-mail: edc@nwrain.net
World Wide Web: http://www.edc-sea.org
Kitsap County
Earle Smith, President
EDC of Kitsap County
4312 Kitsap Way, Ste. 103
Bremerton, WA 98312
(360) 377-9499
FAX: (360) 479-4653
E-mail: edc@kitsap.org
World Wide Web: http://www.kitsap.org

Kittitas County
George Rodriguez, President/CEO
Kittitas Valley Development Council
312 E. 4th Ave.

Ellensburg, WA 98926
(509) 962-3334
FAX: (509) 962-6633
E-mail: georger@ellensburg.com
World Wide Web:
http://www.ellensburg.com/~georger

Klickitat County
David McClure, Executive Director
Klickitat County Public EDA
County Courthouse Annex III
131 W. Court Street
Goldendale, WA 98620
(509) 773-7060
FAX: (509) 773-4521

Lewis County
William Lotto, Executive Director
Lewis County EDC
1611 N. National
P.O. Box 916
Chehalis, WA 98532
(360) 748-0114
FAX: (360) 748-1238
World Wide Web
http://www.econd.org/edcs/lewis/index.htm

Lincoln County
Bruce Vonada, Director
Lincoln County ADO
2008 W. Riverside
Spokane, WA 99201
800-442-9007, ext. 1290

Mason County
Tim Sheldon, Executive Director
EDC of Mason County
103 S. 4th, Angle Bldg., 2nd Fl.
P.O. Box 472
Shelton, WA 98584
(360) 426-2276
FAX: (360) 426-2868

Okanogan County
John Rayburn, Executive Director
OCCED
203 S. Second
P.O. Box 741
Okanogan, WA 98840
(509) 826-5107
FAX: (509) 826-7425
E-mail: occed@televar.com

Pacific County
Jim Lowery, Executive Director
Pacific County EDC
408 Second St.
Raymond, WA 98577
(360) 942-3629
FAX: (360) 942-3688

Pend Oreille County
Jim Jeffers, Executive Director
Pend Oreille Co. EDC
320 S. Washington
Newport, WA 99156-9665
(509) 447-5569
FAX: (509) 447-3709

Pierce County
Erling Mork, President
EDB for Tacoma-Pierce County
950 Pacific Ave., Suite 410
P.O. Box 1555
Tacoma, WA 98401
(206) 383-4726
FAX: (206) 383-4676
World Wide Web: http://www.econd.org

Skagit County
Don Wick, Executive Director
EDA of Skagit County
204 W. Montgomery
P.O. Box 40
Mt. Vernon, WA 98273
(360) 336-6114
FAX: (360) 336-6116
E-mail: edasc@sos.net

Skamania County
Peggy Bryan, Executive Director
Skamania County EDC
167 N.E. Second
P.O. Box 436
Stevenson, WA 98648
(509) 427-5110
FAX: (509) 427-5122
E-mail: scedc@xws.com

Snohomish County
John Thoresen, President
EDC of Snohomish County
917 -134th St. SW, Ste. 103
Everett, WA 98204
(206) 743-4567
FAX: (206) 745-5563
E-mail: jj@intersev.com

Spokane County
Bob Cooper, President
Spokane Area EDC
221 N. Wall, Suite 310
Box 203
Spokane, WA 99210
(509) 624-9285
FAX: (509) 624-3759
E-mail: kolson@palouse.org or
spokedc@palouse.org
World Wide Web: http://www.spokanedc.org

Thurston County
Dennis Matson, Executive Director
Thurston County EDC
721 Columbia SW
Olympia, WA 98501
(360) 754-6320
FAX: (360) 586-5493
E-mail: edc@orcalink.com

Wahkiakum County
Sharon Hart, Executive Director
Lower Columbia EDC
957 Steamboat Slough Rd.
P.O. Box 98
Skamokawa, WA 98647-0098
(360) 795-3996
FAX: (360) 795-3944

Walla Walla County
James Kuntz, Executive Director
Port of Walla Walla
2921 Melrose
P.O. Box 1077
Walla Walla, WA 99362
(509) 525-3100
FAX: (509) 525-3101

Whatcom County
Fred Sexton, President
Bellingham-Whatcom EDC
1203 Cornwall Ave., Suite 103
P.O. Box 2803
Bellingham, WA 98227
1-800-810-4255
FAX: (360) 647-9413
E-mail: bwedc@nas.com

Yakima County
Yakima County Development Assoc.
32 N. Front St., 2nd Fl.
P.O. Box 1387
Yakima, WA 98907-1387
(509) 575-1140
FAX: (509) 575-1508
E-mail: YCDA@wolfenet.com
World Wide Web:
http://www.econd.org/edcs/yakima

Energy Library
The library provides objective, accurate energy conservation and renewable energy resource information to all community sectors. Information is disseminated via newsletters, fact sheets and films. Staff can also access various on-line databases for literature searches.
WSU Cooperative Extension Energy Program
925 Plum Street SE, Building 4
PO Box 43165
Olympia, WA 98504-3165
(360) 956-2076

Employee Ownership Program
Department of Community, Trade & Economic Development
PO Box 48300
Olympia, WA 98504-8300
(360) 586-8984
The program promotes employee ownership and participation, delivers informational resources to worker-owned businesses, and provides technical assistance to owners and employees interested in using employee ownership structures and tax advantages for ownership transitions and to increase business competitiveness.

Federal Laboratory Consortium
Dr. Andrew Cowan, FLC Management Support Office
PO Box 545

224 W. Washington #3
Sequim, WA 98383
(360) 683-1005   Fax: (360) 683-6654   E-mail: andy@zyn.com
The Federal Laboratory Consortium can provide points of contact for the entrepreneur to access technologies, technical expertise and assistance facilities, and cooperative research and development opportunities in more than 600 laboratories and centers of all federal departments and agencies. These contacts may lead to licensing of technologies for new products and processes or to solutions of technical problems crucial to commercialization.

Home-Based Businesses

There are a number of Home Base Business Associations located throughout the state. Their primary goal is to network and share information. Often they also have guest speakers at their meetings or coordinate workshops in their communities. The following is a list of some of the established home base business associations. Other similar associations may be found by contacting your local Chamber of Commerce.

Bainbridge Island Chamber of Commerce
Home-Base Business Roundtable Forum
Sheri H. Mathis, Executive Director
590 Winslow Way East
Bainbridge Island, WA 98110
(206) 842-3700
Home Page: http://www.buslink.com/homebus

Charlie Barb, Rabecca Larson,
Gerri Schaff, co-chairs
Home-Based Business Roundtable
Mercer Isl. Chamber of Commerce
7601 SE 27th Street
Mercer Island, WA 98040
Phone: 232-3404

Linda McCarthy
Craft Networking
2811 S 301st Street
Federal Way, WA 98003
Phone: (206) 839-4747

Steve Veltkamp, President
Olympic Home-Based Business Association
1713 E 3rd Street
Port Angeles, WA 98362
Phone: (360) 452-2418

Connie Hinton
Issaquah Chamber Of Commerce
155 NW Gilman Blvd.
Issaquah, WA 98027
Phone: (206) 392-7024

Jennifer Robichaud
Redmond Chmb of Comm
16210 NE 80th
Redmond, WA 98052
Phone: (206) 885-4014

Innovative Concepts Program

Robin Congers, Program Manager
States Inventors Initiative, Battelle Pacific Northwest Lab
PO Box 999, K8-11
Richland, WA, 99352
(509) 372-4328   (509) 372-4369 fax   E-mail: rl_conger@pnl.gov
Moving an idea from a concept to the marketplace is a long and difficult climb. At each step, trials and pitfalls can hinder an innovators progress. The Department of Energy's Innovative Concepts Program (InnCon) is designed to help guide the inventors and small businesses with energy saving inventions through the process, providing financial, technical and market assistance. The InnCon Program provides seed money to allow innovators to determine if their ideas are technically and economically feasible. InnCon also provides valuable non-financial support by helping innovators find technical partners, commercial sponsors and new sources of funding.

InnCon operates in cycles of roughly 1-2 years. For each cycle an energy related topic is chosen and innovators are invited to submit proposals for funding. Typically 15 inventors are awarded seed money to explore the technical and economic feasibility of their concepts.

Innovation Assessment Center

180 Nickerson St., Suite 207
501 Johnson Tower, Washington State University
Seattle, WA 98109   Pullman, WA 99164-4851
(206) 464-5450   (509) 335-1576

The Small Business Development Center's Innovation Assessment Center provides objective evaluations designed to help inventors and owners of small businesses determine the potential commercial success of a new product, process, or service. A fee of $295 is charged for each evaluation and includes an educational packet, which may be purchased separately for $30. Inventions can be evaluated from the idea phase to fully developed market ready prototypes.

Job Service Center

Washington Employment Security Job Service Centers assist in matching local employer needs for qualified workers with job-ready applicants through job listings, applicant screening and referral, labor market information, tax credits and employer committees. *The Job Service Centers are currently changing many of their phone numbers. In addition, Wetern Washington is also undergoing a change in area codes. Should any of the following numbers be disconnected or out of service, please call 360-902-9585 for clarification.*

Aberdeen - (360) 533-9318	Mount Vernon - (360) 416-3500
Auburn - (206) 833-0102	North Seattle - (206) 440-2505
Bellevue - (206) 990-3770	Omak - (509) 826-7310
Bellingham - (360) 676-1521	Olympia - (360) 407-5100
Bingen -none	Pasco - (509) 545-3001
Bremerton - (360) 478-4941	Port Angeles - (360) 457-9407
Chehalis - (360) 748-2360	Renton - (206) 277-7160
Colville - (509) 684-7444	Seattle - (206) 721-6000
Ellensburg - none	Spokane - (509) 533-2004
Everett - (206) 339-4901	Sunnyside -(509) 837-4904
Interstate - none	Tacoma - (206) 593-7300
Kelso - (360) 577-2250	Vancouver - (360) 735-5000
Lakewood - (206) 589-6350	Walla Walla - (509) 527-4393
Lynnwood - (206) 712-0110	Wenatchee - (509) 665-6605
Moses Lake - (509) 766-2559	Yakima - (509) 574-0100

Office of State Procurement

Department of General Administration, Office of State Procurement
PO Box 41017
Olympia, WA 98504-1017
(360) 902-7400   Homepage: http:\olympus.dis.wa.gov

This Office is responsible for procuring goods and services which include such items as furniture, clothing, fuels, vehicles, office supplies, and janitorial services. There are more than 3,000 types of commodities purchased by OSP and by certain agencies and political subdivisions.

Businesses and individuals wishing to sell to OSP are advised to register on a state bidders' list through the "Suppliers Registration" Packet. To request a packet, you can call (360) 902-7401 or call OSP's Fax on Demand system at (360) 664-2444 and press 1,1,3,1.

SCORE Counseling

The Service Corps of Retired Executives (SCORE) is a program of the U.S. Small Business Administration comprised of men and women business executives who volunteer their time to share their management and technical expertise with present and prospective owners and managers of small businesses. Every effort is made to match a client's need with a counselor experienced in that line of business. Counseling is provided without charge to the client and is confidential. For an appointment, or for information about other counseling locations, call (509) 353-2820. Also, inquire about workshops on Starting a New Business; The Business Plan; Record Keeping; and Marketing which are presented each month for a nominal fee. *See County Listings for the SCORE representative in your area.*

SCORE Bellingham Chapter #591
Bellingham & Whatcom County EDC
1203 Cornwall St.
PO Box 2803
Bellingham, WA 98227
(360) 676-4255 Fax: (360) 647-9413
Counties Served: Island, San Juan, Skagit, Snohomish, Whatcom

SCORE Portland Chapter #11
222 SW Columbia
Portland, OR 97201
(503) 326-3441 Fax: (503) 326-3436
Counties Served: Clark, Cowlitz, Skamania, Wahkiakum

SCORE Seattle Chapter #55
1200 6th Ave, Suite 1700
Seattle, WA 98101-1128
(206) 553-7320 Fax: (206) 553-7044
Counties Served: Clallam, Grays Harbor, Jefferson, King, Pacific

SCORE Spokane Chapter #180
W. 1020 Riverside
Spokane, WA 99201
(509) 353-2820 Fax: (509) 353-2600
Counties Served: Adams, Asotin, Columbia, Ferry, Garfield, Lincoln, Pend Oreille, Spokane, Stevens, Whitman

SCORE Tacoma Chapter #385
C/O Tacoma/Pierce County Chamber of Commerce
950 Pacific Ave, Suite 300
PO Box 1933
Tacoma, WA 98401
(206) 627-2175 Fax: (206) 597-7305
Counties Served: Lewis, Mason, Pierce, Thurston

SCORE Mid Columbia Chapter #590
PO Box 1647
Yakima, WA 98907
(509) 574-4944 Fax: (509) 574-4943

Small Business Development Centers (SBDC's)

Small Business Development Center
WSU- Headquarters, Washington State
501 Johnson Tower
Pullman, WA 99164-4851
(509) 335-6415   harrisj@wsu.edu
E: Mail: true@wsuvm1.csc.wsu.edu

Business Assistance Center - SBDC
Department of Community, Trade and Economic Development
PO Box 48300
Olympia, WA 98504-8300
(360) 586-4854

Funded jointly with state and federal funds, the SBDC provides one-to-one counseling to small business firms, develops educational programs geared to the needs and interests of small business people, and coordinates and conducts research into general and technical small business problems throughout Washington.

SBDC counselors have considerable experience in the private sector, and offer a wide variety of management and technical assistance such as: new venture analysis; business plan analysis; purchase or sale of business; merchandising and advertising; financial records; plant layout; work-flow processing; and loan preparation assistance.

Educational programs are offered through a network of community colleges, four-year institutions and private sector organizations. These seminars and workshops feature instructors who are knowledgeable private sector practitioners. *See Workforce/Training for a list of community colleges and contact the one in your area. Also see County Listings for the SBDC in your area.*

Grays Harbor College
1602 Edward P. Smith Dr.
Aberdeen, WA 98520

Douglas Jones, Business Development Specialist
(360) 538-4021x245 Fax: (360) 538-4299

E-mail: djones@ctc.dtc.edu
Counties Served: Grays Harbor

Western Washington University
College of Business and Economics
308 Parks Hall
Bellingham, WA 98225-9073
Lynn Trzynka,
Business Development Specialist
(360) 676-3899   Fax: (360) 650-4844
E-mail: trzynka@cbe.wwu.edu
Counties Served: San Juan

Centralia College
600 West Locust Street
Centralia, WA 98531
Doug Benoit, Assoc. Dean of Instruction
(360) 736-9391x554 Fax: (360) 330-7504
Counties Served: Lewis

Columbia Basin College- TRIDEC
901 North Colorado
Kennewick, WA 98336
Glynn Lamberson-
Business Development Specialist
(509) 735-6222   Fax: (509) 735-6609
Counties Served: Benton, Franklin

Edmonds Community College
6600 196th St. SW (physical address)
20000 - 68th Avenue W
Lynnwood, WA 98036
Jack Wicks, Business Development Specialist
(206) 640-1435   Fax: (206) 640-1532
Counties Served: Snohomish

Business Development Center - BBCC
Big Bend Community College
7662 Chanute Street Bldg. 1500
Moses Lake, WA 98837-3299
Ed Baroch, Business Development Specialist
(509) 762-6289   Fax: (509) 762-6289
E-mail: edb@bigbend.cdc.edu
Counties Served: Adams, Grant, Lincoln

Skagit Valley College
2405 College Way
Mount Vernon, WA 98273
Peter Stroosma,
Business Development Specialist
(360) 428-1282   Fax: (360) 336-6116
Counties Served: Island, Skagit, Whatcom

OCCED- Okanogan County EDC
Wenatchee Valley College

PO Box 741
203 S. Second
Okanogan, WA 98840
John Rayburn,
Small Business Development Counselor
(509) 826-5107   Fax: (509) 826-1812
E-mail: occed@televar.com
Counties Served: Okanogan

S. Puget Sound Comm. College
2001 Mottman Rd. SW
Olympia, WA 98512-6292
Douglas Hammel,
Business Development Specialist
(360) 753-5616   Fax: (360) 586-5493
Counties Served: Mason, Thurston

Small Business Development Center
102 East Front Street
PO Box 1085
Port Angeles, WA 98362
Kathleen Purdy,
Business Development Specialist
(360) 457-7793   Fax: (360) 452-9618
E-mail: kpurdy@olympus.net
Counties Served: Clallam, Jefferson,
Klickitat,

Small Business Development Center
Washington State University
501 Johnson Tower
Pullman, WA 99164-4851
Joe Harris, Business Development Specialist
(509) 335-6415   Fax: (509) 335-0949
E-mail: harrisj@wsu.edu
Counties Served: Asotin, Garfield, Whitman

Small Business Development Center
180 Nickerson, Suite 207
Seattle, WA 98109
Warner Wong, Business Development
Specialist
(206) 464-5460   Fax: (206) 464-6357
Counties Served: King

S. Seattle Community College
Duwamish Industrial Ed Center
6770 E. Marginal Way South
Seattle, WA 98108
Ruth Ann Halford,
Business Development Specialist
(206) 768-6855   Fax: (206) 764-5838
Counties Served: King

Community Colleges of Spokane

SIRTI Building
655 North Riverpoint Blvd.
Spokane, WA 99202
Mary Alice Brown,
Business Development Specialist
(509) 358-7546   Fax: (509) 358-7680
E-mail: mabrown@wsu.edu
Counties Served: Ferry, Pend Oreille, Spokane,
Stevens

Small Business Development Center
PO Box 1933
950 Pacific Suite #300
Tacoma, WA 98401-1933
Neil Delisanti,
Business Development Specialist
(206) 272-7232   Fax: (206) 597-7395
E-mail: delisant@wsuvm1.csc.wsu.edu
Counties Served: Kittitas, Pierce

Columbia River Economic Development Council
401 W. 13th Street
Vancouver, WA 98660
Janet Harte
(360) 693-2555   Fax: (360) 696-6431

harte@vancouver.wsu.edu
Counties Served: Clark, Cowlitz, Pacific, Skamania, Wahkiakum

Walla Walla Community College
500 Tausick Way
Walla Walla, WA 99362
Rich Monacelli,
Business Development Specialist
(509) 527-4681   Fax: (509) 525-3101
Counties Served: Columbia, Walla Walla

Wenatchee Valley College
1300 Fifth Street
Wenatchee, WA 98801
Jim Montzheimer
(509) 662-1651   Fax: (509) 664-2576
Counties Served: Chelan, Douglas

Yakima Valley College
PO Box 1647
16th & Nob Hill
Yakima, WA 98907
Corey Hansen
(509) 454-3608   Fax: (509) 454-4155
E-mail: yvccsbdc@televar.com
Counties Served: Yakima

Spokane Intercollegiate Research & Technology Institute
Terry Chambers, Coordinator
665 North Riverpoint Blvd.
Spokane, WA 99202-1665
(509) 358-2042   Fax: (509)358-2019
E-mail: terryc@sirti.org   Internet Web Site: www.sirti.org

SIRTI's Technology Enterprise Development Initiative helps start-up, small and medium-sized companies in manufacturing, environmental and information technologies, as well as biotechnologies, to speed commercial development of innovative new products and processes, and to utilize existing technologies to their greatest advantage.

*   **Business Assistance & Commercialization Services–** Help in analyzing industry trends, market niches, business strategies and commercialization steps necessary for small and emerging entrepreneurial activities; seasoned business counsel from experienced developers.
*   **Technical Assistance–** Solutions to technical problems through a network of faculty, scientists, engineers and technicians from area higher education institutions, as well as local industry experts.
*   **Specialized Facilities & Resources–** State-of-the-art laboratories for rent to run simulations, test new products, try-before-you-buy & off-the-shelf technologies; includes biodevelopment, software engineering, digital media and others.
*   **Grant Support–** funding to help move good ideas off drawing boards and into the marketplace on a per project basis. SIRTI Requests for Proposal (RFPs) published regularly.
*   **Training–** Programs in electronic commerce (including electronic data interchange), and fluid power technologies (hydraulics & pneumatics) offered regularly. Call for a schedule. Advanced training in a number of state-of-the-art technologies presented in cooperation with industry sponsors and vendors.

Washington Technology Center

University of Washington
PO Box 352140, Fluke Hall
Seattle, WA 98195
(206) 685-1920

Washington State University
PO Box 641030
Pullman WA 99164
(509) 335-6424

The Washington Technology Center (WTC) is the state's "industry-university" enterprise committed to meeting industry needs in commercially promising research, technology development and transfer. Industry and federal agencies may benefit from collaborative agreements with the Center to develop technologies for specific commercial applications.

Two recent programs, Entrepreneur's Access and Focused Technology Initiatives, offer unique opportunities for entrepreneurs and small-to medium-sized businesses in Washington to participate in proof-of-concept, feasibility or prototype development of innovative technologies. WTC also provides access to cost-centered equipment for use by industry, as well as technology information that can link company needs with development capabilities.

Intellectual properties developed by the Center are licensed and transferred with a priority to Washington businesses capable of creating a commercial success.

Research programs are underway in laboratories at the University of Washington in Seattle, Washington State University in Pullman, and other WSU research and agricultural units throughout Washington in the areas of biotechnology, electronic materials and design, manufacturing technology, bio-materials, applications of virtual reality, computer systems and microsensors.

Export

Center For International Trade In Forest Products (CINTRAFOR)

The Center for International Trade in Forest Products at the University of Washington responds to opportunities and problems related to the export and import of wood products. CINTRAFOR sponsors continuing education and outreach programs such as symposia, seminar series, graduate education, and research on forest product technology, export markets and trade analyses.

City of Seattle Division of International Affairs

Keith Orton, Chief International Specialist
210 Municipal Building
600 Fourth Avenue
Seattle, Washington 98104
(206) 684-8266   Fax: (206) 684-8267

The Division of International Affairs manages the City's international areas of trade, protocol, tourism, and educational and cultural exchange. The Division functions as the city's liaison with the Consular Corp with the public non-profit and business organizations involved in international activities. Other functions include managing Seattle's sister city program and publishing the Seattle Datasheet (an economic and demographic profile of the Seattle area).

Export Finance Assistance Center of Washington (EFACW)

Warren A. Gross, Managing Director & President
Nancy M. Carlson, Vice President
2001 Sixth Avenue, Suite 650
Seattle, WA 98121
(206) 553-5615   Fax: (206) 464-7230

The Export Assistance Center (EFACW) is a private, non-profit corporation which contracts with the State of Washington through the Department of Community, Trade & Economic Development to provide State-paid assistance to established Washington domiciled small and medium sized businesses to become more active in exporting. The EFACW is the "City/State" representative of the Export-Import Bank of the United States and is conveniently co-located with the U.S. Department of Commerce and other federally sponsored trade promotion entities in the U.S. Export Assistance Center in Seattle.

Specifically, the EFACW works with its clients to:
- Identify the risk elements of export transactions and advise on structuring of terms and financing options;
- Locate appropriate lenders, sureties and other financing intermediates to insure, guarantee or fund export financing;
- Assist in the preparation of applications for export-related financing involving both government and private sector resources.

Export Hotline and TradeBank
International Strategies, Inc.
11 Beacon Street, Suite 1100
Boston, MA 02108
(800) 873-9767   Fax: (617) 292-7788 Internet: http://www.exportweb.com
The Export Hotline has business information on 80 countries and 50 industries which is updated twice weekly and includes: trade barriers, financing, distribution, shipping, business etiquette, risks & advisories, key contacts, investment regulation, direct marketing, import issues, trade shows, NAFTA, EU & WTO, government programs, how to export and sample documents. The Trade Bank provides contacts to find new international and domestic trading partners, trade leads, sources and statistics, including:
- Full contact information on 15,000 companies seeking international business.
- U.S. Department of Commerce TOPS leads, updated twice weekly.
- Export statistics for the leading 25 importing countries for the last three years.

These services of the Export Hotline and TradeBank are provided free of charge. The service is underwritten by UPS, AT&T, INC. Magazine, Blenheim Exhibitions, The Journal of Commerce, U.S. Council for International Business and the National Association of Manufacturers, in cooperation with the U.S. Department of Commerce.

Export-Import Bank of the United States (Eximbank)
(See Finance Section for a description of the financing programs offered by the Export-Import Bank, and Export Assistance Center (EFACW) in this Export Section for contact information and assistance in developing proposals and preparation of applications for Eximbank's programs)

Foundation for Russian-American Economic Cooperation
Carol Vipperman, President
1932 1st Avenue, Suite 803
Seattle, WA 98101
(206) 443-1935
Fax: (206) 443-0954
The purpose of the Foundation is to foster economic development and business activities between the Pacific Northwest and the Former Soviet Union (FSU). Specifically, the Foundation provides a resource center for information on busienss development and offers public events and seminars with visiting Russians and U.S. experts regarding trade and the business climate in the FSU.

International Marketing Program
Washington State Department of Agriculture
Meg Van Schoorl, Managing Director

PO Box 42560
Olympia, WA 98504-2560
(360) 902-1915   Fax: (360) 902-2089
The WSDA International Marketing Program assists Washington's food and agriculture companies to sell their products, technologies and services internationally. Export-ready firms can use WSDA's Agricultural Trade Representatives in Japan, Taiwan, Mexico and China to enter markets and connect with qualified buyers. Companies also get hands-on help with export market research, planning and phytosanitary regulations through staff and its network of regional contractors. The department also arranges buyer missions, trade show participation and publishes a directory of 1,300 Washington State food and agricultural suppliers.

International Marketing Program For Agricultural Commodities And Trade (IMPACT) Center

Washington State University, College of Agricultural and Home Economics
A. Desmond O'Rourke, Director
104 Hulbert Hall
Pullman, WA 99164-6214
(509) 335-6653   Fax: (509) 335-3958
Internet Web Site: http://coope.xt.cahe.. wsu.edu/ impact
The IMPACT Center was established at Washington State University in 1985. Its goal is to apply socio-economics and technical expertise to problems and opportunities faced by agricultural exporters. The IMPACT Center supports the work of scientists in many different disciplines. Results of IMPACT Center studies are reported both in scientific journals and in popular media. Information Series reports are designed to be read by the typical farmer or business person and can be purchased from the IMPACT Center. Additional technical reports are available on request.

International Programs

Washington State University, Dr. James B. Henson, Director
328 French Administration Building
Pullman, WA 99164-1034
(509) 335-2541   Fax: (509) 335-1060 E-mail: henson@ wsu.edu
International Programs at Washington State University has responsibility for the international activities of the university. These include a range of on-campus and overseas activities which are student experiences, including study abroad, internships, and associated activities; faculty exchanges and participation; collaborative education, research and public service activities with universities and institutes in other countries; economic development projects, contracts and other development activities in many countries of the world; and a special emphasis on collaboration with private sector organizations in the state of Washington and elsewhere. The university has established and implements geographic education, research, and economic development networks in the Asia/Pacific region; the Middle East; Africa; Western Europe; and the Newly Independent States.

International Trade Institute

North Seattle Community College, Katherine Riley, Associate Dean
9600 College Way North
Seattle, WA 98103
(206) 527-3732   Fax: (206) 527-3729
The ITI is a resource center providing professional training and counseling in the practical aspects of international trade. They offer non-credit seminars, workshops, and a 30-credit certificate program through the Business Division.

Japan-America Society of The State of Washington

Susan S. Mochizuki, Executive Director
1800 Ninth Avenue, Suite 1550 *
Seattle, WA 98101-1332

(206) 623-7900   Fax: (206) 343-7930 E-mail: jassw@us-japan.org
Society Website Location: http://www.us-japan.org/jassw
The Japan-America Society serves as a statewide forum for educational programs concerning the business, economic, political, and cultural relations between the peoples of Japan and the U.S. Programs include lectures, discussion groups, orientation sessions, conferences and seminars on a variety of timely topics. JAS also sponsors Japanese art exhibitions and performing arts events, supports Japanese language programs, provides general information to the public and publishes a monthly newsletter.

Palouse Economic Development Council
AgriTechnics International Program, Paul Hirsch
1345 NE Terre View Drive
Pullman, Washington 99163-5101
(509) 334-3579   Fax: (509) 332-6991 E-Mail: paul@palouse.org
World Wide Web page: http://www.palouse.org/ati/index.htm
AgriTechnics International provides market research and trade development services for eastern Washington agribusiness and forest products companies.

Small Business Development Center/North Seattle Community College (SBDC/NSCC)
SBDC/NSCC U.S. Export Assistance Center
Ann Tamura, Export Development Specialist
2001 Sixth Ave, Suite 650
Seattle, WA 98121
(206) 553-0052   Fax: (206) 553-7253 E-mail: atamura@doc.gov
The Small Business Development Center/North Seattle Community College located at the US Export Assistance Center provides international business counseling, training and related technical assistance to entrepreneurs, small business owners and operators in order to improve their potential for business success in a global economic environment. The SBDC/NSCC, in a unique partnership with the WA State Small Business Center and the US Small Business Administration, accomplishes these objectives through linking resources of Federal, State and local governments, the educational community and the private sector to meet the specialized and complex needs of the increasingly diverse small business community. North Seattle Community College serves the Pacific Northwest with programs offered on the practical aspects of conducting business in foreign markets.

Trade and Market Development
Department of Community, Trade & Economic Development
2001 6th Ave, Suite 2600
Seattle, WA 98121
(206) 464-7143   Fax: (206) 464-7222
The Trade and Market Development Division works to expand targeted export markets. Target markets include Canada, Western Europe, Japan, Mexico, China, Taiwan, Hong Kong, and emerging markets. The division maintains a public trade and business library. The office distributes state trade statistics; publishes *The Export/Import Guide, The Trader*, a bi-monthly newsletter and industry directories; organizes trade missions; participates in trade shows; and manages state offices in Europe, Japan, Russia and Taiwan. One on one counseling is available by appointment.

Trade Development Alliance of Greater Seattle
Bill Stafford, Executive Director
Lisa Seller Fitzpatrick, Customer Service
Sam Kaplan, Communications
1301 Fifth Avenue, Suite 2400
Seattle, WA 98101
(206) 389-7301   Fax: (206) 624-5689
Internet: http://www.pan.ci.seattle.wa.us/business/tda/tda.htm

---

The Trade Alliance is a joint venture between the Greater Seattle Chamber of Commerce, Port of Seattle, Metropolitan King County, City of Seattle and organized labor. Its mission is to promote the Greater Seattle region in targeted foreign and domestic markets as one of North America's premier international gateways and commercial centers.

U.S. Department of Commerce, U.S. and Foreign Commercial Service,

Seattle Office:
Lisa Kjaer, District Director
2001 Sixth Avenue, Suite 650
Seattle, Washington 98121
(206) 553-7251   Fax: (206) 553-7253

Tri Cities Branch Office
Mark Weaver
320 N. Johnson Street, Suite 350
Kennewick, Washington 99336
(509) 737-2751   Fax: (509) 783-3394

The U.S. and Foreign Commercial Service, International Trade Administration (ITA), U.S. Department of Commerce provides businesses with a range of services to help them export. Market identification, assistance with making contacts with foreign buyers, foreign business credit references and checks, information on regulations, workshops, reference library and overseas export promotion are all services provided by the US FCS. There are 125 overseas offices located in major markets worldwide.

U.S. Small Business Administration (SBA)

These offices provide the following export trade development services for potential and existing small business exporters. Counseling and training through our affiliates; Legal assistance program; Macro international marketing information reports; Publications; Referral to other private/public sector international programs; Financial assistance of up to 80% loan guarantee to lending institutions transectional financing for export working capital loan guarantees, and both a Business Information Center in Spokane and a Business Enterprise Center in Seattle with a library of business information and computerized programs available to the public. *See also 1) Business & Technical Assistance Section for information on the Business Information Center and Business Enterprise Center, 2) Finance Section for information on SBA loan export Loan Programs* and *3) Electronic Bulletin Board and Internet Access (Homepage, File Transfer Protocol, Gopher and Telnet).*

U. S. Small Business Administration
Ted Anderson, District International Trade Specialist
601 West 1st Avenue, 10th Floor East
Spokane, Washington 99204
(509) 353-2803   Fax: (509) 353-2829

Pru Balatero, Export Trade Finance Officer
U.S. Export Assistance Center
2001 6th Avenue, Suite 650
Seattle, Washington 98121
(206) 553-5615   Fax: (206)553-5615

Minority and Women's Export Assistance Program

Business Assistance Center
2001 6th Ave, Suite 2700
Seattle, WA 98121
(206) 389-2562   Fax: (206) 464-5868
Minority and Women's Export Assistance Program provides 1) export training and counseling, 2) export market research, 3) referrals to private and public trade professional consultants, 4) coordination of participation in international trade related events, 5) seminars on the export process, and 6) organization and leadership on international trade missions.

Washington State International Trade Fair

Theresa Bagg, Executive Director
999 3rd Avenue, Suite 1020

Seattle, WA 98104
(206) 682-6900
Fax: (206) 682-6190
Washington State International Trade Fair serves the state's business by identifying key international trade shows best suited to sepcific products, by working wiht company principals to prepare for foreign trade shows and by assisting firms mangae the costs and risks associated with foreign trade exhibitions.

Washington Council on Internatioal Trade
Patricia Davis, President
2615 4th Avenue, Suite 350
Seattle, WA 98121
(206) 443-3826
Fax: (206) 443-3828
The Washington Council on International Trade (WCIT) is a private, non-profit association supported by corporate and individual members. WCIT members share a common dedication to maintaining strong two-way trade between the U.S. and its trading parteners. WCIT concentrates on analysis and elucidation of key public policy issues in international trade and economic affairs, and on issues of U.S. trade with individual trade partners abroad. While the Council directs the bulk of its program activity to tis members, it serves the broader public through its work with the media and educational institutions and through public presentations by WCIT staff.

World Trade Center Tacoma
Constance T. Bacon, Executive Director
Peter F. Dodds, Programs and Operations Director
3600 Port of Tacoma Road, Suite 309
Tacoma, WA 98424
(206) 383-9474   Fax: (206) 926-0384
The World Trade Centers Association started in 1970 and has become one of the world's premier international business organizations. There are over 280 World Trade Centers in 80 countries serving over 400,000 businesses around the world.

The World Trade Center Tacoma serves its members by providing hands on custom trade services to small and medium sized businesses with the goal of achieving bottom line outcomes. Services include trade research and information, database access, meeting rooms, business seminars, trade mission assistance, WTC Club membership, access to NETWORK– a closed global computer system for messaging and buying or selling products or services– and skill development for companies to profitably respond to trade opportunities.

WTCTA works one-on-one with companies to connect them to specific trading partners, exchange product data, assist in packaging, arrange financing and offers counsel on cultural issues that might impact successful transactions.

World Trade Club
Cindy Firmani, Executive Director
PO Box 21488
Seattle, Washington 98111
(206) 448-8803   Fax: (206) 448-3531
The World Trade Club provides a forum for the business community to acquire practical skills in international marketing, finance, and import/export procedures, to receive briefings on international trade issues, to expand the understanding of business practices of U.S. trading partners and to develop long term strategic contacts to advance international business.

World Trade Committee Of Greater Vancouver
Greater Vancouver Chamber of Commerce, Cathy Green, President

Vancouver, WA 98663
(206) 694-2588   Fax: (206) 693-8279
The World Trade Committee of Greater Vancouver provides a public forum and an opportunity to exchange information on issues and practical ideas on how to deal in foreign markets.

Finance

Child Care Facility Fund
Department of Community, Trade & Economic Development
PO Box 48300
Olympia, WA 98504-8300
(360) 586-3023
This fund provides financial and technical assistance to businesses to start or expand employer-based child care facilities. Applications for loans and grants are approved by a board with expertise in financing and child care.

Cascadia Revolving Fund
David Kleiber-Associate Director (Loan Information)
Patty Grossman, Executive Director (Investment Information)
157 Yesler Way, Suite 414
Seattle, WA 98104
(206) 447-9226   Fax: (206) 682-4804   E-mail: cascadia@scn.org
Cascadia is a private, non-profit community development loan fund. Socially-concerned individuals and organizations deposit funds with Cascadia which are pooled and lent to small businesses which cannot access traditional sources of credit, especially those owned by women and minorities, businesses located in distressed communities (high unemployment areas) and businesses that restore and/or preserve the environment. Cascadia's Revolving Loan Fund covers all counties in the State of Washington. Maximum loan is $150,000 with no minimum amount (though loans are generally above $5,000). Cascadia is currently developing a Rural Development Investment Fund to make equity investments in small businesses located in rural areas of Washington and Oregon involved in value-added wood products, value-added fish products, alternative agriculture and manufacturing from recycled materials. Investments may be made as preferred stock, subordinated debt or a "Participation Agreement" (low interest loans with a revenue-based "kicker").

Coastal Loan Program
Department of Community, Trade & Economic Development
PO Box 48300
Olympia, WA 98504-8300
(360) 753-0325
This fund was designed to mitigate economic hardships in Jefferson, Clallam, Grays Harbor, Pacific, and Wahkiakum counties. This fund provides business and technical assistance loans to private businesses, local governments, and quasi-governmental organizations. Loans are approved by local loan review boards serving the north and south coast areas. Business borrowers must demonstrate job creation and private investment to qualify for loans up to $150,000. Loans may be used for land, buildings, equipment and working capital, but not to refinance existing debt. The program provides technical assistance loans up to $30,000 for public agencies and $20,000 for businesses. Public agencies and businesses can use technical assistance loans for feasibility studies and planning projects that benefit the community and create jobs, especially for dislocated workers. *See County Listings for the Finance Specialist who can help package loan proposals in your area.*

Community Development Block Grant Float Loan Program
Department of Community, Trade & Economic Development
PO Box 48300

Olympia, WA 98504-8300
(360) 753-0325
This program uses federal CDBG funds as a source of interim financing for business projects that are able to secure an irrevocable letter of credit and are willing to commit to making jobs available to low-income people. To obtain financing, the business must be located in a small cities CDBG-eligible jurisdiction.

Community Development Finance Program
Department of Community, Trade & Economic Development
PO Box 48300
Olympia, WA 98504-8300
(360) 753-0325
The Community Development Finance Program is available to help business secure long-term expansion loans. Five finance specialists work to market public financing programs and to structure small business project applications that leverage private investment, generate tax revenue, and create or retain jobs. They also work with businesses to review project proposal, determine financing alternatives, design a financing structure, prepare and assemble application materials, and present projects to appropriate lending authorities. The program's priority projects include creating employment opportunities in high unemployment and timber-impact areas of the state, creation and retention of family wage jobs and to support minority and women owned business development. Loan Programs are available for real estate, new construction, renovation, major leasehold improvements, machinery, equipment, and working capital.

Community Development Finance specialists assist with the packaging of loans for a variety of programs, including: SBA 504, SBA 7(a), local revolving funds, USDA Rural Development Administration Loan Programs, Bureau of Indian Affairs loan and business development grant programs, WA CDBG Float Loan Program, WA Community Economic Revitalization Board, WA Development Loan Fund, Coastal Revolving Loan Fund, Forest Products RLF, and Industrial Revenue Bonds. Community Development Finance staff are outstationed and regularly call on local Economic Development Councils in rural areas. Contact the Olympia office or *See County Listings for the Finance Specialist in your area:*

Development Loan Fund
Department of Community, Trade & Economic Development
PO Box 48300
Olympia, WA 98504-8300
(360) 753-0325
The Development Loan Fund provides gap financing for businesses which will create new jobs or retain existing jobs, particularly for lower-income persons, in non-entitlement areas of the state experiencing high unemployment. Priority is given to timber-dependent and distressed area projects. DLF may lend up to $350,000, in participation with private lenders, and in special cases up to $700,000.

Town of Almira Revolving Loan Fund
Gene Scammon, Mayor
Box 215
Almira, WA 99103
(509) 639-2601
Trade Area: City of Almira

Rural Development Loan Fund
The Lending Network
Tani K. Allen, Manager
1611 N. National Ave. -PO Box 916
Chehalis, WA 98352
(360) 748-0114   Fax: (360) 748-1238

Trade Area: Lewis, Cowlitz, South Thurston

Joint Development Fund (JDF)
SEED Council, Inc.
Bonita Scherling, Administrator
PO Box 98
Clarkston, WA 99403
(509) 758-5868   Fax: (509) 758-1309
E-mail: bscherl@lcsc.edu
Trade Area: Garfield, Columbia, Asotin, Whitman

Rural Opportunity Fund-
TRICO Economic Development District
Forrest Miller, Loan Director
347 W 2nd, SUITE A
Colville, WA 99114
(800) 776-7318   Fax: (509) 684-4788
E-mail: fmiller@plix.com
Trade Area: Ferry, Stevens, Pend Oreille,
Rural Spokane, Lincoln, Grant, Adams,
Whitman, Garfield, Asotin

Micro Loan Fund
Snohomish County Private Industry
Council
Lynette Chen-Wagner, Loan Officer
917 134th St. SW
Everett, WA 98204
(206) 743-9669   Fax: (206) 742-1177
Trade Area: Adams, Chelan, Douglas,
Grant,
King, Kitsap, Kittitas, Klickitat, Okanogan,
Pierce, Skagit, Snohomish, Whatcom, Yakima

Rural Enterprise Loan Fund
Snohomish County Private Industry
Council
Lynette Chen-Wagner, Loan Officer
917 134th St. SW
Everett, WA 98204
(206) 743-9669   Fax: (206) 742-1177
Trade Area: Island, King, Pierce, San Juan,
Skagit, Snohomish, Whatcom

Okanogan County Investment Association (OCIA)
F. Vern Dwight, Executive Director
PO Box 741
Okanogan, WA 98840
(509) 826-5107   Fax: (509) 826-1012
E-mail: occed@televar.com
Olympic Micro Loan Fund

Clallam County Economic Development Council
Marny Hannan, Office Manager
PO Box 1085
Port Angeles, WA 98361
(360) 457-7793   Fax: (360) 452-9618
Trade Area: Clallam, Grays Harbor, Jefferson,
Mason, Pacific, Thurston,Wahkiakum
Conservation Loan Fund
Shoretrust Trading Group
John Berdes, Managing Director
P O Box 826
Port of Ilwaco, WA 98624

Micro Loan Fund
Ellensburg Business Development Authority
Eve Clark, Executive Director
PO Box 598
Ellensburg, WA 98926-0598
(509) 962-7244   Fax: (509) 962-7141
E-mail: ebdainc@adsnet.net
Trade Area: Kittitas

Cowlitz-Wahkiakum
City of Longview Revolving Loan
Walt Barham, Loan Manager
PO Box 128
Longview, WA 98632
(360) 425-9226   Fax: (360) 577-4014
E-mail: longview@aone.com
Trade Area: Cowlitz, Wahkiakum

Revolving Loan Fund
Skagit Council of Governments
Kelley Moldstad, Executive Director
204 Montgomery St.
Mt. Vernon, WA 98273
(360) 428-1299   Fax: (360) 336-6116
Trade Area: Skagit

Skagit Council of Government Revolving
Loan Fund
Skagit Council of Governments
Kelley Moldstad, Executive Director
204 Montgomery
Mount Vernon, WA 98273
(360) 428-1299   Fax: (360) 336-6116
Trade Area: Skagit

The Washington Entrepreneur's Guide

(360) 642-4265   Fax: (360) 642-4078
E-mail: diane@ecotrust.org
Trade Area: Grays Harbor, Pacific, Wahkiakum

Tri-Cities Enterprise Association
Group Lending Program
Micro Equity Fund
Micro Loan Program
Johan M. Curtiss, Micro Loan Manager
2000 Logston Blvd.
Richland, WA 99352
(509) 375-3268   Fax: (509) 375-4838
E-mail: jcurtiss@owt.com
Homepage: http://www.owt.com/tea
Trade Area: Benton, Franklin

Regional Revolving Loan Fund
Benton-Franklin Regional Council
Tom DiDomenico, Economic Development Manager
PO Box 217
Richland, WA 99352
(509) 943-9185   Fax: (509) 943-6756
E-mail: bfrc@cbvcp.com
Trade Area: Benton, Franklin

Minority and Women's Revolving Loan Program
Northwest Business Development Co.
Rene Werner, Loan Officer
421 W. Riverside, Suite 210
Spokane, WA 99201
(509) 458-8555   Fax: (509) 458-8553
Trade Area: Spokane

Spokane Area Small Business Loan Program
Northwest Business Development Co.
Tony Rund, Administrator
421 W. Riverside Ave., Suite 210
Spokane, WA 99201
(509) 458-8555   Fax: (509) 458-8553
Trade Area: Spokane

Columbia Gorge Small Business Loan Fund
Skamania County EDC
Peggy Bryan, Executive Assistant
PO Box 436
Stevenson, WA 98648
(509) 427-5110   Fax: (509) 427-5122
E-mail: sced@xws.com
Trade Area: Skamania, Eastern Clark

Skamania County EDC Revolving Loan Fund
Skamania County EDC
Peggy Bryan, Executive Assistant
PO Box 436
Stevenson, WA 98648

(509) 427-5110   Fax: (509) 427-5122
E-mail: scedc@xws.com
Trade Area: Skamania, Western Klickitat

CEO Micro Loan Program
Center for Economic Opportunity
Teresa Lemmons, Program Manager
919 South 9th St.
Tacoma, WA 98405
(206) 591-7026   Fax: (206) 593-2744
Trade Area: Pierce

Pierce County Community
Investment Corporation (CIC)
Denise Dyer, Loan Officer
4916 Center St., Suite H
Tacoma, WA 98409-2360
(206) 591-7205   Fax: (206) 596-6604
E-mail: ddyer@co.pierce.wa
Trade Area: Pierce County

Pierce County Revolving Loan Fund
Pierce County Office of Economic Development
Denise Dyer, Loan Officer
4916 Center St., Suite H
Tacoma, WA 98409-2360
(206) 591-7205   Fax: (206) 596-6604
E-mail: ddyer@co.pierce.wa
Trade Area: Pierce County, except City of Tacoma

Tacoma Redevelopment Authority Loan Fund
Tacoma Redevelopment Authority
Patricia Hughes-Raber, Business Loan Specialist
747 Market St., Room 800
Tacoma, WA 98402-3793
(206) 591-5213   Fax: (206) 591-2002
Trade Area: City of Tacoma

Revolving Loan Fund
Mid-Columbia Economic Development District
Steve Schafroth, Loan Program Manager
400 East Scenic Drive, Suite 343
The Dalles, OR 97058
(503) 296-2266   Fax: (503) 296-3283
Trade Area: Klickitat, Skamania

Quest Revolving Loan Fund
Quest for Economic Development
Loan Manager
327 E. Penny Road, Suite D
Wenatchee, WA 98801
(509) 662-8016   Fax: (509) 663-0455
E-mail: quest@televar.com
Trade Area: Chelan, Douglas

Walla Walla Area Small Business Loan Fund-
Walla Walla Area Small Business Center
Richard L. Monacelli, Business Development Specialist
500 Tausick Way
Walla Walla, WA   99362
(509) 527-4681   Fax: (509) 525-3101
Trade Area: Walla Walla and vicinity

Washington Association of Minority
Entrepreneurs (WAME)
Luz Bazan Gutierrez, Executive Director
24 S 3rd Ave
Yakima, WA 98902
(509) 453-5133   Fax: (509) 453-5165
I. YAKIMA COUNTY MICRO LOAN PROGRAM
Trade Area: Yakima County
II. YAKIMA COUNTY REGIONAL
MICROENTERPRISE REVOLVING LOAN FUND
Trade Area: Yakima County
III. SBA PREQUALIFICATION PROGRAM
Trade Area: Yakima County/Eastern Washington area.

Economic Development Councils

Economic Development Councils across the state provide local business assistance resources, community profiles, business seminars, industrial site information, export assistance and finance assistance to small business wishing to expand their operation, and entrepreneurs who wish to start a business. Economic Development Councils also have access to many of the resources in this directory and can often provide written information on programs and provide referrals. *See County Listings for the Economic Development Council in your area.*

Evergreen Community Development Association

506 - 2nd Avenue, Suite #1310
Seattle, WA 98104
(206) 622-3731   Fax: (206) 623-6613
A U.S. Small Business Administration licensed development corporation which provides SBA 504 funding for eligible businesses. *See also U.S. Small Business Administration 504 Program in the Finance Section.*

Export-Import Bank of the United States (Eximbank)

The Export Assistance Center (EFACW)
Warren A. Gross, Managing Director & President
Nancy M. Carlson, Vice President
2001 Sixth Avenue, Suite 650
Seattle, WA 98121
(206) 553-5615   Fax: (206) 464-7230
The Export Assistance Center (EFACW) is the "City/State" representative of the Export-Import Bank of the United States and is conveniently co-located with the U.S. Department of Commerce and other federally sponsored trade promotion entities in the U.S. Export Assistance Center in Seattle. Eximbank is the U.S. government agency that facilitates the export financing of U.S. goods and services. Eximbank helps exporters compete against foreign government subsidized financing in overseas markets. Eximbank offers four major export finance support programs:

- **Lending Programs-** Eximbank's loans provide competitive, fixed rate financing for U.S. export sales of capital equipment and services. Eximbank extends loans to foreign buyers of U.S. Exports and intermediary loans to fund responsible parties that extend loans to foreign buyers. These loans are made at low, fixed rates.

- **Guarantee Program-** Guarantees provide repayment protection for private sector loans to credit-worthy foreign buyers of U.S. goods and services. The guarantees cover for both political and commercial risks.
- **Working Capital Guarantee Program-** This program can help small and medium sized exporters obtain financing needed to produce and market goods for sale abroad. Eximbank also offers guarantees to lenders to encourage loans to businesses to buy, build or market products for export.
- **Insurance-** The insurance program, administered by the Foreign Credit Insurance Association, offers insurance policies to protect U.S. exporters and financial institutions against the political and commercial risks of nonpayment by foreign debtors. Policies exist for small or new-to-export businesses.

Finance Companies- SBA 7a Qualified

There are fourteen SBA QUALIFIED FINANCE COMPANIES which were licensed by the SBA during the Carter Administration. All fourteen can make SBA guaranteed loans and SBA 504 loans anywhere nationally. Historically, the most active has been The Money Store, which is the largest SBA lender in the country. During the last five years, other SBA finance companies have opened offices in the state and entered the Washington market, including AT&T Capital and GE Capital Small Business Finance. These companies compete with each other and banks to make SBA guaranteed loans. They will compete both on interest rate and approving loans which banks may not approve. For a list of all fourteen qualified finance companies, call Jean LaForce, Director of the Financial Institutions Branch of the U.S. Small Business Administration at (202) 205-6493. Below are the finance companies aggressively marketing within Washington State:

AT&T Capital Corporation
Michael H. Brown, Regional Account Manager
2020 Lakewood Drive, Suite 222
Coeur d'Alene, ID 83814
Fax: (509) 325-8762
(208) 666-0502

The Money Store–
Eastern Washington
316 W. Boone, Suite 250
Spokane, WA 99201
(800) 722-3066
Fax: (208) 666-0613

AT & T Capital Corporation-Western Washington
Sam Kerley, Regional Account Manager
22525 SE 64th Place, Room 216
Issaquah, WA 98027
(206) 557-3653
Fax: (206) 557-3605

The Money Store-Western Washington
155 108th Ave. NE, Suite 705
Bellevue, WA 98004
(800) 722-3066
Fax: (206) 646-9327

GE Capital Small Business Finance
12006 98th Avenue NE, Suite 200
Kirkland, WA 98304
(206) 823-1980   Fax: (206) 823-0575   Pager: (800) 209-0470
E-mail: cccef.smorreal@capital.ge.com

Forest Product Revolving Loan Fund

Department of Community, Trade & Economic Development
PO Box 48300
Olympia, WA 98504-8300
(360) 753-0325
These funds provide technical, marketing, and financial assistance to Washington's small and medium sized forest products companies. Loans up to $500,000 are available to secondary wood products companies. The program encourages business development in value-added wood products that better use forest resources.

HUD Section 108 Program
Department of Community, Trade & Economic Development
PO Box 48300
Olympia, WA 98504-8300
(360) 753-0325
This program is used to attract and leverage private sector funds by pledging future state CDBG awards as security for loans which meet established criteria. To qualify, businesses must be sponsored by a small cities CDBG-eligible jurisdiction. In addition, projects must meet CDBG eligibility requirements, demonstrate financing gaps, and produce economic opportunities for low to moderate income people. The federal Department of Housing and Urban Development makes the final decision on the guarantee once the state CDBG pledge is in place.

Local Revolving & Micro Loan Funds
There are numerous local revolving and micro loan funds throughout the state. These are listed in the *County Listing by county served.*

Northwest Business Development Co.
421 W Riverside, Suite 210
Spokane, WA 99201
(509) 458-8555   Fax: (509) 458-8553
A U.S. Small Business Administration licensed development corporation which provides SBA 504 funding for eligible businesses. *See also U.S. Small Business Administration 504 Program in the Finance Section.*

Spokane Intercollegiate Research & Technology Institute
See Business & Technical Assistance Section for SIRTI's grant program to help move good ideas off drawing boards and into the marketplace.

Tax-Exempt Bond Finance- WEDFA
Washington Economic Development Finance Authority
1000 Second Avenue, Suite 2700
Seattle, WA   98104-1046
(206) 587-5634   Fax: (206) 389-2819
Creditworthy small manufacturing and processing companies can access below market-rate financing through the Washington Economic Development Finance Authority (WEDFA)'s tax-exempt bond programs for a maximum of $10 million per project. An equipment-only program can finance purchases as low as $250,000. No governmental funds are involved; the project must be a bankable credit. WEDFA bonds carry a tax-exempt interest rate which provide considerable savings over normal commercial financing sources.

U.S. Department of Agriculture- Rural Development Administration
John Brugger, Program Director
PO Box 2427
Wenatchee, WA 98807-2427
(509) 664-0240   Fax: (509) 664-0258 Fax
The Rural Development Administration (RDA) offers rural development loan assistance to businesses located in areas with a population of 50,000 or less. The Business and Industry Loan Program offers borrowers up to a 90 percent guarantee on loans from commercial lenders. Loan proceeds can be used for acquisition or development of land, buildings, equipment, working capital and refinancing of existing debt. Interest rates are negotiable and the RDA requires a 10 percent equity participation by the business.

U.S. Department of Interior- Bureau of Indian Affairs

Olympic Peninsula Agency
Business and Economic Development
715 Emerson Avenue
Hoquiam, WA 98550
(360) 533-9138

Puget Sound Agency
Business and Economic Development
300-6 Colby Ave, Federal Building
Everett, WA 98201
(206) 258-2651   Fax: (206) 258-1254

Business & Economic Development
PO Box 389
Wellpinit, WA 99040
(509) 258-4561   Fax: (509) 258-7542

The agency goal is to enhance economic self-sufficiency and independence among federally recognized Native American tribal governments and individual Native Americans who are members of these tribal governments within the State of Washington. The law that facilitates this effort is the Indian Finance Act of 1974 as amended in 1984 with leveraging of various other funding sources to structure the selected business venture. Available programs are: Indian Revolving Loan Fund, Loan Guaranty Fund, Indian Business Development Grant Program and Business Technical Assistance.

U.S. Small Business Administration

Seattle District Office- Western Washington
1200 6th Ave, Suite 1700
Seattle, WA 98101-1128
(206) 553-7311 General Information
(206) 553-7070 - Recorded Information
Fax: (206) 553-4155
SBA On Line Electronic Bulletin Board: (900) 463-4636

SBA Internet & Bulletin Board
Information
Home Page: http://www.sba.gov
Gopher: gopher://gopher.sba.gov
File Transfer Protocol: ftp://.sba.gov
Telnet: telnet://sbaonline.sba.gov

Spokane District Office- Eastern Washington
W. 601 1st Avenue, 10th Floor East
Spokane, WA 99204
(509) 353-2800   Fax: (509) 353-2600

Portland District Office
220 SW Columbia St., Suite 500
Portland, OR 97201-6695
(503) 326-2682
          Fax: (503) 326-2808
Wahkiakum, Cowlitz, Clark, Klickitat, Skamania counties

The Small Business Administration (SBA) is a federal agency which provides assistance in the form of direct loans, loan guarantees, counseling, helping small businesses secure government contracts, and acting as a special advocate for small businesses with other federal and state agencies and the private sector. The Small Business Administration has many programs to assist small businesses. A small business is generally defined as any business with less than 500 employees (with certain industry sectors there is also a limitation on annual sales). Generally the limit of SBA risk is $750,000, though some of the programs listed below have higher lending limits.

- The **SBA 7(a) Guaranteed Loan Program** is the most popular program with commercial banks, qualified finance companies and small businesses. It is the SBA's primary loan program. The SBA reduces risk to lenders by guaranteeing major portions of loans made to small businesses. This enables the lenders to provide financing to small businesses when funding is otherwise unavailable on reasonable terms.

- CAPLines is the program under which the SBA helps small businesses meet their short-term and cyclical working-capital needs. A CAPLines loan can be for any dollar amount (except for the Small Asset-Based Line), and the SBA will guarantee 75 percent up to $750,000 (80 percent on loans of $100,00 or less). There are five short-term working capital Loan Programs for small businesses under CAPLines.

- The **International Trade Loan Program** helps small businesses that are engaged in international trade, preparing to engage in international trade, or adversely affected by competition from imports. The SBA can guarantee $1.25 million in combined working-capital and fixed-asset loans. The working-capital portion of the loan may be made according to the provisions of the Export Working Capital Program or other SBA working-capital programs.

- The **Export Working Capital Program** was developed in response to the needs of exporters seeking short-term working-capital. The SBA guarantees 75 percent of the principal and interest, up to $750,000 (80% on loans of $100,000 or less). The EWCP uses a one-page application form and streamlined documentation, and turn-around is usually within 10 days. You may also apply for a letter of prequalification from the SBA.

- **DELTA-Defense Loan and Technical Assistance Program.** If you own a defense-dependent small firm adversely affected by defense cuts, DELTA can help you diversify into the commercial market. The DELTA Program provides both financial and technical assistance. A joint effort of the SBA and the Department of Defense, it offers about $1 billion in gross lending authority. The SBA processes, guarantees and services DELTA loans through the regulations, forms and operating criteria of the 7(a) Program and the 504 Certified Development Company Program.

- The **Minority and Women's Prequalification Loan Program.** If you are a woman or minority who owns or wants to start a business, these programs can help. Intermediaries assist you in developing a viable loan application package and securing a loan. On approval, the SBA provides a letter of prequalification you can take to a lender. The women's program uses only non-profit organizations as intermediaries; the minority program uses for-profit intermediaries as well. Once your loan package is assembled, the intermediary submits it to the SBA for expedited consideration; a decision usually is made within three days. If your application is approved, the SBA issues a letter of prequalification stating the agency's intent to guarantee the loan. The intermediary will then help you locate a lender offering the most competitive rates. The maximum amount for loans under the women's program is $250,000; under the minority program, it is generally the same, although some district offices set other limits. With both programs, the SBA will guarantee up to 75 percent (80 percent on loans of $100,000 or less).

- **LowDoc-The Low Documentation Program** is one of the SBA's most popular programs. Once you have met your lender's requirements for credit, LowDoc offers a simple, one-page SBA application form and rapid turnaround on approvals for loans of up to $100,000. The SBA will guarantee up to 80 percent of the loan amount. Completed applications are processed quickly by the SBA, usually within two or three days. Proceeds may not be used to repay certain types of existing debt.

- The **7 (M) MicroLoan Program** provides small loans ranging from under $100 to $25,000. Under this program, the SBA makes funds available to nonprofit intermediaries; these, in turn, make the loans. The average loan size is $10,000. Completed applications usually are processed by the intermediary in less than one week. This is a pilot program available at limited number of locations.

- The **504 Certified Development Company Program** enables growing businesses to secure long-term, fixed-rate financing for major fixed assets, such as land, buildings and equipment. A certified development company (CDC) is a non-profit corporation set up to contribute to the economic development of its community or region. CDC's work with the SBA and private-sector lenders to provide financing to small businesses. The program is designed to enable small businesses to create and retain jobs; the CDC's portfolio must create or retain one job for every $35,000 of debenture proceeds, provided by the SBA. Typically, a 504 project includes: a loan secured with a first lien from a private sector lender covering up to 50 percent of the project cost, a second loan secured with a subordinate lien from the CDC (a 100 percent SBA-guaranteed debenture) covering up to 40 percent of the project cost, and a contribution of at least 10 percent equity by the borrower. The maximum SBA debenture generally is $750,000 (up to $1 million in some cases). The small business obtains up to 90% financing of their project and the benefit of the debenture's (bond) fixed rate long term financing on 40% of the new debt. *See Evergreen Community Development Association and Northwest Business Development Co. in this section above for contact information on these Certified Development Companies.*

- The **Small Business Investment Company Program**. There are a variety of alternatives to bank financing for small businesses, especially business start-ups. The Small Business Investment Company program fills the gap between the availability of venture capital and the needs of small businesses that are either starting or growing. Licensed and regulated by the SBA, SBIC's are privately owned and managed investment firms that make capital available to small businesses through investments or loans. They use their own funds plus funds obtained at favorable rates with SBA guarantees and/or by selling their preferred stock to the SBA. SBIC's are for-profit firms whose incentive is to share in the success of a small business. In addition to equity capital and long-term loans, SBIC's provide debt-equity investments and management assistance. The SBIC Program provides funding to all types of manufacturing and service industries. Some investment companies specialize in certain fields, while others seek out small businesses with new products or services because of the strong growth potential. Most, however consider a wide variety of investment opportunities.

- The **Surety Bond Program**. By law, prime contractors to the federal government must post surety bonds on federal construction projects valued at $100,000 or more. Many state, county, city and private-sector projects require bonding as well. The SBA can guarantee, bid, performance and payment bonds for contracts up to $1.25 million for small businesses that cannot obtain bonds through regular commercial channels. Bonds may be obtained in two ways: 1) Prior Approval-Contractors apply through a surety bonding agent. The guarantee goes to the surety; and 2) Preferred Sureties are authorized by the SBA to issue, monitor and service bonds without prior SBA approval.

These Loan Programs and others are detailed in the **Quick Reference To SBA Loan Programs** matrix in this directory. See also *1) Business & Technical Assistance Section and Export Section.*

Licenses, Registration, & Permits

Corporate Renewals
Department of Licensing
PO Box 9034
Olympia, WA 98507
(360)753-5589
Provides renewal for all profit corporations registered with the Secretary of State.

Dealer and Manufacturer Control
Vehicle Services Division, Department of Licensing
PO Box 9039
Olympia, WA 98507-9039
(360) 902-3703
Maintains comprehensive and vigorous control over the manufacture and sale of motor vehicles, vessels, mobile homes, the licensing of vehicle salvage operations and the determination and collection of fees and taxes. Provides assistance in complying with the law and obtaining required licensing to motor vehicle dealers, mobile home manufacturers, bulk haulers, transporters, wreckers, scrap processors, registered tow truck operators and vessel dealers. Protects vehicle businesses and individual consumers by identifying and correcting licensee conduct which poses a risk of damage to the vehicle buying public. Investigates and enforces the unlicensed dealer law.

Driver Licensing and Examination Services

Driver Services, Department of Licensing
PO Box 48001
Olympia, WA 98504
(360) 902-3600
Examines and licenses every driver of a motor vehicle on the public roadways of Washington State. Also certifies commercial driving schools.

Master License Service

Department of Licensing
405 Black Lake Boulevard
PO Box 9034
Olympia, WA 98507-9034
(360) 753-4401
The Uniform Business Identifier (UBI) program brought one-stop registration to businesses, which allows a business to fulfill many registration and licensing requirements by completing a three-page Master Application and making a single payment. Provides a centralized source of information concerning licensing, permits and registrations administered by state agencies, and federal, city and county governments. The service is offered statewide at 39 field offices of the departments of Employment Security, Labor and Industries, and Revenue; at the Master Licenser Service in Olympia; at the Corporations Division of the Secretary of State in Olympia; and through the mail.

Allows applicants for certain business licenses to acquire one or more licenses, registrations issued by 10 separate state agencies with one application and one payment at one location. Businesses may also renew the renewable licenses residing on the system at one time and with one payment. The Unified Business Identifier allows businesses to submit applications at 48 statewide service locations, the central offices of the Departments of Revenue, Labor and Industries, Employment Security, the Office of the Secretary of State or at the Master License Service of the Department of Licensing.

A business will be issued a UBI number when a Master Application is received. The actual business license will follow in the mail. If a business need any specialty licenses, such as liquor or lottery licenses, the business will be asked to submit additional information and then must await approval from the regulating agency before beginning business operation.

Permit Assistance Center

PO Box 47600
Olympia, WA 98504-7600
(360) 407-7037
Environmental permit information and permit coordination services are available from the state's Permit Assistance Center. Service is available by phone at (360) 407-7037 or in person at the Department of Ecology's headquarters in Lacey, which is just off Martin Way at 300 Desmond Drive. The center is open Monday through Thursday from 9:00 a.m. to 4:00 p.m.

Professional Licensing Services

Department of Licensing
405 Black Lake Boulevard
PO Box 9034
Olympia, WA 98507-9034
(360) 753-3234
Responsible for the examination, licensing, registration, regulation, investigation and discipline of individuals and businesses in professions and occupations as follows:

Appraiser	Cosmetology Instructor	Funeral Home
Architect	Court Reporter	Landscape Architect
Architect Corporation	Crematoria	Land Surveyors
Auctioneer	Debt Adjuster	Manicurist
Auction Company	Embalmer	Notary
Barber	Employment Agency	Private Detectives
Camp Club	Engineers	Private Security Guards
Cemetery	Escrow Officers & Agents	Professional Athletics
Collection Agency	Estheticians	Real Estate Brokers
Cosmetologist	Firearm Dealers	Real Estate Salespersons
Cosmetology School	Funeral Director	Sellers of Travel
		Time Share

Secretary of State, Corporations Division

PO Box 40234
Olympia, Washington 98504-0234
(360) 753-7115

The Corporations Division is responsible for the registration of all corporations and limited partnerships operating in the State of Washington. Trademarks processed through this office are for intrastate use only. In addition to maintaining corporate records, the division also registers trademarks on the state level. A corporation may file by mail which will take approximately 10 days to process or they can be filed immediately at their office for an expedited fee of $20.00. The Corporations Division also provides a variety of information concerning corporations status, the names and addresses of the corporations officers, and other related information for use by financial and legal services, law enforcement agencies, the IRS and the general public. They also can assist businesses to provide a secure and convenient way to electronically transfer contracts, letters of credit, payments and other formal documents.

Title and Registration Control

Vehicle Services Division, Department of Licensing
PO Box 2957
Olympia, WA 98507-2957
(360)902-3600

Administers the state laws relating to the registration and titling of all commercial and non-commercial vehicles in the state. Coordinates a statewide system of county agents and sub-agents to issue and record vehicle and vessel registrations and vehicle license plates. Through these agents and sub-agents, it issues negotiable titles for each vehicle or vessel owned, thereby providing assurance of title certificates to prospective buyers and lending institutions.

Trade Names Registration

Department of Licensing
405 Black Lake Boulevard
PO Box 9034
Olympia, WA 98507-9034
(360) 753-4401
(900) 463-6000 Trade Name Search

Provides a central location for the registration, discovery and disclosure of the ownership of businesses operating under an assumed name.

Uniform Commercial Code

Department of Licensing
405 Black Lake Blvd.
PO Box 9660
Olympia, WA 98507-9660
(360)753-2523

Protects the lender's interest in collateral used to secure loans by registering secured collateral in a central location. Provides filing and search services to nearly all segments of the business and financial community and to the general public.

Minority & Woman Owned Businesses

Bureau of Indian Affairs
See Finance Section- U.S. Department of the Interior/Bureau of Indian Affairs for Loan Programs available to entrepreneurs who are tribal members.

Black Dollar Days Task Force
116-21st Avenue
Seattle, WA 98122
(206) 323-4701
The mission of the Black Dollars Day Task Force is to effectively address economic issues that impact primarily low income African Americans. The Black Dollars Day Task Force provides a monthly 6 hour workshop "How To Start a Small Business". They also provide classes on business and loan packaging. One on one management and technical assistance is also offered to existing and new business owners to help develop and grow their business. This service is available by appointment after an application is completed.

Cascadia Revolving Fund
This revolving fund places a priority on making loans to minority and women owned business- *See Finance Section for details and contact information.*

Linked Deposit Program
Community Development Finance   Minority and Women's Business Development
PO Box 4830   2001 Sixth Avenue, Suite 2700
Olympia, WA 98504-8300   Seattle, WA 98121
(360) 753-0325   (206) 389-2561
The Washington State Linked Deposit Program is a new financing opportunity for certified minority and women-owned businesses made possible by the 1993 Minority and Women-Owned Business Assistance Act. The Act directs the State Treasurer to operate a program which links the deposit of state funds to loans made by participating financial institutions to qualified minority and women business enterprises.

The deposit of state funds is made at below market rates. The savings are then passed on by the bank to the Linked Deposit borrowers in the form of lower loan rates (generally a 2% savings). To determine if your bank is accepting Linked Deposit loan applications, either contact the loan officer at your bank's local branch office or contact the State Treasurer's Office listed below. For questions on certification, see Office of Minority and Women's Business Enterprises in this same section. For questions regarding credit worthiness of your finance proposal contact:

Local Revolving & Micro Loan Funds
There are numerous local revolving and micro loan funds throughout the state, many of which place a priority on lending and technical assistance to minority and woman owned businesses. *See County Listing by trade area and county served.*

Minority and Women's Business Development Program
Department of Community, Trade & Economic Development
2001 6th Ave, Suite 2700
Seattle, WA 98121
(206) 389-2561

The Minority and Women's Business Development Program provides small, minority and women owned businesses with resources and technical assistance needed to start or expand a business and pursue international opportunities. The strategies behind the program is information and referral, access to capital, direct technical assistance, export assistance, bonding assistance and procurement assistance. The program's Export Assistance section provides seminars on export markets, direct export counseling, and organizes and leads trade missions.

Minority and Women-Owned Business Loan Program
Department of Community, Trade & Economic Development
PO Box 48300
Olympia, WA 98504-8300
(360) 753-0325
This program, a component of the Development Loan Fund, offers loans up to $50,000 to certified minority and women-owned businesses using less restrictive credit standards in lending. Loans can be requested for start-up costs, inventory, working capital, purchase of equipment, real estate, assistance in securing contractor bonding, and technical assistance in such areas as marketing, accounting, and management. Projects must be sponsored by a local government eligible for Small Cities Community Development Block Grant funds.

Office Of Minority And Women's Business Enterprise (OMWBE)
PO Box 41160
Olympia, WA 98504-1160
(360) 753-9693
This office was created in 1983 to increase opportunities for minorities and women to obtain state contracts. It sets annual goals by class of contract and monitors MWBE participation on awarded contracts to businesses owned by women and minorities. A business must be certified by OMWBE to be counted toward an agency's annual goal. The program is designed to:

• Develop, plan and implement programs to provide opportunities to qualified minority- and women-owned businesses.

• Develop and maintain a central minority- and women-owned business enterprises certification list for state agencies, educational institutions and other jurisdictions.

• Identify barriers preventing equal participation. Monitor and perform investigations to resolve unfair business practices.

• Administer the Business Partnership Program (BPP). The BPP is a program that encourages business opportunities for MWBEs in the public and private sectors through contractual partnerships with non-MWBEs. The dollar value of the completed contract may be applied against contracting and procurement goals established by state agencies and educational institutions.

U.S. Small Business Administration
Minority and Women's Prequalification Loan Program- *See Finance Section above for information on this program and SBA contact information.*

Patents & Copyright

Patent Depository Library
University of Washington, Engineering Library
PO Box 352170
Seattle, Washington 98195-2170
(206) 543-0741

The Patent Depository Library at the University of Washington will provide assistance with a computerized trademark search . There is no charge for their assistance. *See Chapter 3,* PROTECTING YOUR CREATIVE ADVANTAGE (Trademarks, Copyrights, Trade Secrets and Patents), *for more information.*

Regulatory Assistance

Alien Employment Certification Unit
Employment Security Department
PO Box 9046
Olympia, WA 98507-9046
(360) 438-4061 and -4064
Employers wishing to supplement their workforce with foreign nationals possessing needed skills may apply to this unit. Admission to the United States must be done through employer sponsorship (the alien cannot apply). The employer must prove or attest that they will not displace nor adversely affect the wages and working conditions of U.S. workers.

Business Ombudsman
Department of Community, Trade & Economic Development
PO Box 48300
Olympia, WA 98504-8300
(360) 586-3022
The business ombudsman serves as an advocate on behalf of small businesses. The ombudsman settles disputes between business and state and local government, manages the business services unit, and provides technical assistance to state agencies on compliance with the Regulatory Fairness Act.

Consultation and Compliance Services Division- Compliance Section
Department of Labor and Industries
(800) 547-8367 or contact local L and I office *(See Regulatory Assistance Section- Department of Labor and Industries)*
The compliance section of the Department of labor and Industries enforces state laws governing workplace safety and health, private sector rehabilitation services, minimum wages on public projects, child labor, family leave construction and other labor laws. It also conducts elevator and boiler inspections, registers contractors and certifies electrical administrators, journeyman and trainees.

Department of Ecology

Central Regional Office
15 West Yakima Avenue, Suite 200
Yakima, WA 98902-3401
(509) 575-2490   (509) 454-7673 TDD
(509) 575-2809 fax

Eastern Regional Office
N. 4601 Monroe, Suite 100
Spokane, WA 99205-1295
(509) 456-2926   (509) 458-2055 TDD
(509) 456-6175 Fax

Northwest Regional Office
3190 160th Avenue SE
Bellevue, WA 98008-5452
(206) 649-7000   (206) 649-4259 TDD
(206) 649-7098 Fax

Southwest Regional Office
PO Box 47775
Olympia, WA 98504-7775
(360) 407-6300   (360) 407-6306 TDD
(360) 407-6305 Fax

Assists businesses in their compliance with state environmental regulations. Assistance is provided through direct contact with the appropriate person within the agency, through informational hotlines, and through distribution of the agency's information booklet on permit requirements.

Department of Labor and Industries- Insurance Services Division
PO Box 44850
Olympia, Washington 98504-4050
(360) 902-5800 or (800) 547-8367
The Department of Labor and Industries provides an array of services to Washington's 5 million citizens, 150,000 employers and 2.1 million workers. Most injured workers receive workers compensation benefits through the Department of Labor and Industries Insurance Services Division. The benefits provide compensation for on the job accidents and occupational diseases. Payment to workers are made from the State Fund, the employee and the employer funded premium pool maintained by insurance services.

The Department is divided and scattered statewide across six regions and 22 service areas. There are offices at the following locations:

Local Labor & Industries Offices

415 West Wishkah St. Suite 1B
Aberdeen, WA 98520-0013
(360) 533-9300

616 120th Ave NE, Suite C201
Bellevue, WA 98005-3037
(206) 990-1400

1720 Ellis Street, Suite 200
Bellingham, WA 98225-4600
(360) 647-7300

500 Pacific Avenue, Suite 400
Bremerton, WA 98337-1904
(360) 478-4921

298 S. Main, Suite 203
Colville, WA 99114-2416
(509) 684-7417

21 C Street SW
Ephrata, WA 98823-1895
(509)754-4608

8625 Evergreen Way, Suite 250
Everett, WA 98208-2620
(206)290-1300

300 West Harrison St.
Seattle, WA 98119-4081
(206)281-5400

500 North Morain, Suite 1110
Kennewick, WA 99336-2683
(509)735-0100

900 Ocean Beach Highway
Longview, WA 98632-4013
(360) 577-2200

525 E. College, Suite H
Mount Vernon, WA 98273-5500
(360) 416-3000

1234 2nd Avenue S
Okanogan, WA 98840-0632
(509) 826-7345

7273 Linderson Way SW
Olympia, WA 98504-4851
(360) 902-5799

1605 East Front St., Suite C
Port Angeles, WA 98362-4628
(360) 417 2700

SE 1260 Bishop Blvd., Suite D
Pullman, WA 99163-0847
(509) 334-5296

901 N. Monroe Suite 100
Spokane, WA 99201-2149
(509)324-2600

Human Rights Commission
Capitol Way, Suite 402
PO Box 42490
Olympia, Washington 98504-2490
(360) 753-6770 (Voice/TTY)

1511 Third Avenue, Suite 921
Melbourne Tower
Seattle, Washington 98101-1626
(206) 464-6500 (Voice/TTY)

West 905 Riverside Avenue, Suite 412
Spokane, Washington 99201-1099
(509) 456-4473 (Voice-TTY)

Washington Liberty Bldg., Suite 441
32 North 3rd Street
Yakima, Washington 98901-2730
(509) 575-2772

The Washington State Human Rights Commission has been given the authority to make legally enforceable regulations which carry out in more specific detail, the provisions of the laws against discrimination and sexual harassment. The commission processes complaints, makes regulations, conducts studies and provides educational and consulting services. Offices are located at the following locations:

Insurance Services Division- Self Insurance Program
Department of Labor and Industries
(800) 547-8367 or contact local Land I office (*See Regulatory Assistance Section- Department of Labor and Industries*)
The self insurance unit regulates and certifies the eligibility for hundreds of companies and government units that use their own resources to insure workers rather than participating in L and I's worker compensation program. They have oversight over self insurers who must provide the same benefits as the State Fund.

Specialty Industries

Daycare *(See also Finance- Childcare Facility Fund)*
Child Care Advantages Program
Department of Community, Trade and Economic Development
PO Box 48300
Olympia, WA 98504-8300
(360) 586-3023
The Child Care Advantages Program provides businesses with financial and technical assistance to develop on-site or near-site child care facilities. The program provides qualified businesses with an opportunity to receive direct loans, loan guarantees, or grants to start or expand child care facilities. Child Care Advantages helps employers develop effective and efficient work family programs.

Film & Video
Washington State Film and Video Office
Department of Community, Trade & Economic Development
2001 6th Ave, Suite 2600
Seattle, WA 98121
(206) 464-7148
This office provides the film and video industry with Washington site location, state permit assistance, writer referrals, and technical assistance. The Office markets the state's diverse locations to filmmakers from out-of-state for use as sites in the production of feature films, television series, TV movies, commercials, documentaries, industrial films and music videos. Local communities benefit by the new revenue which is generated by the production company. These companies hire local crew and talent, rent and purchase local equipment, lease location sites for filming, and house and feed personnel who are in the state temporarily.

Manufacturing
Community Diversification Program
Department of Community, Trade and Economic Development
PO Box 48300
906 Columbia St. SW
Olympia, WA 98504-8300
(360) 586-8973
The Community Diversification Program promotes diversification and improved competitiveness among shipbuilding and ship repair, aerospace and related industries. Activities have focused on supporting creation of over 10 large and small manufacturing networks including ShipNet and the Washington

Aerospace Alliance. These networks have helped companies cut expenses, increase sales utilize new CAD/CAM technology, and become ISO-9000 certified.

Northwest Trade Adjustment Assistance Center
Northwest TAAC
900 Fourth Avenue Suite 2430
Seattle, WA 98164-1003
(206)622-2730   Fax: (206) 622-1105
The center pays up to 75 percent of the cost of hiring outside experts on a contract basis to help manufacturing companies trying to compete with imported products. Up to $100,000 is available to increase sales and profits by modernizing manufacturing techniques and improving marketing strategies. Manufacturers can qualify if their employment and sales or production have declined during the past year due to their customers switching to buy imported products.

Recycle
Clean Washington Center
Department of Community, Trade and Economic Development
2001 6th Ave, Suite 2700
Seattle, WA 98121
(206) 464-7040
The Clean Washington Center was created by the Washington State Legislature to stimulate demand for recycled materials in Washington State. Since then, this state funded program has been working in partnership with business, industry and local governments to reduce solid waste disposal by increasing the use and value of materials recovered from Washington's solid waste stream. Through work with processors, manufacturers and purchasers, the CWC is expanding demand for such recycled materials as paper, plastics, glass, compost, tires, industrial by-products, and construction/demolition/land clearing debris.

Tourism
Tourism Development
Department of Community, Trade and Economic Development
PO Box 42500
Olympia, WA 98504-2500
(360) 753-5600
The Tourism Development office markets the state as a travel destination, and it assists the travel industry develop new visitor attractions and services; i.e., packaging, product development, guiding them to financial assistance opportunities and marketing. Technical assistance is provided to the travel industry through businesses and communities who have identified tourism as a part of their economic well-being. The office provides statistics and research to enhance marketing and economic development objectives, particularly for off-season business. Much of the focus is on entrepreneurial development since 80% of tourism businesses are small businesses.

Taxes & Tax Credits

Community Empowerment Zones, Counties Containing a Community Empowerment Zone Counties and Adjacent to Distressed Counties Deferral Program
Miscellaneous Tax Section, Department of Revenue
PO Box 47477
Olympia, WA 98504-7477
(360) 753-5545
Businesses located in these areas must meet the same requirements as for a Distressed Area Deferral/Exemption covered above, plus must hire one full-time employee for every $750,000 of investment. The employee positions must be new and 75% of the positions must be filled by residents of a Community Empowerment Zone (CEZ), a county containing a CEZ, or a county adjacent to a

distressed county. The level of employment must be maintained during the start-up year, plus seven additional years. No repayment is required if all program requirements are met for the start-up year, plus seven additional years.

Distressed Area B & O Tax Credit

Miscellaneous Tax Section, Department of Revenue
PO Box 47477
Olympia, WA 98504-7477
(360) 753-5545

A company that increases its employment in a distressed area by at least fifteen percent over the prior year may be eligible for a business and occupation tax credit. Manufacturing, computer services, and research and development firms are eligible. This credit also applies to timber impact areas in non-distressed counties. A credit of $2,000 per full-time employee, with a maximum credit of $300,000 is provided. The application must be submitted before hiring begins.

Distressed Areas Tax Deferral/Exemption Program

Miscellaneous Tax Section, Department of Revenue
PO Box 47477
Olympia, WA 98504-7477
(360) 753-5545

This program is designed to stimulate economically distressed areas. A sales/use tax deferral/exemption may be available on buildings, equipment, and machinery used in manufacturing, research and development, or computer-related businesses located in distressed areas. Some areas have specific employment requirements. Applications for the deferral/exemption must be made before construction begins. Taxes on labor performed during construction of an eligible project are exempt from repayment. Once the project is certified as complete and all requirements are met, the deferral becomes an exemption. No repayment is required.

High Technology B & O Tax Credit

Miscellaneous Tax Section, Department of Revenue
PO Box 47477
Olympia, WA 98504-7477
(360) 753-5545

Businesses that perform research and development in Washington in the high Technology categories of advanced computing, advanced materials, biotechnology, electronic device technology, and environmental technology and spend over 92% of their business' taxable amount during that year on research and development may be eligible for this credit. The credit may not exceed $2 million. No pre approval is required. Businesses must complete a High Tech B & O Credit Survey and an Affidavit for the Department of Revenue.

High Technology Sales/Use Tax Deferral/Exemption

Miscellaneous Tax Section, Department of Revenue
PO Box 47477
Olympia, WA 98504-7477
(360) 753-5545

High Technology businesses in the categories stated above may be eligible for a sales/use tax deferral/exemption on machinery and equipment, new structures, and expansion/renovation to increase floor space or production capacity. They must start new research and development, or pilot scale manufacturing, or expand or diversify a current operation by expanding, renovating, or equipping a facility in Washington. If program requirements are met, the taxes do not need to be repaid. An application must be filed before construction begins or machinery or equipment is acquired.

Historic Preservation Tax Certification Program

Department of Community, Trade and Economic Development, Office of Archeology & Historic Preservation
PO Box 48343
Olympia, WA 98504-8343
(360) 753-5010
This program is one of the most useful incentives for encouraging the preservation of our state's historic resources. A federal investment tax credit is available for buildings in Washington state which are listed in the National Register of Historic Places. To be eligible for this 20 percent credit, National Register properties must be income-producing, which may include uses such as commercial, retail, office, rental residential, or industrial.

Manufacturing Machinery, Equipment, Repair, and Installation Sales/Use Tax Exemption

Miscellaneous Tax Section, Department of Revenue
PO Box 47477
Olympia, WA 98504-7477
(360) 753-5545
As an encouragement to preserve and create family-wage jobs in the manufacturing sectors, a sales/use tax exemption is available for qualifying machinery and equipment, its installation, replacement parts with a life of over one year for qualifying machinery or equipment, and repair labor. Businesses must perform manufacturing operations within the state to be eligible. No pre-approval is required. A certificate must be completed and given to the seller at the time of sale or a summary must be completed for the Department of Revenue at the end of the year.

Prorate and Fuel Tax Control

Vehicle Services Division, Department of Licensing
PO Box 48001
Olympia, WA 98507
(360) 902-3600
All interstate fleet operators and other operators of commercial vehicles in this country and Canada who transport goods or people on Washington's public roads are governed by the State's prorate and reciprocity laws which are administered by the prorate and fuel tax division. Individuals or firms using motor vehicle gasoline and other liquid fuels in any manner affected by state taxes placed on those fuels are affected and assisted by vehicle services regulation and audit services.

Taxpayer Information and Education

Taxpayer Information and Education, Department of Revenue
PO Box 47478
Olympia, WA 98504-7478
(800) 647-7706) Nationwide   (800) 451-7985) TTY
This group provides tax information and consultation for prospective and established businesses. It provides informative publications and sponsors tax workshops and business outreach programs.

Workforce

General

Labor Market and Economic Analysis
Department of Employment Security
PO Box 9046
Olympia, WA 98507-9046
(360) 438-4800
Labor Market and Economic Analysis compiles and distributes labor market publications on unemployment, employment, occupations, hours worked, wages earned and significant layoffs.

Washington Service Corps
Dave Broom, Program Manager
PO Box 9046
Olympia, WA 98507-9046
(360) 438-4009
Since 1983, the Washington Service Corps has partnered with the non-profit community to sponsor creative service projects that address critical need at the local level. Administered through the Department of Employment Security, this statewide program serves as a valuable resource to non-profits while challenging young adults with opportunities to develop leadership skills while learning the meaning of citizenship and making valuable contributions to their communities.

Safety

Northwest Disability Business Technical Assistance Center
PO Box 9046 MS 6000
Olympia, WA 98507-9046
1-800-949-4232
The Northwest Disability Business Technical Assistance Center provides information, technical assistance, referrals and training to those who have responsibilities and those who have rights under the Americans with Disabilities Act. Call to discuss your ADA issues with trained advisors; request copies of the latest explanatory or technical materials which have been approved for accuracy by the relevant enforcement agencies; learn about the tax incentives, federal and state programs and other resources available to assist you in implementing the Act; consult their data base on consultants, assistive devices; or arrange training for your business.

The services of the Northwest Disability Business Technical Assistance Center extend to all provisions of the ADA, including employment, state and local governments, public accommodations, telecommunications, public and private transportation, barrier removal and barrier-free design.

Retrospective Rating Program
Department of Labor and Industries
PO Box 44180
Olympia, WA 98504-4180
(360) 902-4851
Offers retrospective ratings to Washington State Fund policyholders. This optional financial incentive program enables employers to receive a premium refund if they are able to keep their claim costs low through safety, accident prevention and claims management programs. The program assesses additional premiums to those employers whose claim costs are greater than expected. Loss Control Consultants are available to assist employers wishing to initiate safety, accident prevention and claims management programs. Each employer is provided with a profile of their workers compensation experience. This profile gives the employer a picture of the impact claims have on their workers compensation premium.

Work Place Consultations Division
Department of Labor and Industries
PO Box 44640
Olympia, WA 98504-4640
(360) 902-5580
This division offers free safety and health consultation to employers. Consultants identify health and safety hazards and recommend how they can be eliminated. Consultation and educational services can prevent accident and worker injuries throughout a business.

Training & Education

Black Dollar Days Task Force
116-21st Avenue
Seattle, WA 98122

(206) 323-0534
The mission of the Black Dollars Day Task Force is to effectively address economic issues that impact primarily low income African Americans. The Black Dollars Day Task Force provides a monthly 6 hour workshop "How To Start a Small Business". They also provide classes on business and loan packaging. One on one management and technical assistance is also offered to existing and new business owners to help develop and grow their business. This service is available by appointment after an application is completed.

Dislocated Workers Program
Department of Employment Security
PO Box 9046
Olympia, WA 98507-9046
(360) 438-4620
Special programs have been established to assist workers, businesses and communities to reduce the negative impact of plant closures and layoffs. In Washington State, a variety of approaches are used in providing services, including plant or industry specific projects that provide services to specific groups of workers; statewide projects servicing a variety of dislocated workers within a specific geographic area; and discretionary projects which provide services to specific groups of dislocated workers under special funds made available on a nationwide competitive basis.

Services provided include resume writing; job seeking skills instruction; personal and financial counseling; skill transferability information; testing; retraining through On-the-Job Training, Institutional Skill Training, or a combination of these two; and financial assistance for relocation, pre-employment interviewing, work enabling equipment, and emergency support.

Employers can gain access to a large pool of experienced, qualified workers, and receive financial assistance for training new employees through on-the-job or customized training. Businesses can obtain assistance without placement or retraining of employees during a partial or complete plant closure.

Electronic Commerce Center
Ed Wilson, Program Manager
4312 Kitsap Way
Bremerton, WA 98312
(800) 478-3933
The mission of the Electronic Commerce Center is to assist companies in understanding and implementing electronic commerce practices. These practices range from e-mail to buying and selling, to full integration of design, manufacturing, finance, inventory control, distribution and maintenance.

The ECRC serves an 8 state region that offers technology demonstrations, education and training courses, technology seminars, conferences, consultation and technical support. These all serve to increase a businesses capability to seek and respond to request for bids, to find and qualify suppliers, to collaborate on product design, to complete financial transactions and to research technical and business issues. In 1995, the ECRC taught almost 3000 students and provided consultation and tech support for over 200 businesses.

Job Skills Program
Workforce Training and Education Coordinating Board
PO Box 43105
Olympia, WA 98504-3105
(360) 753-5676
A state-funded, matching grants program that supports short-term, job-specific training for local business and industry. JSP funds industry/education partnerships that provide customized, quick-start training for specific jobs. By awarding grants to education and training institutions, JSP supports up to one-half of the total cost of training, with industry providing at least 100 percent matching support, in cash or in-kind. Essentially, three activities are eligible for JSP funds: training for prospective employees before a

new plant opens or when existing industry expands; upgrading existing employees to create new vacancies for unemployed applicants; and retraining current employees when retraining is vital to keep their jobs. The business identifies its short-term training needs and selects an education or training institution as a partner. Jointly, the business and institution develop a customized training program, for which the institution prepares and submits a proposal.

Job Service Center
Washington Employment Security Job Service Centers assist in matching local employer needs for qualified workers with job-ready applicants through job listings, applicant screening and referral, labor market information, tax credits and employer committees. *(See Business and Technical Assistance Section for the Job Service Center in your area.)*

Job Training Partnership Act (JTPA)
PO Box 9046
Olympia, WA 98507-9046
(360) 438-3132
JTPA works with local business through Private Industry Councils to tailor training programs to meet the needs of businesses in the community. All Washington employers are eligible. Training activities under this federal program include specialized recruitment and referral of workers to meet the needs of new or expanding employers, wage reimbursements to employers who train new employees under the on-the-job training program, and customized training to help firms obtain workers with new or unusual skills.

Washington State is divided into twelve service delivery areas. Each service delivery area has a Private Industry Council which designs the training programs provided within that area. The actual training is provided on a contractual basis by a variety of agencies.

The Pentad Private Industry Council
Dave Petersen, Director
PO Box 2360
234 N. Mission Avenue
PO Box 9046, Mail Stop 6000
Wenatchee, WA 98807-2360
(509) 663-3091   Fax: (509) 663-5649
Okanogan, Grant, Douglas, Adams

Eastern Washington Partnership
Employment Security Department
Tom O'Brian, Director
Olympia, WA 98507-9046
(360) 902-9393   Fax: (360) 902-9392
Ferry, Pend Oreille, Garfield, Stevens, Columbia, Lincoln, Whitman, Asotin, Walla Walla, Chelan,

Benton-Franklin Private Industry Council
Rich Foeppel, Director
6515 W. Clearwater, Suite 236
Kennewick, WA 99336
(509) 735-8543   Fax: (509)783-5102
Benton, Franklin   (360) 875-7185
Clallam, Kitsap, Jefferson

Kitsap County Personnel and
Human Resources Department
Bert Furuta, Director
614 Divison Street
Port Orchard, WA 98366
Fax: (360) 876-7187

Southwest Washington
Private Industry Council
Beth Taylor, Executive Director
111 West 39th Street
Vancouver, WA 98660
(360) 696-8417   Fax: (360) 696-8999
Clark, Cowlitz, Skamania, Wahkiakum

Northwest Washington
Private Industry Training
Gay Dubigk, Executive Director
PO Box 2009
Bellingham, WA 98227
(360) 671-1660   Fax: (360) 671-4948
Island, San Juan, Skagit, Whatcom

Thurston County/Pacific Mountain Job
Development and Training Department
Mike Kennedy-Director

Yakima County Department of
Employment and Training
Michael Shanahan, Director

719 Sleater-Kinney Road SE, Suite 200
Lacey, WA 98503-1133
(360) 754-4113   Fax: (360) 754-4119
Grays Harbor, Lewis, Mason, Pacific, Thurston

120 3rd Street, Suite 200 A
Yakima, WA 98901
(509) 574-1950   Fax: (509) 574-1951
Kittitas, Klickitat, Yakima

The Seattle-King County
Private Industry Council
Al Starr, Director
Market Place One, Suite 250
2003 Western Avenue
Seattle, WA 98121-2114
(206)448-0474   Fax: (206)448-0484
King

Tacoma-Pierce County
Employment Council
and Training Consortium
Colin Conant, Executive Director
733 Market Street, Room 21
Tacoma, WA 98402
 (206) 591-5450
Fax: (206) 591-5455
Pierce

Spokane City and County Employment
and Training Consortium
Larry Langyai, Director
West 808 Spokane Falls Blvd.
Spokane, WA 99201
(509) 625-6210   Fax: (509) 625-6929
Spokane

Private Industry Council of
Snohomish County
Emily Duncan, Director
917 134th Street, SW, A-10
Everett, WA 98204
(206) 743-9669
Fax: (206) 742-1177
Snohomish

Shared Work Program
Department of Employment Security:
PO Box 9046
Olympia, WA 98507-9046
(360) 902-9350
The Shared Work Program is designed to help an employer who is anticipating a slow down and does not want to lay employees off. Instead, any reduction is spread out between a group of workers. For example, an employer has 10 workers and needs to cut back 20%. Rather than lay two people off, everyone takes a 20% cut in hours. The Shared Work Program then pays those workers 20% of the unemployment insurance benefits they would be entitled to, had they been fully unemployed. The program may also be used to transition employees from full employment to permanent lay off, providing them with an opportunity to seek other employment prior to becoming unemployed.

Trade Adjustment Assistance Program
Department of Employment Security:
PO Box 9046
Olympia, WA 98504-9046
(360) 902-9509
Trade Adjustment Assistance is available to workers who lose their jobs or whose hours of work and wages are reduced as a result of increased imports. A variety of benefits and re-employment services help unemployed workers prepare for and obtain suitable employment. Workers may be eligible for training, a job search allowance, a relocation allowance, and other re-employment services. The benefit to employers is a retrained worker with skills to maintain permanent employment.

State Board For Community And Technical Colleges
PO Box 42495
Olympia, WA 98504-2495
(360) 753-2000   Fax: (360) 586-6440 TDD: (360) 753-3680

Washington's community colleges, technical colleges and vocational skill centers assist employers by providing education and training for new and current workers. Community and technical colleges and cooperating employers can apply for special funding to provide customized job training to suit the requirements of new or expanding businesses.

In addition to regular community and technical college courses that meet business needs, the community and technical college system has entered into a formal contract with the Small Business Development Center to provide education and technical assistance to Washington businesses.

Community Colleges

Washington has 28 community colleges that offer a wide variety of adult education programs, including entrepreneurial skills, management, marketing, computer, accounting, job training, college transfer, basic skills, adult literacy and many others.

Community colleges offer an "open door" to education. They are committed to giving every person the opportunity and the encouragement to succeed, regardless of age, income, background or previous educational experience. Contact the community college in your area:

Bellevue Community College
3000 Landerholm Circle SE
Bellevue, WA 98007
(206)641-0111

Big Bend Community College
7662 Chanute Street
Moses Lake, WA 98837
(509) 762-5351

Cascadia Community College
c/o Northshore Center
22002 26th Avenue SE
Bothell, WA 98021
(206) 487-6779

Centralia College
600 West Locust
Centralia, WA 98531
(360) 736-9391

Clark College
1800 East McLoughlin Blvd.
Vancouver, WA 98663
(360) 992-2000

Columbia Basin College
2600 North 20th
Pasco, WA 99301
(509) 547-0511

Edmonds Community College
20000 68th Avenue West
Lynnwood, WA 98036
(206) 640-1500

Highline Community College
PO Box 98000
Des Moines, WA 98198
(206) 878-3710

Lower Columbia College
1600 Maple
Longview, WA 98632
(360) 577-2300

N. Seattle Community College
9600 College Way North
Seattle, WA 98103
(206) 527-3600

Olympic College
1600 Chester Ave
Bremerton, WA 98337-1669
(360) 792-6050

Peninsula College
1502 East Lauridsen Blvd.
Port Angeles, WA 98362
(360) 452-9277

Pierce College
9401 Farwest Drive SW
Tacoma, WA 98498
(206) 964-6500

Seattle Central Comm College
1701 Broadway
Seattle, WA 98122
(206) 587-3800

Everett Community College
801 Wetmore Ave.
Everett, WA 98201
(206) 388-9100

Shoreline Community College
16101 Greenwood Ave. North
Seattle, WA 98133
(206) 546-4101

Grays Harbor College
1620 Edward P. Smith Dr.
Aberdeen WA 98520
(360) 532-9020

Skagit Valley College
2405 East College Way
Mount Vernon, WA 98273
(360) 428-1261

Green River Community College
12401 SE 320th Street
Auburn, WA 98002
(206) 833-9111

South Puget Sound Comm College
2011 Mottman Road SW
Olympia, WA 98512
(360) 754-7711

South Seattle Community
6000 16th Ave SW
Seattle, WA 98106
(206)764-5300

Spokane Community
N. 1810 Green Street
Spokane, WA 99207
(509)533-7000

Spokane Falls Community
West 3410 Ft. George Wright Dr.
Spokane, WA 99204
(509)533-3500

Tacoma Community
6501 South 19th
Tacoma, WA 98466
(206)566-5000

Walla Walla Community
500 Tausick Way
Walla, Walla, WA 99362
(509)522-2500

Wenatchee Valley College
1300 Fifth Street
Wenatchee, WA 98801
(509)662-1651

Whatcom Community
237 West Kellogg Td.
Bellingham, WA 98226
(360)676-2170

Technical Colleges

The technical colleges will develop a curriculum specifically directed to meet the needs of a business, or they will modify a training plan that an organization already has. Training can be offered at the college, at the business site, or elsewhere:

Bates Technical College
1101 South Yakima Avenue
Tacoma, WA 98405
(206) 596-1500

Lake Washington Technical College
11605 132nd Avenue NE
Kirkland, WA 98034-8506
(206) 828-5600

Bellingham Technical College
3028 Lindbergh Avenue
Bellingham, WA 98225-1599
(360) 738-0221

Renton Technical College
3000 Northeast Fourth Street
Renton, WA 98056-4195
(206) 235-2352

Clover Park Technical College
4500 Steilacoom Blvd. SW
Tacoma, WA 98499-4098
(206) 589-5800

Seattle Vocational Institute
315- 22nd Ave South
Seattle, WA 98144
(206) 587-4950

Vocational Skills Centers

Washington also has eight high school vocational skills centers that offer specific vocational skill training, producing students with high entry-level job skills for high school students:

Clark County Vocational Skills Center
Evergreen School District #114
12200 NE 28th Street
Vancouver, WA 98682-7858
(360) 604-1050

Sno-Isle Vocational Skills Center
9001 Airport Road
Everett, WA 98204
(206) 353-8810

Kitsap Peninsula Vocational Skills Center
101 National Avenue N
Bremerton, WA 98312
(360) 478-5083

Spokane Vocational Skills Center
4141 North Regal
Spokane, WA 99207
(509) 353-3363

New Market Vocational Skills Center
7299 New Market Street
Tumwater, WA 98501
(360) 586-9375

Tri-City Area Vocational Skills Center
5929 W. Metaline
Kennewick, WA 99336-1494
(509) 736-2500

Sea-Tac Occupational Skills Center
18010 8th Avenue S
Seattle, WA 98148
(206) 433-2524

Yakima Valley Skills Center
1116 South 15th Avenue
Yakima, WA 98902
(509) 575-3289

Order Form

for additional copies of *The Washington Entrepreneur's Guide*
or
Financial Software

Name _____

Organization _____

Address _____

City _____ State _____ Zip _____

Phone _____

Enclosed please find: Check _____ Government PO# _____

VISA/MASTERCARD # _____

Expiration date _____ Signature _____

Please send:

_____ copies of *The Washington Entrpreneur's Guide* $19.95
         plus shipping and handling $ 3.50
_____ copies of 3 1/2" IBM Financial Templates $ 5.00
_____ copies of *How to Write a Questionaire* $ 7.00

                                          Total   _____

Mail to: McElroy Business Development Corporation
           1719 Dearborn
           Missoula, MT   59801

or call: 1-800-243-6840